ADH 1503 °

The

HORIZON
COOKBOOK

and Illustrated History of
Eating and Drinking
through the Ages

The
HORIZON
COOKBOOK

and Illustrated History of
Eating and Drinking
through the Ages

by

WILLIAM HARLAN HALE

and

THE EDITORS OF HORIZON MAGAZINE

EDITOR IN CHARGE

WENDY BUEHR

RECIPES EDITOR TATIANA McKENNA

HISTORICAL FOODS CONSULTANT MIMI SHERATON

PUBLISHED BY

AMERICAN HERITAGE PUBLISHING CO., INC.

BOOK TRADE DISTRIBUTION BY

DOUBLEDAY & COMPANY, INC.

TABLE OF CONTENTS

HORIZON
BOOK DIVISION

EDITORIAL DIRECTOR
Richard M. Ketchum

GENERAL EDITOR
Alvin M. Josephy, Jr.

Staff for this Book

EDITOR IN CHARGE
Wendy Buehr

ART DIRECTOR
Mary Ann Joulwan

FOOD EDITOR
Meryle R. Evans

COPY EDITOR
Brenda Savard Bennerup

ASSISTANT EDITORS
Nathan Adams
Margot Price Brill
Jane Hoover Polley

PICTURE RESEARCHER
Sara Hunter Hudson

TEXT RESEARCHER
Nancy Simon Kaufman

ART ASSISTANT
Carol Fogel

EDITORIAL ASSISTANTS
Pam Meacham Ross
Shelley Benoit

EUROPEAN BUREAU
Gertrudis Feliu, *Chief*
Mary Jenkins

AMERICAN HERITAGE
PUBLISHING CO., INC.

PRESIDENT
James Parton

EDITORIAL COMMITTEE
Joseph J. Thorndike, *Chairman*
Oliver Jensen
Richard M. Ketchum

SENIOR ART DIRECTOR
Irwin Glusker

PUBLISHER, HORIZON MAGAZINE
Paul Gottlieb

FRONTISPIECE: *For guidance in good party giving, hosts might do well to follow the example of the gods, as shown by the seventeenth-century Fleming, Hendrick van Balen the Elder.*
MUSEE DES BEAUX ARTS, ANGERS; GIRAUDON

PART ONE

Illustrated History
of Eating and Drinking
through the Ages

INTRODUCTION

"A clever cook," Erasmus observed, "can make . . . good meat of a whetstone." "A fine sauce will make even an elephant or a grandfather palatable," added the irreverent gourmet, Grimod de La Reynière.

Today, with quality meats, fresh vegetables, and succulent fruits available in most American and European markets, the cook is seldom called upon to practice such magical arts. But throughout history and in many less fortunate parts of the modern world, creative cooking has played a crucial role in making limited food resources the stuff of nourishment, ritual, and communal celebration.

The ancients, for whom eating and drinking were chief public divertisements, devoted a great deal of thought to the place of the cook in the cosmos. Cooks, they reasoned, were only slightly lower than the gods in divine gifts, for they had brought men from cannibalism to civilization with their sauces. A *Coquus Gloriosus*, it was said, was the first earthling to master the Promethean fire, the first to wear the victor's crown at the Olympian games; it was a cook from whom Bacchus was descended and a cook, one Cadmus of Phoenicia, who taught the West the alphabet. Is it any wonder that a fish, exquisitely prepared by one of that noble profession, was seen to smile with satisfaction as it simmered in the pan?

The Greeks were so enamored of the dinner hour that they could make it last for days on end (the dialogue of one symposium of enthusiastic eaters recorded by Athenaeus fills fifteen books). The Romans would as soon have read recipe books as odes. On the other side of the world, men no less than Confucius and Lao-tse turned their deepest thoughts to the kitchen. As

Brillat-Savarin, the ideological descendant of these classical gourmets observed in the eighteenth century, "the pleasures of the table are of all times and all ages, of every country and of every day."

The pursuit of these pleasures has changed the face of the earth. In search of better, more reliable food sources nomadic man matured into farmer and husbandman, history's first technologist; and his ventures to sea as fisherman emboldened him to set sail for exotic spices, turning once-legendary lands into familiar market places. In all this Europe has been both prime mover and principal beneficiary. Rice from the Orient and corn and potatoes from the Americas have long since become staples of the Western diet. Coffee, tea, sparkling wines, and distilled liquors have provided the *raison d'être* for new rituals of hospitality. New kinds of public eating and drinking establishments have evolved to serve a more sociable, leisured population. And as foods of better quality and more variety have become available, so, too, cooking techniques have become more sophisticated.

Much remains to be solved before all the world will share in these good things. Cockaigne, that secular Paradise where the rivers flow with wine and there is cake enough for everyone, is as much a dream as the ancient Greek Elysium. But as the Roman Persius wisely predicted some twenty centuries ago, the palate has truly been "the teacher of art and the giver of ingenuity," and for all anyone can guess in this year, new foods and flavors may lie still untapped in the laboratories. It is a thought which would have tantalized Erasmus and the good Grimod, who knew—and as this history will tell—a clever cook can conquer almost anything.   *The Editors*

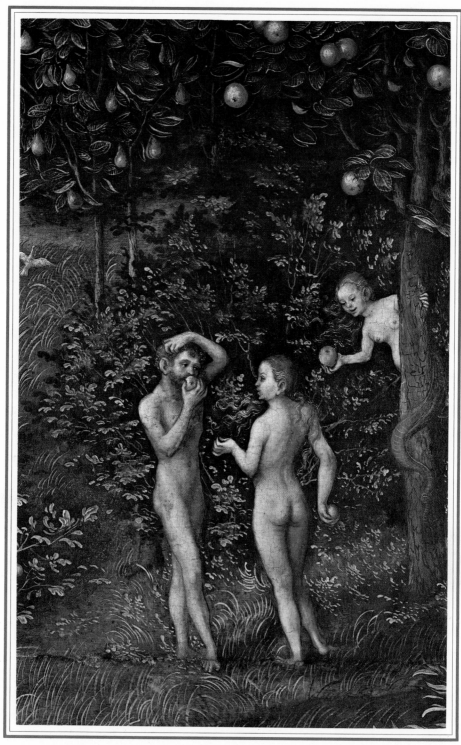

Original sin—and food—from a 1530 painting by Lucas Cranach

FIRST
THE
APPLE

Man lives by food and in great part by its festivities. Beasts forage or prey until they have a bellyful, but man very early invented that basic social rite, the meal. The meal gave rise to the feast, often shared with his gods, and the feast one day was to evolve into the massive nineteenth-century Sunday dinner of Western peoples.

Innumerable occasions, religious and secular, over the centuries have called for a ceremonial board—birthdays, harvest days, holy days, even death days. In the *Iliad* King Priam ends the funeral for his slain son Hector with a banquet—the first wake known to literature. The custom of the birthday party, the historian Herodotus tells us, was well established among ancient Persians of rank, who liked to observe their anniversaries "with a dinner of special magnificence," having "an ox or a horse or a camel or a donkey baked whole" for the event. Man's very calendar, with its survivals of seasonal celebrations, describes his ancestral absorption with the gathering of his crops and the rebirth of spring. At harvest time ancient man approached his deities with sacrifices or first fruits; we have Thanksgiving and recall, if we do not practice, the custom of grace before meat. The ancient Hebraic rite of the consumption of the paschal lamb along with unleavened bread at Passover stands in close relation to that most solemn observance of Christendom, Easter, and both suggest some elements of the ancient festivals that marked the beginning of the planting season. The Occidental New Year, which is widely celebrated today with tin horns and all-night cavorting, was (before Caesar's Romans reformed the calendar and declared wintry Januarius to be the first month) marked in many cultures by rites of atonement and purification followed by feasts for the encouragement of fertility and new crops. The Babylonians, the Western world's first astronomers, reckoned the year from either the seedtime moon of March or the harvest moon of September, and they observed the first days of their new year somewhat as earnest Christians keep the Lenten season.

In the beginning there was fire, and when primitive man learned to capture and use it rather than flee from it in terror like the other animals, a profound distinction arose between his way of life and theirs. Having provided himself with a source of warmth and light against the cold and dark, he learned before long to throw killed game upon the flame rather than devour it raw, and so laid the basis for an entirely new diet (and for the gradual recession of his huge jaws). Just when the hearth came into being remains a matter of conjecture; recent dis-

coveries in the Durance valley in France date man-made fires back some 750,000 years. Probably it was the hearth, with the clan eating their cooked kill around it and protected by its glow against hostile beasts, that served to turn primeval man into a social animal.

Yet for aeons he remained only the most elementary sort of cook. Down

Paleolithic meat, by a Lascaux cave painter

through paleolithic times—that is, to some twelve thousand years ago—the only method of cooking was that of roasting over the open fire. (The pleasure so many urban and suburban men in our time find in staging a cookout or a barbecue may reflect a primordial instinct—besides which, there are few delights finer than a cut of beef raising its savor over a bed of charcoal and hickory.) A more varied diet was to arise only with the invention of indirect, or "off-the-fire," cooking, which involved utensils—a slab for frying, a pot for boiling, and an oven for baking.

Early man discovered that the hard kernel of wild grasses, all but indigestible to him in its raw form, could be made palatable if its husk were cracked open by fire. Experiments were no doubt made with "popping" hard grains by throwing them on the coals, but there was no way to retrieve them from the fire; a stone slab placed over the flame was a logical improvement. It would transmit heat to the kernels gradually and permit them to be recovered. This was the first frying pan. A related discovery, also originating with the use of stones as a heat-transmitting agent, involved water as the softener and cooking medium. Long before earthenware or iron vessels came into being, prehistoric man hit upon the scheme of lining a pit with stones preheated by prolonged direct contact with fire and filling the pit with water. When the water rose to a boil, he would immerse the kernels. To this day the cooking pit survives in the New England coastal ceremony of the clambake, with shellfish steamed by the juices of sea grasses tossed upon hot stones embedded in sand. For prehistoric man the pit was the vessel for his first crude gruels or mashes. What he had created was neither an efficient cookpot nor an oven, but it foreshadowed the principles of both. Along the way he may also have witnessed for the first time the chemical process of fermentation, since kernels when watered and heated and left to stand awhile under warm conditions become affected by the converting yeasts. Aeons later the yeasts were to make man both a baker and a brewer. Which came first is uncertain.

Yet cookery could not progress beyond its simplest stages without containers—above all, the vessel able to hold liquids and solid foods over continuing heat. Stewing, porridge- and soup-making, pickling in brine, controlled fermentation—all these processes involving extraction and preservation of food flavors—required a pot. The rise of culinary art began, in effect, with the bowl of clay. Clay also went into that other major late-prehistoric invention, the oven—of all man's cooking containers perhaps the most valuable since it provided his daily bread. First constructed of packed clay, later of brick, it provided the dry, even heat that made baking possible.

Man's outburst of inventiveness in cooking techniques and utensils coincided with a period that saw fundamental change in his estate. Indeed, these innovations were a basic part of that change, often called the neolithic revolution. The era beginning some eight millennia before the time of Christ saw men gradually shifting from simple hunters and gatherers of food to shepherds, stockmen, and cultivators. The revolution—perhaps more accurately evolution—proceeded at different paces in various areas of the neolithic world, with herding an intermediate stage along the way to civilization. Man's nomadic ways would continue even after he had domesticated animals, but farming meant settlement and the creation of fixed communities. Grain, grown from seed, had to be sown on prepared soil at the proper season and harvested at the

Sumerian chafing dish with ornamental legs

The Gift of Fire

From his lofty vantage atop Mount Olympus, Zeus had been noting man's progress with jealous alarm. To keep the social climber in his place, he decided to withhold the precious element of fire, decreeing that raw meat should be man's diet. But Zeus had not figured on the meddlesome Prometheus. This self-appointed champion of mankind promptly lit a torch from the fiery chariot of the sun, hid its glowing ember in a fennel stalk, and brought the gift to earth. Having outwitted the tyrannical Zeus once, Prometheus was emboldened to test his strength further. He took man aside and showed him how to prepare his sacrifices so that the gods might be tricked into eating the tougher joints while leaving the most tender fillets for the cook. For this and other effronteries, so the Greek legend goes, Zeus finally had the young Titan bound to the highest peak in the Caucasus with a hungry vulture as his sole companion. Of small comfort to the beleaguered Prometheus, man has never ceased to be grateful. Fire festivals no less than harvest celebrations were among the first rituals of civilizing man, and many continue to this day in forms altered to suit the doctrines of religions that have superseded them.

From China, where the three-day "eating of cold food" was observed in April, to Peru, where the summer solstice was greeted by fasting, the custom of extinguishing the old flame and kindling the new has universally symbolized man's search for rebirth. The New Year, Easter, May Day, Midsummer Night, Halloween, Christmas—all can trace some part of their ritual to celebrations of fire which banished their enemies, purged their fields of blight, forged their metals, chased away the cold and damp, and baked their festive cakes. In Rome a temple was built to Vesta, goddess of the hearth (the goddess of the oven rated only a festival), and the ceremonial flame was maintained there by a sorority of patrician virgins, the only mortals deemed suitably pure to perform the sacred tasks of relighting the fire on the first day of the new year, March 1. Appointed for terms of thirty years and paid a small salary for their services, the vestal virgins were expected to remain chaste, under penalty of being buried alive should they stray from their appointed rounds—keeping the state's flame alive as their own fires dimmed.

proper time. Seed had to be preserved for the next season; against a hand-to-mouth existence, granaries, with a continuing capital of food, were needed. The possibilities for leisure and the crafts this increasing security afforded

Ornamented Iranian bowl

laid the basis for stable life and civilized societies. It replaced a haphazard existence with opportunities for ritual, religion, and social cooperation. It provided time to develop better agricultural tools and techniques. (The potter's art and a rudimentary calendar were among the first results. In observing the cycle of the year—floodtime, seedtime, harvest—for his own practical necessity, man learned to watch the movement of sun, moon, and stars.)

The wild upland grasses of regions such as Anatolia and western Persia were parents of the wheat, barley, and rye of early Mesopotamia, where man's first cities arose. In neolithic China the first crop was millet, to be followed by rice perhaps a long time after the cultivation of rice had begun in India; the first written Chinese mention of rice dates back to only 2800 B.C. The ancestral wild herds of the Middle East gave rise to that region's plentiful stock of domestic sheep, goats, and cattle, with the result that stock raising could be combined

with farming. A man's wealth might then be counted in kine. (Thus Job in his prosperity could boast of "seven thousand sheep, and three thousand camels, and five hundred yoke of oxen, and five hundred she asses," which made him "the greatest of all the men of the east.") Other areas remained poor in meat, and their cultures—those of China and Japan in particular—developed largely on a vegetarian basis. In the pre-Columbian civilizations of Central and South America, there were almost no domestic animals for meat, milk, wool, or burden (the Andean llama and alpaca coming closest in usefulness), but there was extremely varied domestication of plants: in addition to bringing corn to a high state of cultivation, the Indians raised the indigenous potato, numerous forms of beans, gourds, and squashes, and such other produce unknown in the Old World as the tomato, the peanut, the green pepper, chocolate, vanilla, chili, the guava, the avocado, and the pineapple. Indeed, as one leading scholar, Richard S. MacNeish, writes, by the time their European conquerors arrived in the sixteenth century A.D., Indians "had made agricultural advances far beyond those of the Old World."

Ultimately the New World's cornucopia of vegetables and fruits was to be brought to Europe to augment the diet of the Old World, one of the most notable contributions being the potato, which became the staple of the German and the Irish diets. At the same time, Europe was to introduce into the Americas its cattle and sheep, thereby providing (along with the horse) entirely new

15

bases for American existence. Yet this exchange, while particularly dramatic, was only one peak of a process of food migration and development that had been going on since neolithic times. Every food plant important to man was not only growing in that early era, but many were already spreading far from their places of origin, undergoing important genetic changes as they took root in new soils and climates.

Not only were wheat, barley, and rice on the move. A species of broad bean

Assurbanipal partying with his Assyrian queen

was spreading from western Asia over much of Europe and was used in Bronze Age Troy, Egypt, and even Spain. The lentil, possibly native to lands near the Himalayas, was known to Assyrians and early Egyptians and was brought to the neolithic Balkans and southern Germany by Danubian peoples. Cabbage, which may have originated in the Mediterranean area, appears to have been raised by Bronze Age lake dwellers beside Lake Zurich. A form of spinach, perhaps related to the types in distant Turkistan and Afghanistan, was consumed in central Europe at about the same time. The peach spread from Persia; the plum perhaps from Russia or the Balkans. The Roman gastronome Lucullus is reported to have brought back the cherry tree from the Black Sea; meanwhile, the apple tree had long been flourishing north of the Alps, while the vine sacred to Dionysus had been transplanted from Asia Minor to lands as remote as Punjab and Kashmir.

The history of rising civilization is intertwined from the start with man's far-ranging pursuit of food and the usages, rituals, and pleasures he has derived from it. At the outset it might be remarked that man is omnivorous. He is also voracious. At the same time he tends to be ceremonious about eating. The story of his relationship to food is therefore complex. Other animals are highly selective in their diets, some being only red-meat eaters, others only plant eaters, still others partial to insects or spawn of the sea. But man—barring occasional food laws and taboos—will and does ingest almost every edible substance that nature provides. Included on man's menu are blubber of seal (among the Eskimos), sheep's eyes (an Arab specialty), frogs' legs (among the French), larks' tongues (favored by the Elizabethans), hippopotami (particularly in Uganda), water lilies (among the Chinese), animals' intestines cooked into a pudding with gruel (enjoyed by ancient Greeks), the organs of sheep mixed with suet, onions, and oatmeal (the Scotsmen's "haggis"), and domestic cats stewed in sherry (a favorite among the Basque workmen).

The intensity of man's quest for food has left its mark upon the entire globe, which he has scoured and often despoiled in the pursuit. In northwestern China, vast areas of the once-rich "yellow earth" that supported an advanced Bronze Age culture and gave rise to Chinese civilization have long since been eroded and reduced to rubble and wind-blown loess—the result of a process of overuse that may have begun some four thousand years ago. Ancient Sumerian tablets tell that the lords of Lagash garnered for their tables, and for those of their gods, such Mesopotamian bounty as goats, sheep, oxen, doves, chickens, ducks, fish, figs, dates, cucumbers, butter, oil, and grain; but the country around ruined Lagash today is largely barren wasteland. Only broken monuments survive in sandy Libya to testify that here once lay the most ample granary of imperial Rome, despoiled by human locusts.

Wars have been fought and whole subcontinents won not only for the sake of more meat or fish or grain, but for the very spices and condiments with which to preserve and flavor them. The Apocrypha of the Old Testament speaks of salt as "basic to all the needs of man's life." It had become an essential from the time man learned to cook and to try to preserve his foods, and it was accessible to many early peoples in the form of deposits such as those of Syrian oases, Dead Sea shores, Nile delta lakes, and Alpine outcrops. Early Iron Age men cut into the salt-bearing strata around Hallstatt high in the Austrian mountains; and the Roman historian Strabo writes that the salt mines of Spain's Sierra Nevada were being worked more than five centuries before Christ. But

the Western world's urge for more and finer spices helped set in motion adventures that were ultimately to encircle the globe. Saffron and myrrh could be had from Mesopotamia; ginger was sought from Arabia; the quest for pepper and cloves, nutmeg and cinnamon, led—once Arab and Ottoman interference with the trade had been broken—to the opening and colonizing of the Far East. The hunt for new fisheries in the Atlantic, particularly after the Hansa seaports had monopolized North Sea and Baltic grounds

A hurried meal at an Assyrian army kitchen

in the fourteenth century, had much to do with the exploration of the New World; the search for a Northwest Passage undoubtedly was bent as much on spices as it was on the rumored gold and rubies of Cathay.

At the same time, while lusting for his food, man has revered its sources. From the start he has seen it not only as the result of his hunt or toil, but as a gift bestowed (and sometimes withheld) by powers greater than himself. Man's gratitude to his gods for the fruits of the earth has taken many forms. The Indians of southwestern Yucatán,

Gold ewer from Mesopotamia

where maize ("Indian corn") had been developed from a wild pod-enclosed kernel into a cereal grain, demonstrated this humility well. Anthropologists Robert Redfield and Warner Lloyd have written of their agriculture:

"It is not simply a way of securing food. It is also a way of worshipping the gods. Before a man plants, he builds an altar in the field and prays there. He must not speak boisterously in the cornfield; it is a sort of temple. The cornfield is planted as an incident in a perpetual sacred contract between supernatural beings and man. By this agreement, the supernatural yield part of what is theirs—the riches of the natural environment, to man."

In other cultures the supernatural donors not only had to be propitiated but also fed—sometimes, as among the Aztecs, with human sacrifice, although usually an animal would do. Herodotus relates that among the Egyptians a bull was ceremonially slaughtered after libations of wine and invocations to the gods; it then was disemboweled, stuffed with bread, honey, raisins, figs, frankincense, myrrh, and finally was burned. The men who offered the sacrifice preserved a fast until the ceremony was completed, after which they dined on what was left of the carcass.

Among its basic beliefs, the ancient world abounds in stories of beneficent earth and fertility spirits, many of whom tend to disappear with the death of winter and are resurrected with the first shoots of spring. A generic myth is that of a primordial earth mother or grain goddess who has a child god or goddess of vegetation who comes and goes with the seasons. Innumerable changes were rung on this theme. In Egypt the deity Osiris, broadly the god of death and resurrection, but also the god of grain, vanishes with the Nile's annual decline, to be mourned by his consort Isis until the river rises once again, renewed by her tears. An old pyramid inscription speaks of him causing "the fields to flourish with golden corn" even though his handsome form remains in the realm of the dead.

The Greek Persephone, daughter of Demeter, the earth goddess who first bestowed grain to mankind, is doomed through her abduction by Hades to spend the fallow months of each year in the underworld, until the earth's reawakening restores her to her fields and hills. The Eastern civilizations cast their players similarly: Adonis, coupled in ancient Syrian cult with Astarte, and Attis joined Cybele in Phrygian mythology, to revive as a vegetation spirit with the vernal equinox. Dionysus, a god very likely of Thracian origin, whose worship entered Greece in connection with fertility rites and mystery cults, is the most famous of all the fruit-bringing deities as the provider of wine and the

Belshazzar

When Belshazzar gave a dinner party, nothing was too much trouble. The guest list was enormous—the "four hundred" then numbered many times over when all the warriors and priests essential to maintenance of domestic tranquillity were invited. The table service to accommodate the crowd could have bought a small kingdom. The din of laughter and music was such that a whole city might collapse unnoticed around the revelers. And that, according to Daniel's account in the Bible, is precisely what happened. As "Belshazzar the king made a great feast to a thousand of his lords and drank wine before the thousand," Darius and the Persian armies slipped into the capital and promptly ended Babylonian supremacy in Mesopotamia. One can imagine the luxury of the evening—the lords were seated on high chairs, their feet off the floor as was the custom, at rows of long tables ranged in the palace courtyard. The sweet perfume of blossoming fruit trees filtered down from the Hanging Gardens nearby, to join with the wailing of reed flutes, the clashing of cymbals, the handclapping of dancing maidens, in a farrago of sensual delights. Eunuchs served dark red wines poetically labeled "Divine Liquid" and "Unguent of the Heart," brought from the palace of Nabonidus, Belshazzar's father, or from the far-off vineyards of Assyria. A heady brew of barley and a wine of date palms stiffened with honey were also offered, and at a signal from the king, the meal began in earnest. As a first course, they might have sampled a salted river perch garnished with locusts and seasoned with ginger and coriander, followed by roasted ducks and geese from royal farms, sauced with mint and mustard. A profusion of vegetables—turnips, leeks, carrots, and onions—and a salad of cress, lettuce, and endive were also brought round. So it must have gone until the profligate host, over a dessert of honeyed barley cakes, glanced up and saw a hand write upon the wall, "God hath numbered thy kingdom and finished it. . . . Thou are weighed in the balances, and are found wanting. Thy kingdom is divided, and given to the Medes and Persians." Belshazzar's life was ended, and with it a thousand years of sophistication, not only in the art of cooking but in man's ability to draw sustenance from a baked and parched land.

patron of its joyous, sometimes frenzied, festivals; he too is a seasonal god, doomed to die each autumn, when the vine must be cut back to bare stock after the harvest of the grapes. In his honor the Greeks erected numerous theaters where festivals were celebrated. The Athenians began with the *Oschophoria*, or vintage rites of October, followed in December with the *Rural Dionysia;* made sacrifices at the January *Lenaea*, or feast of the wine vats; observed a giddy three-day *Anthesteria* in February when the casks were opened; and with the com-

Joseph distributing grain to his brethren

ing of spring in March, held their splendid *Great Dionysia*, with its processions and the performance of new tragedies and comedies.

From Sumer of the third millennium before Christ, a frieze has survived that depicts priests milking, straining, possibly making butter, at a sacred dairy farm of the Sumerian mother goddess Ninhursaga. The first Mesopotamian farmers also built shrines that included granaries for the storing of produce (some of it set aside as offerings to the gods), the valuable agricultural surplus that would serve to sustain the people

until their next harvest. Thus, the service of food and that of its divinities have gone hand in hand.

The Old Testament from the outset describes the Israelites as a people profoundly concerned with both, and with all the forms, laws, feasts, and restraints that should govern them. In Leviticus, Moses consecrates Aaron and his sons to the Lord and oversees the ritual consumption of the sacrificial calf and ram; there follows his pronouncement of those prohibitions against the use of "unclean" foods (particularly swine, animal blood, along with certain fish and birds) that have governed Jewish dietary laws ever since. Yet the well-provided table also offers great pleasure: we read of the Canaanites who at harvest "went out into the field and gathered their vineyards, and trode the grapes and made merry, and went into the house of their god, and did eat and drink." Moses commands the children of Israel to keep three great feasts a year, among them that of the Tabernacles, with the produce of threshing floor and wine press, in memory of the years spent wandering through the desert in search of the Promised Land: "Seven days shalt thou keep a solemn feast unto the Lord thy God . . . because the Lord thy God shall bless thee in all thine increase, and in all the works of thine hands, therefore thou shalt surely rejoice."

Food and food taboo, like feast and abstinence, have also been long interlinked. Many ancient kings and priests were required to limit their flesh diet to a few meats and to abstain from pork and goat in particular, perhaps on hygienic grounds. But there were other foods, especially the mushroom, on which they had a monopoly, deeming such delights too good for the common man. The Greek historian Herodotus describes a diet for Egyptian priests, which consisted of "bread made for them out of the sacred grain, and a plentiful daily supply of goose-meat and beef, with wine in addition. Fish they are forbidden to touch; and as for beans, they cannot even bear to look at them, because they imagine they are unclean (in point of fact the Egyptians never sow beans, and even if any happen to grow wild, they will not eat them, either raw or boiled)."

By contrast, the heroes of Homer are almost always feasting when not fighting or sulking. The *Iliad* describes a banquet given by the King of Lydia that lasted nine days and nights. We are told, too, that worshipers of the grain and fruit spirits Cybele and Attis were permitted the upper, "ascending," parts of vegetables but not the seeds, or "de-

Demeter blessing man and his harvest

scending" roots, at their festivals, while they could eat some meat—though not pork or fish. The art of making dough rise by the use of a yeast or other fermenting substance was known all over the Middle East by about 1500 B.C., but among the Israelites it became and remained the subject of religious restrictions under which the use of leaven was wholly forbidden during the Feast of the Passover and for most offerings at the altar—fermentation being to them a symbol of corruption. Jesus declared, "Beware of the leaven of the Pharisees," and Saint Paul urged the Corinthians, "Let us keep the feast . . . with the unleavened bread of sincerity and truth." The Roman *flamen Dialis*—the high priest who was regarded as the living embodiment of the chief god Jupiter—could eat neither leavened bread nor wheaten flour nor raw meat.

In India of the early Brahman period described in the *Rig-Veda* some fourteen hundred years before Christ, a pastoral society existed that counted its wealth in cattle and enjoyed nothing more than a great feast of beef. Yet later Hindu doctrines led to the prohibition of flesh food on the basis of ideas of transmigration. All animals might embody human or divine spirits; the cow, for example, was recognized as a direct descendant of Kamadhenu, a sacred spirit with the face of a beautiful woman. As a consequence, its milk was highly valued and its life protected. Dairy foods were, in fact, important in the diets of a large part of the ancient world—introduced by the Aryan Indians whose migrations in search of grazing lands for their herds took them westward. And because milk

21

soured very quickly in warm climates, butter and cheese were probably the most common forms in which dairy products were eaten. Agitated in a simple churn or carried in bags made of animal stomachs where the natural enzymes that cause milk to clot could work, the transformation was easily accomplished. Man thus discovered how to make dairy foods that stored better than milk and had a high nutritive value.

The people of China, on the other hand, have shown a traditional distaste for dairy products and particularly for cheese, apparently thought unclean. Unlike the Aryans, the agricultural Chinese could not support herds of milk cattle, while their long-standing foes, the nomadic herders of the steppes to the west of them, fed on milk and cheese. It has been thought by one authority that the Chinese disaffection for dairy products distantly reflects this ancient enmity. On a quite different level of taboo—"homeopathic," anthropologists call it —we learn of the avoidance of pork by Carib Indians for fear of acquiring "pigs' eyes," and of tortoises for fear of becoming as clumsy as they.

But while certain foods have been avoided in one or another place for reasons varying with time and culture, other foods have enjoyed special and joyous esteem wherever found. In the Near East and eastern Mediterranean area, a particular affection was bestowed on native honey and the olive, and above all, on the product of the vine.

Honey, ancient man's first and basic sweetener, was a gift of innumerable bees buzzing over flowering slopes long before man's first attempts at agriculture, and very early it acquired a special importance in his mind. Mesopotamian folklore saw it as a magical substance, with medicinal or purifying powers: gods drinking it were made immortal and immune to illness. Babylonians and Assyrians fermented it for the mead of their libations when they dedicated new shrines. The Promised Land of the Israelites was described as one "flowing with milk and honey." Dionysus the wine god is said to have found the streams of Mount Parnassus running with honey when he established himself there. In practice, mead-making may have arisen even earlier than neolithic times, and in Egypt honey was fermented with the juice of dates to produce a syrup of high alcoholic content. When mixed with flour and oil, it also produced the honey cake, an ambrosial treat offered to the gods of ancient Mesopotamia, and still a favorite sweetmeat of the Near East. The Romans are described as having consumed amounts of honey "out of snow-white jars" in observance of their New Year.

The evergreen olive tree, possibly native to southwestern Asia and cultivated in the Near East and eastern Mediterranean since the Neolithic Age—five

Sumerian priests at work in the temple creamery

Tributes of butter for the Persian Xerxes

thousand years ago or earlier—was also surrounded by a special aura. From time immemorial it was associated with ideas of peace and reward. Noah's ark brought back an olive branch from Mount Ararat, and the city of Athens received its name from Athena, who won a contest among the gods for the honor of naming the city by striking the ground and bringing forth the olive tree as the most valuable gift to man. Its fruit certainly was unique in value: thriving on lean and sandy soil, it yielded almost all the oil used in antiquity, for cooking, lighting, and cleansing; and the advancing diet as well as economy of the Mediterranean would have been inconceivable without it.

That particularly beloved growth, the grape-producing vine plant (*Vitis vinifera*), may have been cultivated before 4000 B.C. (or even, it has been suggested, well before 6000 B.C.) by tribesmen in Transcaucasia, to which it was indigenous. Either date takes us back to the very early days of agriculture, and testifies to man's ancestral predisposition toward alcoholic drinks. Fermenta-

tion of grain had already produced beer, probably no later than the production of bread itself, if not before. In Mesopotamia, the Oxford *History of Technology* estimates, at one time about 40 per cent of cereal production was for brewing. Fermented milk drinks, such as the *koumiss* of Asian plainsmen, probably followed in time the development of fermented honey and date juices. The South American Indians were to have their *paiwari*, converted from manioc, or cassava; the Aztecs, their *pulque*. But no crop was attended by more ritual and care than the grape and its yield. It was known in prehistoric Mesopotamia and was brought to Egypt before 3000 B.C.; a Sumerian record of 2400 B.C. describes a temple garden planted "like a mountain with vines." In Egypt irrigated vineyards produced as many as half a dozen varieties of grapes from white to deep red, and individual wines were named by origin and graded by inspectors. In Palestine cultivation of the grape was exceeded only by that of the olive and the fig. The Assyrian king Assurbanipal interested himself enough to make a wine list of the best growths.

Ancient mythology, poetry, and symbolism invest the fruit of this scraggly vine with vast generative and regenerative powers, in which the physical is coupled with the metaphysical. The product could be misused—or overused, as Noah, the Bible's first vineyardist, discovered to his grief. One day the forgiveness of God was to be pictured by the image of a flourishing vine. On a temporal level, meanwhile, the spreading use of wine did much to raise the standard of pleasure and taste at the tables of many Mediterranean peoples, even when it was mixed with honey, resin, or other substances that would make it almost unpalatable today.

Even by the time of ancient Sumer and Babylonia, there were ample agricultural resources and traditions of food and table. An Assyrian herbal of about the eighth century B.C. discusses some 250 plants both as to their dietetic and medicinal values. It speaks of lettuce as having "a narcotic principle"; of garlic as good "to chew and fumigate"; of leeks as having some value "against gray hairs"; of the cherry (*karšu*, or *cerasus* as it was to become in Latin) as having "a pleasant fragrance." The energy of Babylonians and Assyrians in irrigating and diking their lands greatly increased their yield. Herodotus remarks that "as a grain-bearing country Assyria is the richest in the world. . . . As for millet and sesame, I will not say to what an astonishing size they grow, though I know well enough . . . people who have not been to Babylonia have refused to believe even what I have said already about their fertility." Their diet ranged over a wide variety of cereals and fruits, some meat and river fish. From their resources and love of feasting one might construct a banquet menu somewhat as follows:

Garlic in Sour Cream
Barley Soup
Tigris Salmon
Roast Pig or Lamb
Goat Cheese
Honey Cakes
Dates and Pomegranates

But it remained for the Egyptians, blessed by the unique phenomenon of

Hieroglyphic seal motifs for Egyptian wine jars

the Nile floods that annually renewed their lands with fertile topsoil and enriched their vast delta in particular, to convert nature's food gifts into a cuisine. This astonishing people, as inventive as they were self-indulgent, made the most of everything edible within reach. From early, or Old Kingdom, times, they possessed a vigorous African strain of longhorn cattle; later they imported other strains from Asia. They grain-fed their steers to produce a good rib of beef, and force-fed their fowl to produce plump roasting birds, along with the makings of something resembling a *pâté de foie gras*. They relished pigeon, quail, and duck, and dined also on watermelon, artichokes, cucumber, lettuce, endives, leeks, radishes, beans, peas, dates, figs, apples, apricots, and cheese. An inscription of the Twentieth Dynasty mentions thirty different forms of breads and cakes in use. Another cites forty-eight varieties of baked meats and twenty-four of drinks. The basis of such amazing gastronomic totals remains obscure; evidently fine points of difference in preparation were being taken into account. In drink there appears to have been almost boundless choice: there were many grades of wines, along with five different types of beers—some of a strength equal to that of wine—along

The Ageless Olive

"*I*t is easier," the Talmud says, "to raise a legion of olive trees in Galilee than to bring up one child in the land of Israel." It probably was, for herein lay the secret of the olive's success in the harsh, arid lands of the ancient world—it flourished with a minimum of care where less hardy fruit trees would wither and die. The roots of the olive tree go far back in history and lie deep in the stony soil of Asia Minor. According to the Bible, the Hebrews found the olive growing wild in the land of Canaan, and there is evidence that the tree was first cultivated in neolithic Crete. Early records reveal that the Minoans carried on a prosperous trade in olive oil with Phoenicia and Egypt. By then the olive had become to the Mediterranean world what butter is to northern Europe today—the basis of all cooking. No other fruit was as versatile as the olive. In Palestine, where every kitchen was equipped with a press for extracting oil, the olive provided food and lamp fuel as well as cooking oil. Even the hard wood of the tree was of great value. All that was needed to make the olive orchard grow was patience and time. Ten years were required to produce the first harvest—thirty years to produce the best. The Greeks, who anointed not only their salads with olive oil but also their bodies, arrived at a mythical explanation for the tree, as they did for so many other wonders of their world. It was a gift from Athena, they said; and they promptly installed a sacred olive tree at the Acropolis to honor the occasion. It was nearly as much a sacrilege as an economic disaster when, during the Peloponnesian War, the Spartans destroyed the olive groves in Attica. The Greeks worshiped

the olive, but the Romans exploited it. In Cato's day, the average profit from an olive plantation was 6 per cent of the capital invested. In Spain and Portugal olive oil has been an important export since the time the Phoenicians introduced the tree there, as early as 1700 B.C. Unlike the world around it, the olive and its cultivation has remained unchanged throughout history. In the words of Lawrence Durrell: "The whole Mediterranean . . . the wine, the ideas . . . seems to ride in the sour pungent taste of those black olives. . . . A taste older than meat, older than wine. A taste as old as cold water."

with palm wine, date wine, a fermented pomegranate drink imported from Palestine and resembling hard cider, and many innocuous fruit juices.

The Egyptian feast, in length and elaborateness, became somewhat overwhelming. Garlands of lotus blossoms or other foliage were draped around the wine jars to keep away the flies. As course followed sumptuous course, dancing girls, harpists, and amorous singers moved among the guests, even at banquets supposedly in tribute to the dead. A typical aristocratic tomb, that of the architect Kha, a favorite of the Kings Amenhotep II and III, shows on its painted walls an array of provisions for the repose of his soul that includes butter, meat, oil, wine, milk, dates, and raisins, along with a complete set of kitchen utensils. Yet by the Eighteenth Dynasty—midway in ancient Egypt's history—celebration had reached a point where guests themselves consumed much of the funerary tribute and, moreover, drank too much. "Give me eighteen cups of wine, behold I should love drunkenness," reads an inscription attributed to a Seventeenth Dynasty Egyptian lady of position.

Sweet are the grapes of Horus,
Sweeter the song-filled night.
The lips of thy beloved
Are washed with honey.

So ran an old Egyptian chant, to the accompaniment of dinner instruments imported from the East. Rome in its time was to outdo Egypt in the amplitude and elegance of its table, in scents and revelry; and a later Western world was to exceed them all in the sheer scope of consumption. Neither a Pharaoh nor a Caesar could match the grandeur of King Edward I of England, who in 1274 was to order his sheriffs to provide 278 bacon hogs, 450 porkers, 440 fat oxen, 430 sheep, and 22,600 hens and capons for his coronation feast. Nor was Nefertiti the equal of Catherine de' Medici, the heiress who arrived in France in 1533 with her Florentine chefs to be married to the future King Henry II. She entertained in 1549 with a dinner for fifty that included 30 peacocks, 33 pheasants, 21 swans, 90 cranes, 66 guinea fowl, 30 capons, 90 pullets, 99 quail, in addition to a massive supply of hares, rabbits, and pigs. Neither the Pharaoh's guests nor those of King Edward or Catherine needed anything like the amount of food they ate festally, but ancestral memories of far hunts, lean years, and slender pickings may have lingered in their minds. Man's fare from the dawn of time has been determined not only by his sources of supply but by the means he has found to convert raw nature. The great fire, the ample feast, the noble libation, the glittering table, are all symbols of what he sees as his advancement. As late as 1939, in a part of the world that had supposedly overcome both scarcity and the temptations of gluttony, the President of the French Republic and Madame Lebrun were to be regaled during a state visit to the Court of St. James's by a three-day round of luncheons and dinners that overwhelmed them with dozens of courses (from *consommé quenelles aux trois couleurs* to *bombe glacée Victoria*) accompanied by twenty-one wines, not to mention after-dinner port and punch.

FOOD
OF
THE
PHARAOHS

Cakes, figs, and fowl for the goddess Isis—from a Nineteenth Dynasty relief

From sowing to reaping to the recording of the annual harvest on its way to government granaries.

The Staff of Life

While barbaric tribes of northern Europe were still subsisting on raw meat and wild plants, the Egyptians were enjoying no fewer than thirty varieties of breads and cakes. It was in the Nile valley that the oven was first invented and the process of leavening discovered. Housewife and royal baker alike daily performed (with full credit to their deities) the miracle of transforming soggy dough into fragrant, nourishing food. As staples in the Egyptian diet, bread—and the heady beer brewed by steeping spiced loaves in water

Bakers' tasks were well organized and highly specialized, beginning with the milling, left, and

the grain crops of the Nile valley were always under the watchful eye of the Pharaoh's lieutenants.

and allowing the broth to ferment—had their monetary value as well. The workers who built the pyramid of Cheops were paid a daily wage of three loaves and two jugs of beer, both probably consumed upon receipt. Taxes and tributes to officials rendered in loaves of bread were not so quickly digested. One can only guess how stale and unpalatable the nine hundred wheat loaves and the thirty-six thousand flat loaves distributed annually to one such officer must have been by the time they reached the tables of his dependents.

A Hebrew bread stamp

moving by gradual stages to the kneading board, the ovens, and, finally, the brewing vats, right.

The King's Pleasure

This duck-hunting scene, a panel taken from a gilt shrine dedicated to Tutankhamen and his queen, shows that the comforts of the home and table had not succeeded in completely destroying the royal zest for the more strenuous pursuits of the outdoors. In the Nile valley, the plains and marshes abounded with a great variety of wild game and fowl, and while hunting had become by then more a matter of sport than of sheer survival, it provided an important part of ancient man's diet.

Oasis in the Sun

32   *A garden, c. 1400 B.C., from a Theban wall painting*

Trained baboons gathering figs

Force-feeding a goose

The scented walks and shady groves that graced most private gardens in ancient Egypt must have been a source of inspiration to poet and cook alike, for it was there in their own back yards, a few steps from the kitchen, that fruits, vegetables, fish, and fowl—almost every food but red meat and cereals—were raised. In the garden at left, orchards of date palms, pomegranates, and vineyards grow along the borders; plots of vegetables and herbs grow within. Fish, as well as lotus, cress, and other water greens, share the pond which doubled as a reservoir for a complex irrigation system.

Beekeeper and hive

Watering and weeding onions

Slaves harvesting okra from trellises

Fruit
of
The Vine

Temperance was not a virtue in Egypt.
It was said of the Luxor vineyards that
production was "more plentiful than the
water of the Nile at its highest mark";
and there were few temple gardens or
private estates where scenes of the harvest and the trampling of the grapes—
often to music (opposite)—did not oc-
cur. Wines were stored in earthen jars
which were bedded on large pallets.
Each jar was carefully labeled by vintage.
Even dates were pressed and mixed with
honey to obtain a strong, syrupy drink.
Still, consumption outran supply, and
huge quantities of potent beer (sucked
through reeds by visiting Syrians above)
were needed to slake the national thirst.

The Brimming Cup

A good wine deserves better than an earthen cup, and throughout the ancient world, vessels were fashioned to honor the grape as well as the occasion. Most were made from silver or gold, but as early as 1600 B.C., the Egyptians had learned to make glass from quartz sand, tinting it with copper or iron. Tutankhamen drank from the calcite goblet shaped like a lotus flower, above.

Dainty draughts and elixirs for an Eighteenth Dynasty queen of Egypt might have filled the blue, threaded glass vase, right. At lustier celebrations in the royal banquet halls of ancient Persia and Assyria, ringing toasts were likely raised in sturdier vessels: the griffin-handled rhyton of silver and copper above, and the lion-headed cup below.

37

A Matter of Tastes

The Egyptians either feasted or nibbled; there was no middle ground. Breakfast was an eat-as-you-go affair, a buffet of bread and meat washed down with a beer chaser. But a feast, whether it was the simple family celebration below or the boisterous, three-day marathon with dancing topless waitresses opposite, tested the endurance of everyone involved—cooks, servants, and guests alike.

Two brace of thrushes and a bowl of eggs, from a Pompeian fresco

WHEN
EATING
BECAME
DINING

The chronicle of dining in classical antiquity begins with the robust aroma of Homeric oxen roasted on the outdoor spit and culminates in the perfumes and perversities of the banquets of Nero and of such even more outrageous Roman emperors as Domitian and Elagabalus. It embraces almost a thousand years of changing mores as well as sustenance. But along the way, from simplicity to decadence, the men of Greece and then of Rome raised the art of the table to the highest level of cultivation to be known in the West until that of eighteenth-century France. The West retains their legacy.

The primeval Homeric dinner, to be sure, did not always consist of red meat. Though the heroes preferred it, and the ancient commentator Eubulus rhetorically asks: "I pray you, where in Homer is the chief Who e'er eat fish, or anything but beef?" Homer himself tells of many occasions on which their fare was only a rudimentary mess of pottage. Such were the dishes of grated cheese and white barley mixed with wine prepared for Nestor by his captured Trojan girl slave; the comparable dish sweetened with honey and soporifics which Circe served to stupefy Odysseus and his sailors; and "the great pudding, stuffed with fat and blood," offered to the returning hero by King Antinous. Along with the feasting, the Homeric dinner was also a sociable affair. Thus when Odysseus is within a short sail of Ithaca after his ten years' wanderings he remarks, looking ahead to what may greet him, "There is no greater fulfilment of delight than when joy possesses a whole people, and banqueters in the halls listen to a minstrel as they sit in order due, and by them tables are laden with bread and meat, and the cup-bearer draws wine from the bowl and bears it round and pours it into the cups."

From that world of blood puddings, bards, and meals of friendship, a vast distance and several centuries take us to the most notorious table in all Rome —that of the boy emperor Elagabalus in the third century A.D. This painted wastrel liked to shower his guests with aromatic blossoms (a few unfortunate guests are said to have smothered) while they savored tongues of peacocks and nightingales and to arrange banquets according to a color sequence (one evening everything from the plates to the food itself was green, the next evening iridescent, the third blue). Once the brains of six hundred ostriches were provided as a delicacy. The chronicle known as the *Historia Augusta* relates that, on occasion, he would serve "twenty-two courses of extraordinary viands, and between each course he and

his guests would bathe and dally with women." After three rollicking years Elagabalus was murdered in a latrine and thrown into the Tiber.

Between these extremes lies a long evolution of tastes in food, drink, and manners of the table; and both early Greek and later Roman literature tell us much of a civilization evidently greatly taken up with them. One of the earliest of Greek lyric poets, Anacreon of sixth-century Asia Minor, wrote verses in praise of wine:

Water bring and bring me wine,
Bring the wreaths where flowers entwine;
Hasten, lad; our fists we try,
Matched together, Love and I.

Come, a wassail I would keep,
Drinking pledges flagon-deep.
Pour me wine, five measures, lad;
Measures ten of water add;
So good manners shall remain
In your Bacchant, foxed again.

Drink, good fellows, drink no more
With a clutter and uproar;
Thus, when Scythians hold a bout,
Wine goes in and tongues let out.
Gentlemen, observe a mean,
Tippling with good songs between.

Plato's famous dialogue, the *Symposium*, deals with a banquet at the house of the poet Agathon, made brilliant by the presence of a duly washed and brushed Socrates, and made memorable by the clamorous arrival of an inebriated Alcibiades who enters shouting, "Hail friends. . . . Will you have a very drunken man as companion to your revels?" Refusing the goblet of wine offered, he orders a wine cooler, "a vessel holding more than two quarts," which he promptly fills, empties, and refills. The intruder then launches into a diatribe against Socrates saying, "What follows I could hardly tell you if I were sober," excusing his candor with the Greek equivalent of *in vino veritas*. After the arrival of a second band of revelers, the drinking gets out of hand, and if Socrates' response was a discourse extolling the virtues of sobriety, not even

Faience cup from Cyprus

Aristodemus was in any condition to hear him. Upon awakening, Aristodemus notes, "There remained only Socrates, Aristophanes, and Agathon, who were drinking out of a large goblet which they passed around, and Socrates was discoursing to them."

Socrates' other disciple, Xenophon, in his own *Symposium*, provides a fanciful account of an even livelier banquet. When one of the guests orders an onion for his drink, his neighbor comments, "Niceratus is intent on going home smelling of onions to make his wife believe that no one would have even conceived the thought of kissing him." The master, who called the feast a perfect dinner, obliges with a song, after which

a clown, a girl acrobat, a citharist, and a flute player entertain. The banquet ends with a risqué skit about the wedding of Bacchus, the Roman Dionysus.

Plato himself, though disdainful of the pleasures of the table, pauses in another of his dialogues to mention his favorite food suppliers and advisers: Thearion the pastry cook, Mithaecus, who wrote a treatise on Sicilian cooking, and Saramus the wine dealer. The poet Aeschylus, usually concerned with bleak destiny, gives away a touch of his own humanity when he says:

But I will place this carefully fed pig
Within the crackling oven; and, I pray,
What nicer dish can e'er be given to man?

The loosening of restraints at a vinous spring festival is the subject of *The Frogs*, a sardonic tale by Aristophanes. Ever the critic of urbane Athenian ways, in a later work he lingers more approvingly over a simple countryman's luncheon—three olives, two onions, a loaf of bread, and a small goatskin of wine.

The Roman Horace dwells in his odes on the prandial pleasures of his Sabine farm, his tastes in wine, and his occasional surrender to its heady effects:

. . . Welcome, the sweet delight
Of danger! Lord of Wine
Lead on! I follow garlanded with vine.

And in a satire he relates the precise order of dishes and seating at the banquet of one miserly Nasidienus that overwhelmed the guests, particularly when a canopy over the table collapsed. And, in case the guests might fail to appreciate the supreme efforts to which their host has gone, he all but numbs them with copious commentary on the geographic origins of the foods set before them and the time of day and phase of the moon when the ingredients of each dish were found.

Much later Macrobius, a philosopher of sorts and chronicler of manners, described a formal dinner for high priests of state given in Julius Caesar's time that began with oysters and other shellfish in several forms and went through game pies, fillets of wild boar, sows' udders, pigs' heads, and ragouts of hare and fowl. He also took pleasure in recalling that at a banquet of the emperor Septimius Severus a splendid sturgeon (a fish then found chiefly in the Rhone and the Po) was borne in by crowned attendants to the sound of flutes. Martial, author of epigrams, delighted in giving out brief gastronomic hints, such as a recipe for cooked eggs ("If a white liquid surround the saffron-colored yolks, let the sauce of Spanish mackerel season the eggs."), and grew so enamored of truffles that he wrote of them in the first person: "We truffles that burst through the nurturing soil with our soft heads are of earth's apples second to mushrooms."

But for sustained and intensive interest in the subject of food, nothing in literature can approach the ambitious compendium written by Athenaeus, an Egyptian Greek of the third century A.D., under the name *The Deipnosophists,* or "The Banquet of the Learned." This unique work, cast at the outset in the form of a Platonic dialogue, purports to record the knowledge displayed on a multitude of subjects at a several-day symposium comprising philosophers, grammarians, physicians, a prominent jurist, a poet, and a musician, most of them hailing from Hellenized and Romanized Egypt and Asia Minor. They discuss many matters of literature, law, music, and history, but it soon becomes apparent that their primary interest is the table, and for the greater part of the fifteen books of text that survive we are treated to a banquet of ancient gastronomic lore.

Some of the information is medicinal and at times cautionary. Of mushrooms: they "are good for the stomach and pass easily through the bowels, and are very nutritious." Of asparagus: "They are remedies for every kind of internal disorder." Of cabbage: "At Athens [it] used to be given to women who had just

Hoof-shaped mug depicting Greek farming

been delivered, as a sort of medicine." Of almonds: "There is nothing which is a greater provocative of drinking." Of carrots: "This vegetable is harsh, says Diphilus, but tolerably nutritious . . . it is indigestible, diuretic, and not without some influence in prompting men to amatory feelings." Of eggs, onions, et cetera: "One must set bounds to much eating, especially of such things as have anything glutinous or sticky about them; as, for instance, eggs, onions, calves' feet, snails . . . for they remain in the stomach a long time, and form a lump there, and check the natural moisture."

Much of the lore also falls into the category of helpful advice to the cook and marketer. Thus, of cabbage: "The finest and most delicious . . . is grown in Cyme; in Alexandria it is bitter; and the seed which is brought from Rhodes to Alexandria produces sweet cabbage for one year, after which time it degenerates again, from the nature of the soil." Of eggs: according to the food expert Heraclides of early Syracuse, "The best of all eggs are peacock's eggs; the next best are those of the fox-goose; and the third best are those of common poultry."

The speakers are particularly engrossed with sea food and its preparation, and they discourse at length on innumerable marine species, citing Aristotle for instance on the habitat and qualities of tuna and turning for practical guidance to the work of one Archestratus of Athens, a follower of Epicurus, who toward the end of the fourth century B.C. wrote a gastronomic tract under the title *The Luxurious Way of Living*. The fragments of this treatise that survive in *The Deipnosophists* include perhaps the first recipes set down in writing.

Thus Archestratus writes that "a boiled ray is good about midwinter. Eat it with cheese and assafoetida [a foul-smelling palm resin which was, unaccountably, favored as a condiment by the Romans]." When roasting a dogfish, strew it with cummin, be sparing of salt, and add nothing else but "some sea-green oil"; when boiling it, "add what fragrant herbs the garden gives," and be careful

of the heat of the fire: stir frequently, "lest the meat should catch, and spoil your dinner so, before you know it." And further:

*I counsel you always to boil a harp-fish
If he is white and full of firmish meat;
But if he's red and also no great size,
Then it were best, when you have prick'd him o'er
With a new sharpen'd knife, to roast him gently.
Sprinkle him then with oil and plenteous cheese,
For he does like to see men liberal,
And is himself intemperate.*

Such counsel, from so old a source, held the attention of Athenaeus and his learned table half a millennium after. The diners of course had ample experience of newer and more sophisticated cookery; thus one speaker tells of a whole pig being served one half roasted and the other half boiled ("[we] all marvelled at the cleverness of the cook") and moreover stuffed with such dainties as slices of sow's womb, the yolks of eggs, the entrails of birds with their ovaries, and fanciful seasonings. But while greatly respecting the genius of chefs, they sometimes wondered whether elaboration might not go too far. Again they looked to that older authority, Archestratus, who had stated with certitude, "Many are the ways and many the recipes for dressing hares; but this is the best of all, to place before a hungry set of guests a slice of roasted meat fresh from the spit, hot, season'd only with plain, simple salt. . . . All other ways are quite superfluous, such as when cooks pour a lot of sticky, clammy sauce upon it."

By the time the deipnosophists convened, the art of cookery in the Mediterranean world had progressed far beyond "sticky, clammy sauce." For detailed knowledge of its development, posterity is indebted to another author—a certain Apicius, believed to have been the writer of a compendium sometimes known as *De Re Coquinaria*, "The Art of Cooking."

Apicius' actual identity is uncertain; there were several Roman personalities by that name, one of them a rich courtier and epicure in the time of Augustus and Tiberius who wrote about food. Pliny called him *altissimus gurges*, or "sublime gullet," and it was said that when Apicius one day found that he had spent a hundred million sesterces of his fortune on food and had only ten million left with a prospect of starvation before him, he poisoned himself. This may well have been the Apicius who compiled what has come down as the Western world's oldest surviving cookbook.

More accurately, the recipes of Apicius comprise only a part of a fourth- or fifth-century-A.D. manuscript compiled by some anonymous editor from several Greco-Roman sources. *De Re Coquinaria* describes a culinary tradition based on the extraction and enhancement of flavors. It involved the basic art of preserving the best in meat, fish, and vegetables by cooking them in their own juices; of creating sauces to enrich these foods by the use of stock (or, as a modern chef would say, of making a court bouillon); of providing additives in the form of numerous spices, garnishes, and cooking wines. Thus the Romans developed a basic sauce called *garum*, or *liquamen*, from the entrails of fish cast into brine

and combined with condiments, water, wine, or vinegar. They boiled down wine or "must" for cooking purposes, creating *defrutum* and, when sweetened with honey, *mulsum*. These substances figure prominently in Apicius' recipes, which range from crayfish and mussels to venison, fried eggs, and a classic casserole of crane or duck with turnips, presented as follows:

"Wash and truss the bird and boil it in a large saucepan in water, salt, and dill, until half done. Cook the turnips so that they lose their pungency. Remove the duck from the pan, wash again, and put into another saucepan with oil, liquamen, and a bouquet of leek and coriander. Put over it one washed and finely chopped (uncooked) turnip, and braise. When it has been cooking for a while add *defrutum* to give it color. Then prepare the following sauce: pepper, cummin, coriander, assafoetida root, add vinegar, and some of the cooking-liquor; pour over the duck and bring to the boil. When it boils thicken with cornflour and add to the turnips. Sprinkle with pepper and serve."

But much of the pleasure of advanced cookery consisted in the game of intermixing flavors, textures, and even shapes with total disguise the goal. Apicius provides a recipe for a *"patina* [or mold] of anchovy without anchovy," in which other fish and jellyfish were used instead: "At table no one will know what he is eating." A leading comic dramatist of the Roman Republic, Plautus, mocked these trickster cooks as men "who serve you up whole pickled meadows in their patinae—men who make cows their messmates, who thrust herbs at you,

Lucullus

"*A*nd, indeed, Lucullus' life, like the Old Comedy, presents us at the commencement with acts of policy and war, at the end offering nothing but good eating and drinking, feastings and revellings, and mere play." History has all but forgotten the "acts" that earned Lucius Licinius Lucullus this grudging praise from Plutarch and the wherewithal to indulge his middle-aged appetites. As a general, Lucullus campaigned in Asia Minor, conquering the Persians and, more importantly, discovering the sophisticated cuisine of the East. Even then his strategy was aimed directly at the enemy's mid-section, stressing, as Plutarch observed, that "the seat of war [is] in the belly." The fabled Lucullan feasts that would forever link his name with high living began after his triumphal return to Rome; following a gigantic feed for the entire city, he gave up the public arena for the dining room. Tubero, the Stoic, possibly because he never made the guest list, was so scandalized by his extravagance that he called him, after the Persian potentate, "Xerxes

in a gown," but such political notables as Cato, Cicero, and Crassus were delighted to attend any banquet, large or small, that their friend might prepare. Leading poets, philosophers, and ranking foreign dignitaries also turned up regularly at the Lucullan table. At one such banquet, when the guests of honor protested their host's generosity, Lucullus replied self-indulgently, "Some of this, indeed my Grecian friends, is for your sakes, but more for that of Lucullus." According to Plutarch, even *en famille* this early gourmet demanded the best. Once when he was dining alone and was presented a simple supper, the general snapped at his cook, "What, did you not know, then, that to-day Lucullus dines with Lucullus?" He maintained several dining halls, from the sumptuous "Apollo," to more intimate chambers, and he had only to name the room to indicate to his chief steward how lavish the service should be. To keep his larder well stocked with delicacies befitting all occasions, he shopped the length and breadth of the Mediterranean world and kept wondrous gardens at his sprawling villa. Even the mighty Pompey, when he craved out-of-season or exotic fowl, was not above raiding the special fattening coops kept outside Rome by his former officer. When Lucullus died in 56 B.C., it was said in the senate that half of Rome suffered indigestion.

then proceed to season these herbs with other herbs." Later, the satirist Petronius remarks in praise of the ingenuity of his master chef, "he will make you a fish out of a sow's belly."

The chefs of Athens were never as artful nor as ambitious in the meals they prepared as were the Romans. The ten-hour banquet was unknown in Attica before the arrival of Alexander and the Macedonians sometime before 323 B.C. At this late period in Greek history, Attic dining customs resemble in extravagance those of the full-blown Empire. Witness the orgiastic feast once staged by the Macedonian conqueror, an alcoholic who enjoyed prancing about besotted and in costume. The party began with hors d'oeuvres of chickens, ducks, ring-doves, geese, hares, pigeons, turtledoves, partridges, and young goats. An intermission for entertainment by naked girl dancers was followed by a pig stuffed with "thrushes, ducks, warblers, peas purée poured over eggs, oysters and scallops. . . ." While the guests were digesting these entremets, a troupe of acrobats were brought in, some of whom "performed tumbling acts among swords, and blew fire from their mouths," so Athenaeus recounts. Then further rounds including skewered boars were served, and the drinking began in earnest, accompanied by more dancing girls decked out as nymphs and Nereids and staging erotic tableaus.

Obviously, the image of Greek simplicity contrasted with Roman self-indulgence is a gross oversimplification. For the two cultures, both setting forth from simple ways and diets, developed some strikingly similar customs of meals

and hospitality during their independent rises toward affluence. In the late stages of the Empire the Romans far surpassed their Greek mentors, becoming what the poet Vergil hoped they would be —*rerum dominos,* masters of the world. In fact, Rome was still a small and uncertain state beside the Tiber when a strong taste for luxury was first brought to southern Italy in the eighth century B.C. by the more sophisticated Greek colo-

Bronze pastry wheel from Gaul, c. 200 A.D.

nizers, many of them hailing from old cities in Asia Minor. Their settlement of Sybaris on the Adriatic coast became legendary for its pleasures, and one of the tyrants of Syracuse, Nysaeus by name, was notorious for his gluttony, drunkenness, and debauchery with boys and women alike.

Spartans, Athenians, and Romans all were very prone to look down on the self-indulgence of others. "The Attic race is quick and eloquent, and they eat little," wrote the Greek Eubulus; "but the Boeotians eat enormously." To "drink like a Scythian" was a term of obloquy in Athens. Anyone so foolish as to take his wine neat in Scythian fashion was, in the opinion of Herodotus, likely to go mad.

The Medes and Persians were viewed with particular disfavor. A typical story told was that of the Persian Cantibaris, who, whenever his jaws were weary with eating, had his slaves hold them open to pour more food into his mouth. It was also said that the Persians loved their wine so much that any important political decision that was made when their leaders were sober was reconsidered when they were drunk. Herodotus, at the climax of his history of the Persian Wars, relates that after the rout of Xerxes at Plataea the commander of the victorious Greeks, Pausanias of Sparta, entered a tent abandoned by one of Xerxes' Median officers to be astonished by the "gold and silver couches all beautifully draped, and gold and silver tables, and everything prepared for the feast with great magnificence." The Greek commander ordered that the feast be served to his officers, but ordered a simple Spartan meal to be served also, exclaiming as his men came to view the two boards, "Gentlemen, I asked you here in order to show you the folly of the Persians, who, living in this style, came to Greece to rob us of our poverty."

Republican Romans, for their part, held in contempt the ways of their neighbors to the north, the Etruscans, a race inordinately bent on the delights of table and sex. Surviving Etruscan figures on sarcophagi show their men to have been distinctly potbellied—indeed, the Roman nickname for an Etruscan was *obesus*. One Roman chronicler writes of their "unbridled luxury and indolence," adding with apparent envy that "twice a day they have tables sumptuously dressed and laid with everything that can contribute towards delicate living; they have coverings embroidered with flowers and are served wine in quantities of silver bowls." Another, Theopompus, writes that at the conclusion of Etruscan family parties of eating and drinking, servants bearing torches brought their masters female prostitutes, boys, or their own wives, and that multiple love-making went on in public.

On the side of virtue and restraint, there are equally impressive examples among the Greeks and Romans. Just as the Greeks had their Spartans, whose regimen included communal messes where the appetites of all male citizens were scrutinized, so there were Romans who prized nothing more highly than a virtuous and thrifty household. In the second century B.C., the Stoic philosopher Posidonius emphasized the frugality of meals as a particular quality of the Roman way of life before the state grew in size and wealth.

Sallust, who as one of Julius Caesar's tribunes must have shared in the new prosperity, thought the change came after the destruction of Carthage and Rome's other great adversaries. He added that the people were overcome by riches and leisure, and had become *dediti ventri* —slaves of their stomachs. Livy also emphasized that a love of luxury had entered Rome with Asiatic influences. No more vivid example of this trend exists than the emperor Claudius, a mighty drinker and feastgiver of the first century A.D. who often had as many as six hundred guests at his table and, according to Suetonius, rarely left it until utterly gorged and sozzled.

Yet not all late Roman emperors were excessive in their tastes either; the successor to Claudius and Nero, the middle-class Vespasian, was known for his frugal tastes at board, and Tacitus writes that it became the fashion during his rule for high society to emulate him.

Sumptuary laws were passed at various times to enforce moderation. The cost of a meal, the number of guests, the variety of dishes, were legislated—and were consistently ignored by the aristocracy. Cato the Censor ordered that an *eques* (knight) be deprived of the public horse that was his perquisite, if he were too corpulent to ride it. Leading the conservative faction, he warned constantly against the incursion of Greek manners as a menace to the moral fiber of the Republic; and the struggle between Cato and his archenemies, the influential philhellenic tribe of the Scipios, convulsed the state and contributed to the rise of military dictators and to the end of the Republic.

In contrast to their banquet fare, the daily subsistence of both the post-Homeric Greeks and the Romans was largely a diet of grain dishes made more palatable by honey and wine and, whenever possible, supplemented by pork. Cretans long before them had raised sheep, goats, and hogs, had hunted hare and deer, had fished for tuna, lobster, crab, and had grown apples, quinces, and pears. The Mycenaeans, as we know from the decipherment of their tablets, had cultivated figs, olives, peas, and had raised coriander, celery, cummin, fennel, and mint. Later Greece and Rome continued to enjoy an adequate supply of cereals, fruits, and vegetables, but the plentiful cattle on which Homer's heroes feasted had declined to scattered herds on the meagre, eroded, and overgrazed grasslands of Attica. Red meat had be-

come a luxury. The Spartans had their black broth, a stew of pork, barley, salt, and vinegar. The Athenians consumed barley kneaded into a sort of porridge with water—"noble cakes," Plato called them—and griddlecakes. Hog puddings and sweetened sausages were very popular in Athens; "the stuffed paunch of an ass" was a delicacy. The early Romans boiled barley and wheat into a paste.

Though Rome had no commercial bakeries before the second century B.C., Athenaeus reports that there were at one point as many as seventy-two kinds of bread in Greece, and we can assume that the Romans must have known how to prepare many of these at home. The Romans also had their *placenta*, a honey-sweetened cake resembling that of Near Eastern cookery, and a traditional fruit-cake was the *satura*, a mixture of barley mash, dried raisins, pine kernels, and pomegranate seeds laced with condiments and honeyed wine—a dish from whose name two interesting words derive. One is "satire," the Romans who invented and named this literary form looking upon it as a mixture or hodge-podge of many ingredients, sweet and sour; the other is "saturated."

The Greek peninsula—for the most part rugged and riverless, with its chains of mountains enclosing plains that lie sere during the long months of summer and autumn—was not hospitable to cultivation or cattle raising. Barely a fifth of it was (and is today) arable. The fisheries of the Aegean and eastern Mediterranean, too, were meagre, due to a lack of plankton in those transparent waters adequate to support large schools of fish. Many days, the small fishing boats returned to port with only a paltry catch of sardines, anchovies, squids, and octopi in their holds.

The Romans, however, were better favored, particularly as they expanded beyond their spare homeland in the Alban hills. They sought out the nearby plains of Etruria, finding the region "rich in [wheat], cattle and everything"—and it was from there, in the area between Fiesole and Arezzo, that the fine wheat came which was used as the basis of confectionery and what we know as pasta. Rome's greatest culinary advantage, as

Roman mosaic of a breadbasket

the state grew and prospered, lay in the very variety of the regions it incorporated and conquered, and in the efficient trade and transport network which fed back to the capital. There was game from the Laurentine forests, cheese from the herds of Tuscany, good wine from Campania (the best, that from Falernum); there were pickles and wine from Spain, pork from Gaul, apples and pears from Chios, lemons and pomegranates from Libya, plums from Damascus, apricots from Armenia, and peaches from Persia. And always important to the ancient world

was the oyster. To insure a constant supply, the Romans began seeding the salt ponds around Baia (Naples) about 100 B.C. Soon after, a richer supply of *ostreae* began coming in from faraway Britain, where the Roman invaders uncovered the great natural beds of Colchester and other estuaries of East Anglia. "Poor Britons," the historian Sallust remarked in 50 B.C., "there is some good in them after all—they produced an oyster."

Whatever the scarcity or abundance of foods, a remarkable similarity of customs of the table persisted between Greeks and Romans for many generations. Two meals a day, for instance, was the general rule, though some Romans did take a morning *jentaculum*—a piece of bread dipped in wine or eaten with honey or cheese or olives. A light meal (the *ariston* of the Athenians or the *prandium* of the Romans) consisting often of just a bowl of barley, perhaps a cut of cold meat, and a flask of wine, was eaten about midday and was frequently consumed standing up or *sine mensa*—without a set table, or cafeteria style. The main meal, the Greek *deipnon* or the Roman *cena*, took place in mid or late afternoon, preferably after exercise and a visit to the baths. (Nero was much criticized for sitting down to dinner as early as noon in his banquet halls "with fretted ceilings of ivory, whose panels could turn and shower down flowers and were fitted with pipes for sprinkling the guests with perfumes.") At dinner the practice among the gentry of both Greece and Rome was to recline on couches placed around the table. The couches were constructed with an incline at one end, so that the head of each diner rose

An Acquired Taste

*A*ll Gaul owes a huge debt to its ancient conquerors, for wine was most prob-ably introduced into France by the Greeks, who left great stacks of *amphorae* about Marseilles as evidence. The Romans, too, found Gaul a ready market for their wines. Diodorus of Sicily wrote, "[The Gauls] have a real passion for wine . . . and, their greed leading them to drinking heavily, they get so drunk that they either fall asleep or become wild. This is why so many [Italian] merchants, impelled by their habitual cupidity, profit from [them]." When the natives discovered that they could cultivate the vine locally and even sur-pass Rome's production, the senate passed laws inhibiting competition, re-stricting foreign viticulture to the estates of wealthy colonists. The law seems to have had little effect, and by the end of the first century A.D., the grape was widely cultivated in Gaul, Sicily, and Etruria, where the *bucchero* or drinking horn, below, was used. Indeed, cereal production was so badly neglected that the Emperor Domitian decreed, again without much success, that no new vine-yards should be planted in Italy and that half of those in the provinces should forthwith be uprooted and replaced by other crops. From contemporary writ-ers, we know that classical wines were developed for a taste very different from that of today. They were rich in sugar, strong in alcohol, and concentrated in taste, due largely to the custom of leaving the grapes on the vine for several

weeks after they had ripened—bringing about *la pourri-ture noble*, or "noble rot"—a practice still followed by the vintners of Sauternes. The wines were further adul-terated with herbs, saffron, anise, flower scents, and (according to one writer who took a dim view of the practice and compared the vintners to pharmacists) sometimes colored with smoke. The wines of Vienne, among the most prized of modern growths, were resin-ated in Martial's day (and were called *vinum picatum*)

as were those of Greece; and Pliny, whose oenological enthusiasms were second only to his interests as a naturalist, so admired the slow and careful processing of wines from the vineyards of the Ardèche region north of Avignon, that he studied the technique. He observed that after the vintagers had twisted the stem, "Some times they cut the entire branch and let it hang for a while, with the grapes still attached. Other farmers pick them when ripe, but before press-ing them, they spread them out to dry in the sun or else dry them on hot bricks."

above the level of the board; the diner rested on his left arm and reached for food and drink with his right.

The Greeks, eating with their fingers, wiped their hands on morsels of bread that were then tossed to the dogs beneath the table; it remained for the Romans, who dipped their fingers in bowls of perfumed water between courses, to introduce the custom of the napkin. Often the guest would bring his own, using it to carry home what tidbits he could not finish at the table.

In Athens wives and children dined apart from their husbands and sat on straight chairs, often in another room; in Rome women were eventually admitted to the men's dining chamber, perhaps as a result of the influence of the more sociable Etruscans, who always considered feminine companionship essential to a good dinner. In either instance, the privilege of the dining couch was a mark of social distinction, and the lower orders of freedmen and educated slaves were not normally admitted to it.

Meticulous rules of precedence as to seating at a formal dinner were developed, particularly in Rome. There the practice was to group the couches around three sides of a rectangular table, leaving the fourth side open for service. To insure the liveliness of the conversation, the table was customarily set for no fewer than three—the number of the Graces— nor more than nine—for the nine Muses; the place of honor was the right-hand couch opposite the empty side of the table. A *nomenclator*, or usher, announced the names of the guests, who had duly washed hands and feet on entering, and assigned them to their places. Food service then began—far more elaborate in later Rome, to be sure, than in Periclean Greece—the meal being divided into a series of courses beginning with a *gustatio*, or hors d'oeuvres of preliminary dishes, and going through one or more main engagements (*mensae primae*) to a climax of dessert.

Both Greek and Roman custom divided the formal dinner into two parts— the first in which one primarily ate, and the second in which one primarily drank, talked, and otherwise amused one's self and those assembled. In Greece the *symposium* (literally, drinking party) properly began with the end of eating and the offer of prayers and libations, particularly to Dionysus. So Xenophon writes of an exuberant evening with Socrates "when the tables had been cleared away, and the libations were made and a paean chanted." A *symposiarch*, or lord of the feast, might be appointed to lead a conversation on a given theme. Or he might oversee the bouts at wine: this happened for instance when Alcibiades, already well along in drink, invaded the famous symposium of Socrates with his revelers and made himself master of the evening. Had the group been able to stay awake, there might have been charades, parlor games, matches of wit and storytelling, throwing of knucklebones and dice, with tidbits of cake, dried fruit, grilled beans, and such to accompany the wine. In addition to the custom already established in Greece of bringing in entertainers ranging from jugglers to would-be Nereids, the Romans introduced the *commissatio*—a ceremonial drinking match at which a master of ceremonies dictated how many cups of wine each guest was to consume at one draught, and of what size and strength, and in what sequence around the table.

Such feasts, particularly as they took on ever greater length in Roman times, imposed considerable strain upon the digestive system. Vessels for self-relief were sometimes placed beneath the table. Belching, as a sign of satisfaction, was accepted and approved (as it is among certain Arab tribes to this day). Many rude jokes were made about breaking wind. In some circles there was resort to a *vomitorium* to purge the system and ready it for another round of food and drink. The poet-philosopher Seneca, himself on a strict diet, spoke with distaste of Romans who *"vomunt ut edant, edunt ut vomant,"* referring to a cycle of gorging and disgorging. But in general, vomiting appears to have been reviled by men of good taste, who preferred a bath and a massage, if need be, between stages of their banquet.

Perhaps the sharpest critique of overindulgence in later Rome, and certainly the liveliest, appears in the famed *Satyricon* by the first-century-A.D. author Petronius. Only portions survive of this work, sometimes called the first novel—a picaresque tale of the exploits of a band of wastrels taking their pleasure with new money. The ringleader, a Syrian freedman named Trimalchio, decided to stage a blowout of colossal proportions. At this boisterous affair, heralded by stewards and assisted by servants who first administered a pedicure to the guests, proceedings began with appetizers of fantastic design, including dormice (small rodents) rolled in honey and poppy seeds, and hot sausages laid on a

silver grill under which "black damsons and red pomegranates had been sliced up and arranged so as to give the effect of flames playing over charcoal." A donkey cast in Corinthian bronze stood on a side table; on its back were two panniers, one holding green olives, the other

Distributing the public grain supply in Ostia

black. While the guests were sampling these, a fanfare of trumpets announced the arrival of the host, "carried in propped up on piles of miniature pillows," as the American translator William Arrowsmith renders the scene, "in such a comic way that some of us couldn't resist impolitely smiling." A platter was borne in containing a peahen made of wood, with wings outspread as when setting. "Warbling waiters" thereupon plucked from the straw around her a pastry egg for each guest; inside were fat orioles seasoned with pepper. Jars of Falernian wine were passed around accompanied by dishes related to the guests' individual signs of the zodiac—chick-peas for Aries, a slice of beef for Taurus, a pair of testicles and kidneys for Gemini, the belly of a virgin pig for Virgo, a crawfish for Scorpio, and so on —followed by a flourish from the musicians and the entry of slaves bearing "fat capons and sowbellies and a hare tricked out with wings to look like a little Pegasus" accompanied by "four little gravy boats, all shaped like the satyr Marsyas, with phalluses for spouts."

Next was the presentation of "a wild sow of absolutely enormous size. . . . Perched rakishly on the sow's head was the cap of freedom which newly freed slaves wear in token of their liberty, and from her tusks hung two baskets woven from palm leaves: one was filled with dry Egyptian dates, the other held sweet Syrian dates. Clustered around her teats were little suckling pigs made of hard pastry, gifts for the guests to take home. . . . The slave who stepped up to carve . . . whipped out his knife and gave a savage slash at the sow's flanks. Under the blow the flesh parted, the wound burst open and dozens of thrushes came whirring out." This was followed by the presentation of a boiled calf with a helmet on its head, which was attacked and carved by a slave brandishing a sword and dressed up as Ajax. After this came a dessert designed by the confectioner in a large priapic shape surrounded by every kind of fruit. But this was not the end: Trimalchio invited all his guests to take a hot bath, after which a second service of courses began in another dining room, while those who felt they had better shift entirely to wine could drink in accordance with the rites of the *commissatio*.

Although this was written as burlesque, Petronius was not wildly exaggerating. Immense wealth was spreading among the newly rich. Favored by a corrupt court with all manner of supply contracts and trading monopolies, many of these men could and did emulate emperors in their magnificence. Rich *novi homines* had ice and snow, embedded in straw, transported all the way from the Alpine Ticino to their country estates around Rome in order to provide refrigeration. Fish ponds, or *vivaria*, were laid out amid their gardens to insure a constant and private supply of fresh trout, sturgeon, and carp. A single farm in the Sabine hills, so the historian Varro writes, brought in as much as sixty thousand sesterces in one year alone from the sale of thrushes raised in its aviaries for the luxury trade. Meanwhile, chefs skilled in handling the proliferating banquets became increasingly prized and costly. Livy recalls that while in early times a cook was considered "the lowest and least useful of slaves," a good one had since become "of prohibitive price." Only a very rich man could afford a first-class chef; Pliny remarks that "today . . . a cook costs as much as a triumph" (meaning the great public celebration honoring a returning military victor).

Almost all classical antiquity drank wine both at meals and at other festivities, and this fact has caused later censorious writers, particularly of Protestant and prohibitionist persuasion, to relate the eventual decline of the ancient, pagan world to its overuse. Actually, the wine consumed then, of a heavy, rather sweetish quality that would be unpalatable to most diners today, was almost universally diluted with water, the proportions leaning to five of water to three of wine. The Minoan Cretans drank wine in astonishing quantities, as their ruined cellars attest, though the studies of Sir Arthur Evans, the great archaeologist of Crete, leave some questions as to when. The Mycenaeans definitely savored it—we read in the *Iliad* of "Arne rich in vineyards," of "Epidauros full of vines"; and the recently discovered wine cellar thought to be that of the Homeric Nestor at Pylos could have accommodated six thousand liters. The Greeks especially enjoyed their wine at the annual festivals of Dionysus—the Haloa and Lenaea celebrations of winter, and the Eleusinian mysteries of the fall—and the Romans were partial to it at all times, first raising the grape in their own Alban hills and later also cultivating it in Spain, Syria, the Rhine valley, and especially France. Martial speaks of the excellent wine from *vitifera Vienna*—not, to be sure, the great Vienna of European history, where the Romans had an outpost too, but little Vienne along the banks of the Rhone (celebrated in our time by the presence there of one of the most hallowed restaurants of France, La Pyramide, and by the vineyards of Côte Rôtie and Hermitage).

It was surely not an abuse of wine that undid classical taste after it had reached its height. It was sheer gluttony and the lavish expenditure of men and money in its service. One Roman emperor, Vitellius, is said to have sent out a whole fleet to scour Mediterranean coasts for the makings of a single dish compounded of flamingo tongues, pike livers, pheasant brains, and lamprey milt. Great estates were converted for the production of peacocks, cranes, and pheasants for rich tables, leaving the emperors of Rome to provide handouts to the poor in the form of daily doles of grain.

Innumerable causes have been offered, particularly from the writings of Edward Gibbon on, for the decline and fall of Roman leadership and estate. One of the most curious causes, recently suggested by the American sociologist Seabury Colum Gilfillan, is that Roman aristocracy died off in large part from lead poisoning, induced by the use in wealthy circles of leaden cooking vessels. Wine or "must" that was boiled down to a syrup to make sauces and to sweeten wine, seems to have absorbed an especially heavy dose of lead, with a high frequency of sterility among this class the result. The poor, meanwhile, using ordinary earthenware that lacked a comparable chemical reaction, were spared. If this be true, the *defrutum* and *mulsum* prized by Apicius as elements of fine cuisine may have played some part in the dissolution of the Empire.

As the Roman Empire declined, so too did the influence of its cuisine, apparently throughout the Mediterranean. Enter the Visigoths, the Ostrogoths, the Vandals—peoples far removed from the cult or culture of the oyster, the sauceboat, and the pastry cook. Enter also the Christian converts, men and women from eastern Tarsus to the Appenines and Alps and beyond, who in many cases cast off all association with the pleasures of the pagan table. To them a meal, reflecting that holiest meal of their faith, was a ceremony of brotherhood—recalling Hebraic origins. The church father Tertullian of Carthage said that a man should eat only to the measure of his hunger. And amid the disarray of the world of A.D. 400 and after, great hunger lay ahead.

SALAD DAYS
OF
THE CAESARS

A cargo of Cyrenaic herbs readied for export, from a vase painting c. 550 B.C.

A shrine dedicated to lares, *gods of the Roman household*

Luxury Begins at Home

Dining at home, as depicted in a tomb relief

The *triclinium* was the favored room of the Roman household, and much time and care was lavished on its decoration. The extraordinary mosaic opposite was uncovered in the ruins of Pompeii, where it had once served as a dining room floor. It illustrates the wide range of sea food common to the classical diet: lobster, skate, eel, octopus. A *lararium* like the corniced shrine above was common to houses of every class. In return for offerings of wheat, salt, and wine, the gods blessed kitchen and table.

Behind the scenes at a Roman dinner, a small army of cooks and assistants was needed to prepare a meal

The Cook's Domain

A good cook was a household status symbol and could be worth his weight in sesterces. Most cooks considered themselves artists rather than galley slaves and had inflammable temperaments to match. The mistress who meddled in the kitchen risked having dinner sabotaged.

suitable to gracious living. In the next room, stewards kept the wine and the conversation flowing.

The Roman kitchen was crowded, simple, and smoky. Wood or charcoal burned on a raised brick hearth which was seldom equipped with a chimney. Many a cook toiling over his fire must have cursed Fornax, the goddess of the oven, and anyone else in earshot, every *jentaculum*, *prandium*, and *cena*. His pots and pans, which rested on grates above the fire, were usually of earthenware or iron. Implements like the Etruscan ladle, far left, and the strainer whose punctures form a Bacchic face, above, were also heavy, requiring a firm hand to manage them.

Homemaking was a skill acquired with time, patience, and energy. A mother and her daughter perform the age-old rite of the cooking lesson, as shown in the sixth-century-B.C. Boeotian terra cotta above.

Caveat Emptor

Imperial Rome was the supermarket of the Mediterranean world. Into the city's shops and stalls flowed the bounty of an empire: grains from Africa and Egypt, venison from Gaul, the cured meats of Andalusia, and rare spices from the East. One market, which was built by the Emperor Trajan, housed 150 shops; and more than 250 mills throughout the capital supplied flour to countless bakeries similar to the Pompeian shop shown in the wall painting opposite. The baker, perched atop his open-air stand to watch for prospective customers, makes a sale.

Vendors sell cutlery from open stalls.

A matron shops for a plump goose destined perhaps for the evening's meal.

63

In Vino Veritas

 The deceptively innocent but glassy-eyed mask in the insert at left belongs to Dionysus. He was not only the Greek god of wine but an entire religion unto himself. Intoxication was thought to wrest the human spirit from the mind's control. Wine, then, became everywhere in the classical world a medium of religious experience. The bronze sculpture above shows one true believer, minus spirit, sagging on the arms of two servants who are attempting to guide him homeward after a hard night's worship. Even the noble Socrates, himself a sometimes bibber, was moved to say, "So far as drinking is concerned, you have my hearty approval; for wine does of a truth 'moisten the soul' and lull our griefs to sleep." But he warned, "If we pour ourselves immense draughts, it will be no long time before both our bodies and our minds reel, and we shall not be able even to draw breath, much less to speak sensibly." These parting words of fatherly advice, though well meant, were seldom heeded.

The footed wine jar above—which was designed to stand inside a cooler—shows Satyrs during an orgy. For the Greek on the *kylix* below, the party is over.

OVERLEAF: *A detail from a vase painting, c. 400 B.C., depicts revelers lounging on couches. The* krater *resting at their feet was used for mixing the wine.*

65

Trade and Table

Aelius Aristides, in his impressions of second-century Rome, wrote: "So many merchantmen arrive here with cargoes from everywhere, at every season and with each return of the harvest, that the city seems like a common warehouse of the world." Undoubtedly, this was an accurate description, for the state of Rome's stomach relied, in great part, on the wealth of her colonies. Nearly half a million tons of wheat annually passed through Rome's great port of Ostia which was located only a short, two-day sail from the granaries of North Africa. Roman colonists who had settled and farmed the conquered lands provided the Empire with a steady flow of foodstuffs. Opposite, an early mosaic shows sailors carrying a menagerie of live game —an ostrich, a gazelle, and a trussed-up boar—aboard a ship which is about to sail for Rome and her hunting preserves.

Half the wines served in Rome were produced in Spain. But many came from Gaul, where boats filled to the gunwales with wine casks, top, plied the rivers of the fertile Moselle valley. The last leg of the long trip to Roman tables was accomplished by carts, above.

69

The War on Hunger

The imported wines and exotic birds of peaceful commerce were for the rich. It took enormous tributes of cattle and wheat, received annually from captive lands, to fill the tables of the public at large; and as the population swelled past a million, even these food sources were insufficient. Under the Empire, Rome's armies not only waged war but were responsible for shipping food back to the home front. Trajan sought to increase local productivity, too: veterans were forbidden to emigrate, and under a plan called the *alimenta*, they were settled on tenant farms around the capital. A program of public assistance, the *annona*, provided monthly doles of grain to the urban proletariat; and *tesserae*, or ration cards, were issued. By Trajan's time a third of Rome was on welfare.

As the Roman armies reaped victories, so too did they reap grain in the fields of their enemies. Above and at left, engravings after bas-reliefs on a column celebrating Trajan's campaigns show troops plundering fields of the Dacians of eastern Europe and returning to camp with the spoils.

As Rome's supply routes reached farther into the interior of the continent, they were increasingly exposed to attack by marauding barbarians. The scene above shows a fortified city on the northeast frontier under siege. While troops repel the enemy at the wall, cohorts bring food to the fortress.

Time of Uprighteousness

It was a glutted world that faced the lean times of the Christian era. The centuries of banqueting were drawing to a close. While pagan Rome had feasted horizontally from couches, the early Christian meal was eaten upright and with solemn dignity—at least in the retrospective version of the Biblical "Marriage at Cana," below.

ANDRE HELD

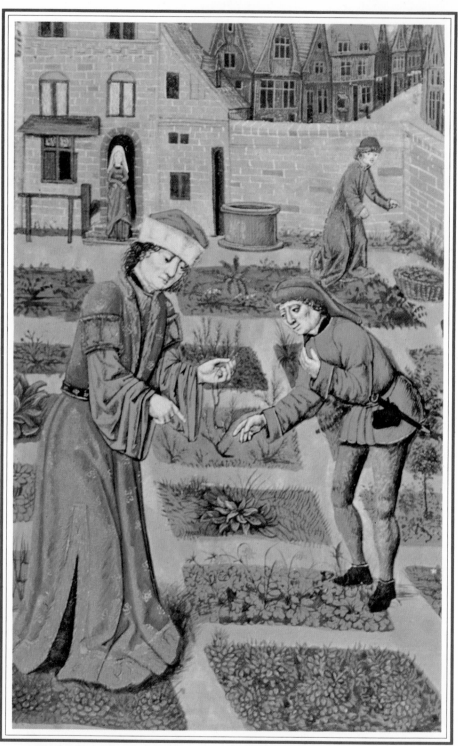

Lord and serf arguing a fine point of horticulture in the well-tended herb garden of the manor

MEDIEVAL
FEAST
AND
FAMINE

A millennium is a long time to wait between first-class dinners. Yet even more time was to separate the last great tables of antiquity from those of the Renaissance, whose influence began spreading from Italian cities to France and beyond soon after A.D. 1500. The vast intervening epoch was by no means one of little taste. The medieval centuries presented a profusion and confusion of tastes—some advanced, some rudimentary, some ample, some ascetic—and these reflected the turbulence of the age, its new ethnic mixtures, and its insecurity. It was a time in which feast alternated with famine; plenty with scarcity; the king's peace with baronial anarchy; crusader with brigand (often united in the same person); a Saint Francis with Gargantua. It saw a return to mud huts and near savagery in areas where proud Roman cities had flourished along the Rhine and the Danube; in Spain it also saw the incursion of a Moorish culture of great refinement. The age suffered depopulation through barbarian invasions, plagues, and chronic famines, of which some of the earliest were so terrible that sporadic instances of cannibalism are recorded. France endured ten famines during the tenth century and twenty-six in the eleventh and twelfth; and England, it has been estimated, averaged one famine every fourteen years in the same period. The bubonic plague decimated the Eastern Roman Empire in the sixth century and spread to Sicily and southern Italy in the eighth, reaching its most virulent stage in the "Black Death" of fourteenth-century Europe. The age was also one of mighty influx of new blood, as Teutons and Slavs mixed theirs with that of older

Wine rations for William the Conqueror's men

Western stock. It saw Europeans almost constantly at war, fighting off Saracens in the south, viking raiders in the north, Huns, Avars, Bulgars, and Slavs in the east. Crusades and the recurrent struggles between partisans of emperors and partisans of popes also disturbed the Continent. Peaceable Christian life was preserved chiefly by the monasteries, those great refuges of both learning and practical craft for a Western world fallen into ignorance and disarray.

The first to suffer under such conditions was the poor peasant, subsisting in bitter seasons on a diet of groats if he were lucky, and making a "feast" (so the fourteenth-century poem *Piers the Ploughman* by William Langland has it) of "a farthing's worth of mussels or a farthing's worth of cockles." There were better days for him, too:

> *"I have no penny," quoth Piers*
> *"Pullets for to buy*
> *Nor neither geese nor piglets*
> *but two green cheeses*
> *A few curds and cream*
> *and an oaten cake*
> *And two loaves of beans and bran*
> *to bake for my little ones*
> *And besides I say by my soul*
> *I have no salt bacon*
> *Nor no little eggs, by Christ*
> *collops for to make*
> *But I have parsley and leeks*
> *and many cabbages*
> *And besides a cow and a half. . . ."*

At the same time, the age found barons surfeiting themselves on tankards of mead and trenchers of spitted game in the smoky Great Halls of their castles, entertained by jongleurs, or minstrels, somewhat after the fashion of Homer's heroes. It was an era of hearty and often gross sexuality, culminating most visibly in the exhibitionist codpieces of the fifteenth century. It was also an age of tender romances—of Abelard and Héloïse, of Dante and his Beatrice, and the exquisite "courts of love," presided over by Eleanor of Aquitaine, with their cult of adoration and physical restraint.

Beginning with rawness and ruin, and only a shattered remembrance of things past, the age evolved a social system, based on feudal ownership of land, that for a time, roughly the twelfth century,. brought relative stability and moderation to much of Europe. This tempered life was, however, short-lived. In the centuries that followed, the Lucullan dinners of abbots and other high clergy were judged particularly scandalous. The enthronement in 1467 of George Neville, the Archbishop of York and Chancellor of England, was celebrated by a feast that included (according to a kitchen list that has survived) 300 huge loaves of bread, 300 tuns of ale (about 75,000 gallons), 100 tuns of wine, 105 oxen, 6 wild bulls, 1,000 sheep, 304 pigs, 304 calves, and 400 swans. It took sixty-two cooks to prepare the meal. This kind of clerical indulgence caused much social unrest and led the reforming Archbishop Cranmer, in the next century, to inveigh against clerical extravagance. He ruled that an archbishop must not consume at one sitting more than six flesh dishes, and not more than four "second" dishes; a bishop could have only five of the first and three of the second; archdeacons and deacons were to be allowed only four and two respectively; and so on down. When Cranmer was condemned to be burned at the stake for his heretical beliefs, there were few friends to come to his defense.

Feast, famine, gluttony, temperance —there were correspondences between the cycles of life of the Middle Ages and those of Rome. Yet the contrasts were profound. The Roman Empire, even when overrun by invaders from the northeast and east in the fifth century A.D., still occupied about one fourth of the entire European continent, including almost all its most fertile areas. The Ro-mans had cleared vast forest lands, drained marshes, built a network of over ninety thousand miles of roads, developed advanced techniques of stock-breeding and crop management, and brought together peoples from Britain to Asia Minor and from Gaul to Africa under the aegis of Roman law, language, and trade. Rome had also exported its civilized ways at table. We read of fifth-century festivities at which Romanized Gauls reclined on cushioned divans (though a few Gauls, disdainful of Roman indolence, preferred chairs, benches, stools, or wooden seats, covered with rugs). The guests ceremoniously wash their hands before and after the first course, don special robes and slippers, spread napkins which they have brought, and embark upon a repast that begins with a drink of heated wine mixed with honey, to be followed by fresh eggs, quarters of beef, mutton, and pork, all highly seasoned with pepper, pickles, caraway, and poppy seeds, saffron, aromatic balsam, honey, and salt. For the serious eaters there was also boar meat with a garniture of cooked apples, deer, roebuck, hare, and even the urus, "that wild buffalo whose horns become at once a cup and a trophy."

But gradually such scenes of dining extravagance disappeared as the peoples Rome had conquered and assimilated were in turn overwhelmed by rough tribes of Goths in Spain, Franks in Gaul, Angles and Saxons in England, and Norsemen along the northern seacoasts. Under these barbarian successors to the Roman proconsuls, such imperial centers as Arles, Reims, Trier, London, Cologne, Aix-la-Chapelle, Utrecht, Mérida, Cartagena, Vienna, and great Rome itself sank into oblivion. Wealth, splendor, and power survived for another six hundred years in Byzantium, the eastern part of the Empire; but in central and western Europe, almost all semblance of social order vanished, and civilization halted. The new barbarian kings were little more than local tribal chieftains; bands of brigands roamed the countryside; roads fell into disrepair, bridges collapsed and were not rebuilt, trade and communications almost came to a standstill; the successors to many productive estates were primitive communes whose peasants worked strips of land with crude plows. One traveler speaks of the desolation of the once-rich Danubian plain, where "not a laborer is to be seen." Vast areas cultivated by Romans and their *coloni*, or tenants, reverted to forest, marsh, and wasteland—the haunt of bears, boars, deer, and aurochs. By the tenth century, woodland had recovered a third of England, much of Spain, Italy, and the greater parts of fertile Gaul and the Low Countries.

Amid this decay, communities were economically isolated, their life one of sheer subsistence. In the event of crop failure or shortages of cattle, draft animals, or manpower, outside help was rarely available. Moreover, lack of enough fodder to tide animals over the winter (in turn the result of poor governance of soil) made it necessary to kill off most of the livestock in the fall. A great slaughter usually occurred at about Martinmas (November 11), with some of the unseasoned meat being served immediately and the rest salted or dried. This practice, which continued through

A yeoman's feast in slaughter season

most of the Middle Ages, resulted in a dismal winter diet made palatable only by resort to many herbs and spices. In addition, the livestock tended to be stunted and lean, since the art of selective breeding had been lost, and sick and healthy animals interbred. Then, if the meagre supply of winter meat ran out, even the few remaining brood cattle might have to be slaughtered—assuring more shortages of animals for plowing, breeding, and eating in the future.

Despite the disorder we associate with the term "Dark Ages," forces were stirring to restore a modicum of good life to western Europe. The feudal idea— that of the banding together of lords and tenants, masters and workers, for mutual protection and with mutual social and economic obligations—began to emerge even before the reign of Charlemagne. After having been crowned Holy Roman Emperor in the year 800, the Frankish king became through the power of his personality and his office one of the great unifying forces of European history. An inspired organizer, he brought local chieftains to order. He sought to turn the barbarian from the sword to the plowshare. He promoted efforts to reclaim lands become barren, and in 812 he issued *De*

Villis, a remarkable ordinance concerning the management of the royal domains of Aquitaine. It set forth a model scheme of imperial workshops and agricultural enterprises, listing everything from the number of millers, bakers, butchers, weavers, smiths, and fullers needed to an inventory of the specific vegetables and herbs he wished to see raised. In this, he was acting in concert with the power that had crowned him—the church of Rome, possessed now of more than a third of western Europe's land holdings under the stewardships of its bishoprics, abbeys, and monasteries.

Monasticism, with its ideals of asceticism and withdrawal, had come from the Christianized East to Italy in the fourth century. There it met with initial hostility, but by the seventh and eighth centuries, monasteries had established themselves as centers of stability in the European countryside. Major houses arose in places as distant as Jumièges in Normandy, Malmédy in Belgium, Bury St. Edmunds in England, St-Gall in Switzerland, Kempten and Fulda in Germany, Santiago de Compostela in Spain, and along the Scottish borderlands and Baltic marches. In France King Clovis founded the abbey of Ste. Geneviève; Dagobert endowed St-Denis; and Sigismund established St-Germain-des-Prés.

Peasants reaping and binding sheaves of grain

Many barons, thinking of prestige and heavenly reward, also provided lands and money for monastic communities. "From the seventh century," writes the modern historian Ferdinand Lot, "there was not a single nobleman or bishop who did not wish to ensure the salvation of his soul by a foundation of this kind." At the end of the tenth century, there were 543 abbeys with monastic enclosures in France alone.

Far more than retreats, these institutions became communities of advanced farming and industry. The church, through such voices as the reforming Benedict of Nursia, founder in A.D. 528 of the first monastic order in western Europe, took exception to the earlier ideal of the withdrawn and contemplative hermit. To the Benedictines of Monte Cassino, he proclaimed a gospel of manual labor as a Christian duty. Hard work (besides subduing the weaknesses of the flesh) would lead to the productivity Europe so desperately needed. Wide areas of wasteland were reclaimed by tonsured men working under their abbots. Bogs were drained, new fields seeded, gardens and orchards re-created, vineyards revived. (The wines of the Côte d'Or of Burgundy, well known in Roman times, became prized again in the seventh century.)

The monastery, as a model farm capable of surviving hard times, emerged as a storehouse of food to feed the surrounding populace. It was also the wayfarer's perennial inn, offering him lodging and a good meal by the refectory fire. Monks, some of whom may have heard of Apicius, were among the very few who had some notion of Roman cuisine. Indeed, until the Renaissance the monastery appears to have been the chief transmitter of higher forms of cookery. It was also the center of communal life and culture, providing miracle plays and rough games that diverted the peasants of neighboring manors.

The Benedictine monastery of St-Gall on Lake Constance, for example, was a town unto itself—a self-contained center of civilized living even in A.D. 830. Enclosed by walls, it possessed in addition to the all-important abbey thirty-two buildings, several gardens for herbs and vegetables, a central fountain, and a courtyard surrounded by cloistered ambulatories reminiscent of a Roman villa. There were rooms for baking, brewing, drying fruit, and preserving; sheds for various breeds of animals; and quarters for the craft of cooper, wood carver, shoemaker, saddler, and smith. St-Gall had a herb, or "physic," garden that yielded roses, water cress, sage, rue, pennyroyal, peppermint, cumin, lovage, savory, rosemary, and fennel; a kitchen garden that grew such staples as cabbage, beets, parsnips, carrots, leeks, shallots, celery, parsley, and garlic; and an orchard that produced apples, pears, plums, quinces, peaches, and even figs. As its wealth increased, St-Gall extended its holdings to broad tracts in Swabia, Neustria, Alsace, and even Italy, with as many as four thousand "manors" of greater and lesser lands bound to it as fiefs. Each was obliged to supply an annual quitrent in the form of produce—another stimulus to agriculture.

But far greater than the enterprise of the Benedictines was the mighty colonizing work of the Cistercian order,

founded in 1098. Expanding rapidly from its mother abbey in Cîteaux south of Dijon, it settled on the northern moors of England, along the sandy wastes of the Bay of Biscay, amid the bogs and forests of Germany, and in the gorges of the high Vosges. In the Bordeaux country, and along the Rhine and Neckar rivers, Cistercians grew grapes for wine; in Normandy, they grew apples for cider; in Germany, Flanders, and England, they farmed the staple cereals for malt and ale. East of the Elbe, they raised horses. They mined large salt deposits. They successfully bred cattle, pickled the meat, and tanned the hides. They constructed dikes against the northern seas and drained the swamps to reclaim areas usable for meadow and pasture, for sheep runs and goose farms, and for the grazing of the Low Countries' scanty herds of cattle.

From such industry Europe was to acquire productive skills again. There remained severe limitations on the commerce of food, as of all other products. Apart from the half-ruined road system and the constant threat of marauders and pirates, there were tolls and local customs duties that impeded the passage of goods. There was a jumble of local laws and local currencies (even abbots at times minted their own money) that made business beyond the barter level difficult. There was virtually no investment capital. There was a language barrier—one part of Europe spoke in tongues descended from Latin, the other in German dialects. Yet travel, production, and trade gradually revived. The Celts of Wales and Ireland had long fared out to sea in their small boats to

In Praise of Folly

*I*n an era that idealized courtly love, swallowed whole the heroic *chansons de geste*, and listened patiently to somber admonitions to prepare for the afterlife, poetry celebrating the joys of wenching and wining was something of an anomaly. The poets of this uncommon verse came from the ranks of defrocked monks, itinerant scholars, and medieval equivalents of beatniks, and their verses were often audacious Latin parodies of the rhyme, rhythm, and melody of church liturgy: "Paternoster of the Wine," "Gospel According to the Silver Marks." Dubbed "goliards," a term derived from the Latin *gula* for "gullet," or perhaps from the Biblical Goliath, these merry mendicants hicced and hiked around the European countryside, with only their ribald songs for baggage. In exchange for bed, bread, and beverage (preferably alcoholic), the goliards would provide their host with an evening's entertainment. Not surprisingly, ecclesiastical authorities soon moved to suppress these "low strollers," and by the beginning of the fourteenth century they had all but silenced them. Their bawdy zest for living is heard in the song below, from a collection of *cantiones profanes* known as the *Carmina Burana*. The ballads, translated by the medieval authority George Whicher, were hidden under cloak and key in the Bavarian cloister of Benedictbeuern until their discovery in the nineteenth century.

Hircus quando bibit,	*When he drinks the lewd clodhopper*
que non sunt debita dicit,	*Uses language most improper;*
cum bene potatur,	*When he's altogether pickled,*
que non sunt debita fatur.	*Then by uncouth deeds he's tickled.*
Cum bene sum potus,	*When I'm in my cups my curse is*
tunc versibus effluo totus.	*That I simply slobber verses;*
Cum sicco siccor,	*But I'm quickly sick of* hic or
nec in hic, nec in hec, nec in hoc cor.	Haec or hoc *when lacking liquor.*

transport their salted meat and hides to the Continent in exchange for its salt, oil, wines, and cloth. By the eleventh century a modest international market was centered in Lombardy (particularly in Pavia and in Florence), the future seat of Italian banking. In the Low Countries, as new towns developed, a cloth industry based on sheepherding came into being. Soon Europe was to see great annual fairs, especially those of the Champagne region at Troyes (origin of troy weight standards), and of Provins and other centers near Paris, at which the goods of Flanders were exchanged for those of Italy, and the wines of France for spices from the East.

As they grew, such fairs and lesser local markets stimulated a formidable interchange of produce, and therewith an enhancement of the medieval diet. Normandy and Picardy exported apples. The south of France and eastern Spain again abounded in orchards. Oils, chestnuts, plums of southern Italy, were widely sold. Roquefort cheese was mentioned in 1070 in the records of Conques, a monastery on the pilgrimage route to Santiago de Compostela. Cheese from Gorgonzola was part of a bequest made to the school of St. Ambrogio by the Bishop of Milan in 879. As early as 1200 the hard cheese of Parma was also cured. Rice from Spain appeared on the market, as did Spanish saffron, ginger, sesame, figs, quinces, the first cultivated strawberries, and the lemons raised by its Moorish masters—though north of the Pyrenees citrus fruits remained a luxury for all but the richest men.

The fisheries of the Atlantic, too, expanded enormously under the stimulus

of trade and profit. Coastal peoples of far northern waters had long risked their lives in pursuit of seal, porpoise, and whale. Now herring, one of the cheapest and most nutritious fishes, traveling in schools of millions from the Shetland Islands in the spring to Yarmouth in the fall, made that port into a great trade

A French cheese merchant

center. There and in other North Sea ports huge catches of herring were brought in, salted down, barreled, and shipped to markets all over the Continent. Fishing fleets of several realms also pursued cod and haddock off the Dogger Bank, Iceland, and Norway. The Hanseatic League, a powerful mercantile confederation that originated among several free coastal cities including Germanic Lübeck, Hamburg, and Bremen, built much of its trade with the Baltic on the exchange of East Prussian wheat and Russian furs for fish and Scandinavian dairy products.

The Thames, still unpolluted, was itself a major source of supply for a people that strictly observed fifty-two weekly "fysshe dayes" in the year and moreover relied heavily on fish during Lent, which came providentially at a time when supplies of winter meat were running low. As Thomas Tusser put it neatly in his description of the "fermers dailie diet":

A Plot set downe, for fermers quiet,
*   as time requires, to frame his diet;*
With sometimes fish, and sometimes fast,
*   that household store, may longer last.*

Let Lent well kept, offend not thee,
*   for March and April breeders be.*
Spend herring first, save saltfish last:
*   for saltfish is good, when Lent is past.*

The Seine also had a profitable fish trade, and numerous breeding enclosures were built along its banks. Fish such as salmon and trout were especially prized; monasteries and noblemen's manors had their own "stews," or fish ponds, recalling Roman vivaria, to provide fresh carp, eel, and tench; and a noble sturgeon, wherever caught, became—like the whale—royal property subject to the disposition of the king.

In this agricultural revival, great prosperity came to the monastic foundations that had done so much to inspire systematic food production. While the rules of some orders—the Cistercian in particular—forbade them to sell produce in secular markets or to participate in fairs, large quantities were sold at the monastery doors. One critic suspicious of all this trafficking declared, "Flocks and fleeces, crops and granaries, leeks and potherbs, drinks and goblets are nowadays the reading and study of monks."

Gradually, actual labor on the land passed from the monks to serfs, acquired as the monasteries won more and more estates. Since the orders were in later centuries largely populated by sons of the feudal aristocracy, for whom manual labor could hardly have been an article of faith, the church proclaimed that "vicarious" labor, of monk supervising serf, was a suitable substitute. The Cistercian Caesar of Heisterbach wrote that the richest houses of his order were equipped to feed five thousand persons every day if need be. His Welsh brother in the church, Giraldus Cambrensis, known for his caustic criticism, explained with unusual tolerance, "this greed of theirs . . . arises from the hospitality which the members of this order, although in themselves the most abstemious of all others, indefatigably exercise, in their unbounded charity to the poor and to strangers." The thirteenth-century abbot of Leubus complained, "Scarcely a month passes by, nay, scarcely a day in which it is not necessary for the abbot to give away something. . . . One demands money . . . another grain, the one bread, the other hay, and he takes at the same time 100 head of sheep . . . the seventh would like to have his jug filled; the eighth demands fish; the ninth requests a measure of large cheese; the tenth, seed-cake; the eleventh, apples . . . but it is far worse when the huntsmen come with their servants and dogs. . . . They are as hungry as wolves and a loaf of bread for one of them is too small."

The outcome in any case led to a vast improvement in the daily board, though dishes tended to be heavy and robust rather than accomplished in any Roman sense, save on occasion at the high table of a leading abbot or great lord. The peasant's daily bread was coarse-grained and dark, made most commonly from barley, rye, or bean flour. The wealthy townsman or squire bought fine wheaten flour for the making of white loaves, cakes, or pastry; and as a treat for the tenant on a feast day or when he had finished some "boon-work," the lord might contribute one of his own white loaves, along with a joint of meat. Bakers and millers were licensed and were considered so essential to the economy as a whole that at one point Louis IX, the sainted king of thirteenth-century France, ordered that they be relieved of the military watch duties expected of his other subjects in Paris, in order not to interrupt their work.

It was an age of stews, thick broths, pies, and soups. Long-stored, salty, stringy meats were, as we would say, "tenderized" by hashing, mincing, and pounding, and were then served up with an admixture of wine or honey. A fish stew known as *chaudemer* was the ancestor of chowder. There was herring pie, a stew composed of pickled fish, raisins, currants, dates, and cinnamon placed in a "coffin"—that is, a pastry blanket—and baked. A truly royal pie is described by a chaplain in the fourteenth century court of Charles VI of France. It consisted of three partridges, six quails, a dozen skylarks, thrushes, and diced bacon mixed with *verjus,* a kind of vinegar made of green grapes or apples. There was a dish called venison frumenty, popular in fifteenth-century England, in which strips of deer meat were put into a soup made of wheat boiled in milk, to which the yolks of eggs, sugar, and salt were added. Sometimes several different stews or soups were served and consumed at one meal.

Amid Europe's forests, there had always been game in plenty, though hunting and venery became the prerogative of landlords who enclosed their demesnes as private parks; and poaching became a capital—but very prevalent—crime. The right to fish rivers and streams also belonged to the lord, though the peasant devised ways of trapping and spearing that readily escaped the keeper's eye. Hogs, which foraged for acorns in the woods, were particularly valued when cattle and fodder were scarce. The best flesh went into pickled "souse"; the trimmings, including parts of the head, feet, ears, tongue, tail, bones, and gristle, were set to simmer with an accompaniment of vegetables, sage, and other herbs to become "brawn"—a great favorite of people of moderate means.

Hawking for game birds was the pleasure of those who could afford falcons and hounds, but a great deal of "fowling," involving the use of nets and snares, was done by the peasants, who also became the custodians of flocks of poultry as barnyard domestication increased. Pheasants' eggs were a delicacy, but ordinary hens' eggs were commonly eaten fried or poached. A thirteenth-century Englishman counseled, "A fried egg does not need instruction, but dig not at it with your thumb turned down —move it about with the point of your knife." Advanced cooks managed to produce that challenge, the omelette.

Despite the growing variety of the fare, the common diet—except for those seasons and places in which absolutely fresh produce could be obtained—continued to be based on preserved meat and fish, and this led to a heavy impo-

Taillevent

When Guillaume Tirel was a mere scullion, scrubbing pots and tending fires, French cooking was still a relatively brutish, almost hazardous affair. The huge open kitchen hearth was better designed for warming drafty halls than for cooking dinners; and the chef's battery consisted of a few iron and copper pots suspended by chains, a turnspit or two, and a pair of andirons, occasionally fitted with crude braziers. Foods were either mercilessly boiled over a high flame or skewered for roasting, and the cook who approached his steaming pots to stir or add that certain something did so at his own peril. Tirel, or Taillevent as he called himself, had the good fortune to be born just as kitchens and the cook's estate were improving: oval-shaped ovens were built into the wall, and damping devices to control the heat were developed. He used his opportunities well. After several years of service to Philip VI of Valois and the Dauphin, he was summoned to the court of Charles V where he became "first squire and master of the kitchen garrisons." Around 1375 Taillevent put off his aprons long enough to write *Le Viandier*, the oldest French cookbook on record. The manuscript, which gives a detailed picture of the tastes and manners of the medieval court, enjoyed a phenomenal reputation not only in Taillevent's lifetime but in succeeding centuries, when it became one of the first books to be printed. Like all French chefs after him, Taillevent was much occupied with the secrets of making a fine sauce, a culinary innovation which was now literally within the reach of the clever cook. In the seventeen sauces described, including such classics as *cameline* and *sauce Robert*, the master recommends as thickening agents plain and grilled breads—flour as a binder was still unknown. Bread also figured in the popular "sops," etymologically and gastronomically the forerunner of puréed soups. Sops were made of milk flavored with wine, saffron, honey or other sweeteners. Slow-cooked *ragoûts*, *galimafrées*, *mortreux*, and *hochepots*, all newly fashionable, were explained; Taillevent even offered recipes for vegetables. (The very fact that he coaxed the king to eat his first cabbage was recorded as a matter of historical interest.) When Taillevent died in 1395, at the age of sixty-nine, he was buried beneath a tombstone portraying him in the honorary dress of a sergeant at arms, complete with helmet and mace. Fittingly, his shield was emblazoned with three cooking pots.

sition of sauces and seasonings to cover up the briny, stale flavors. Royal sauces relied on exotic flavors—Edward I of England ran up a spice bill of £1600 in one year—the equivalent of $100,000 today. But every household boasted an herb garden—even the peasant usually had a small plot of his own.

Salt, fundamental in the curing of meats and fish and in the disguising if not improving of flavors, was honored by a special place on the board. Often it was contained in a monumental salt-cellar placed just a little below the center of a lord's high table—whence comes the pejorative reference to guests seated "below the salt." The London Guild of Salters, aware of their importance, early coined their own motto: *"sal sapit omnia"* ("salt savors everything").

Hardly less prestigious were the Pepperers, who organized themselves as a guild in England in the eleventh century, when this common condiment was most widely imported. It had been brought to Europe by Arabs, though many Englishmen who traded for it were unaware of its origin. Cinnamon, and cloves as well, had begun to enter France as early as the eighth century, transported from China, India, and Indochina along the few tenuous trade routes then surviving in the Middle East. All but cinnamon were very expensive.

Crusaders who encountered sugar cane growing in Tripoli, where it had spread from Syria, delighted in sucking on the stalks and encouraged its importation as an improvement over the traditional sweetener, honey. But in large part Europe still relied on its own condiments. There was anise for meat jellies and

Abbey kitchen wing

liqueurs, and bay for soups, omelettes, and fowl stuffing. Caraway for bread and cakes also had medicinal value, along with dill, which "assuageth the rumbling in a man's womb," and sage, "also . . . good for venom or poison."

What came out of the pot was sometimes a mixture that to us would seem as foreign as anything in Homer: for example, *maumenye ryalle,* a stew of strong wine, cinnamon, soft pine cones, cloves, almonds, ale, and pulped hog's brawn. Saffron, ginger, salt, and more sweet wine completed the stupefying concoction. The English then as now were partial to a strong sauce of mustard. Chaucer's Frankeleyn, a rich freeholder in the *Canterbury Tales* and "Epicurus' owne sone," kept a year-round open house of food and drink:

> *With-oute beke mete was never his hous,*
> *Of fish and flesh, and that so plentyous,*
> *It snewed in his hous of mete and drinke,*
> *Of alle dáyntees that men coude thinke.*

His cook was charged with all manner of hearty dishes, varying in particulars "after sondry seasons of the year"; and "he coude roste, and sethe, and broille, and frye, Maken mortreux, and wel bake a pye"—but woe unto him if the mustard sauce was not "poynaunt and sharp."

Herbs and condiments, in addition to being thrown into stewpots, medical preparations, and witches' brews, also played a major part in the medieval salad. A recipe for "salat" from *The Forme of Cury*, an important early cooking manual compiled by the master cooks of Richard II of England around 1390, advises, "Take parsel, sawge, garlec, chibollas [young onions], oynons, leek, borage, myntes, porrectes [a kind of leek], fenel, and ton tressis [cresses], rew, rosemarye, purslarye [purslane]; lave, and woisshe hem clene; pike hem, pluk hem small with thyn [thine] honde, and myng [mix] hem ind raw oile. Lay on vynegar and salt, and serve it forth."

Generally, customs and manners of the table were as bluff as the fare. Before the twelfth century, kitchens as such were a rarity. Food was prepared either at the hearth of the "hall" that served as the household's one meeting and dining space, or on the floor below, or in a separate building. By the fourteenth century, manors and castles were equipped with kitchens sometimes as spacious as the halls themselves, with high-domed roofs to let the steam and smoke escape. Large ovens bearing iron doors were built into the thickness of the wall. There were pantries, butteries (after *boutelle* for the bottles stored there), and pits for disposal of wastes. Occasionally, small dining rooms were built separate from the hall, but in great houses the custom of large numbers of people eating together persisted. The head of the household sat on a dais often under a canopy of embroidered

silk or wool; he was surrounded by his family and guests, who were ranged along the cloth-covered head table in order of precedence, while retainers sat at lower, trestle tables, food being sent down to them after those at the high table had taken their choice of the best cuts presented. In the twelfth century, typically, every two diners shared one large bowl or wooden trencher (so named for the *tranche*, or slice of stale bread, which had still earlier served as the dish) for their stews or meats. Everyone also was given a cup or mug for his wine or ale, though in poorer houses

Mother and child at work

and on ceremonial occasions everywhere, a single cup was passed around. Etiquette demanded that hands be washed before eating, that weapons be left at the door, and that hands remain above the board (except when tossing scraps to the dogs) as evidence that the guest carried no concealed dagger. Grace was said either before or after meals.

In royal and other great houses, a marshal was in charge of the arrangements. He supervised the airing of the hall, the freshening of the rush-strewn floor, the cleaning of the tables. He was protocol officer, too, designating the order of seating and the planning of entertainments. He was assisted by a butler who saw to the distribution of wine and bread—just the proper quality for each rank of diner, from fresh loaves for the master to four-day-old bread for the lowest table. The butler in a royal household also performed the rites of assay, tasting everything for possible poison before serving. A sewer (steward), a cupbearer, squires, pages, and various other assistants brought the dishes into the hall for presentation by squires and pages on bended knee. To carve before one's lord or noble father was part of a knight's education. Even great lords did table service to their liege: when Rudolf of Hapsburg was crowned Holy Roman Emperor at Aachen in 1273, the seven electors waited upon him as recalled in an ode of Friedrich Schiller: . . . *Die Speisen trug der Pfalzgraf des Rheins, Es schenkte der Böhme des perlenden Weins* . . . ("The Palatine duke proffered the dishes, The lord of Bohemia served sparkling wine").

In the Middle Ages one ate with a knife, a spoon, and with one's fingers, and numerous directives were offered on the proper use of each:

Let not thy spoone stand in the dysche
Whether thou be served with fleshe or fishe
Also eschewe, withouten stryfe
To foule the borde clothe with thy knyfe. . . .

Thus, do not leave your spoon in the bowl or wipe your knife on the tablecloth. Another: "With mete ne bere thy knyfe to mouthe," evidently meaning

that the food-bearing knife should not touch the tongue. One person who mastered the art of dainty consumption was Chaucer's aging Prioresse, the provincial Madame Eglentyne, whose painstaking table manners are described in one of the poet's most famous tongue-in-cheek passages:

At mete wel y-taught was she with-alle;
She leet no morsel from hir lippes falle,
Ne wette hir fingres in hir sauce depe.
Wel coude she carie a morsel, and wel kepe,
That no drope ne fille up-on hir brest.
In curteisye was set ful muche hir lest.
Hir over lippe wyped she so clene,
That in hir coppe was no ferthing sene
Of grece, whan she dronken hadde hir
*   draughte.*

England in Chaucer's time was regarded by Continentals as an unsophisticated region, at the outskirts of trade

Stewards at a lord's table

and taste, and unfamiliar with what remained of the light of antiquity. Yet England shared with the Continent, among other things, a quite new fashion in mealtimes. Throughout western Europe the main meal of the day, once reserved for afternoon or evening, was advanced to the morning, the hour varying with place and period. We learn of

Frenchmen rising before dawn, dining at nine A.M., and supping at five:

> *Lever à cinq, diner à neuf,*
> *Souper à cinq, coucher à neuf,*
> *Fait vivre d'ans nonante et neuf.*

For an Englishman during the Yorkist age, however, this early dinner was only an epilogue to his traditional hearty breakfast, often taken at six. We read of Edward IV breaking his fast after very early Mass with ale, bread, and boiled beef, mutton, and herring.

While many ancients had contented themselves with two meals a day, only one of them substantial, now there were often four, the English in particular favoring a post-supper "livery" at about eight in the evening—or what we would consider a late buffet or formidable bed-time snack. A Venetian traveler visiting England during the disordered period of the Wars of the Roses commented on the huge amounts of food and drink Englishmen consumed, adding that even "when war is raging most furiously, they will still seek for good eating and all their other comforts. . . ." He noticed, also, a predilection among the English for drinking in public taverns—institutions new or strange to a proper Continental, more accustomed at that time to the abbot's table or the prior's garden if he went forth to dine and wine.

The pleasures of the medieval board were united with the observance of religious feast days, of which there were many, some carried over with new meanings from the pagan calendar. There was the solstitial Christmas, with its boar's head borne in on a garlanded platter and its mince pie, all enjoyed to the accom-

Jolly transactions at an English mill

paniment of carols; there was New Year's Eve and Twelfth Night, or the Feast of the Three Kings, with its proverbial "cakes and ale"—actually a "wassail bowl" (a concoction of ale and roasted apples spiced with cloves, ginger, nutmeg, and cinnamon) and spicecakes. Another ceremony connected with the Twelfth Night was the election of the King and Queen of the Bean. A cake containing a pea and a bean was portioned out and the happy recipients of the prizes crowned. To the frugal Spaniards, the *Fiesta de los Tres Rejes* was the day of greatest feasting.

There was Easter and Hocktide (the second Monday and Tuesday after Easter), observed with the first harvest of winter fields, duly blessed; and there was Michaelmas with its geese. Whitsuntide was marked with morris dances, cakes, and Whitsun ale, brewed from malt contributed by the parishoners and sold to raise money for the church. The summer solstice festival known as Saint John's Eve, or Midsummer Night, was celebrated with fires on hilltops (to symbolize the height the grain would reach) and much carousing; and so around to Sheepshearing Supper and Harvest Home. Yet almost any occasion, sacred or secular, provided an excuse for conspicuous consumption if the makings were available. Betrothals, burials, enthronements, or just visits among clans —any event would do.

A twelfth-century visitor to the high table of the Prior of Canterbury recorded that he had often seen sixteen or more very costly dishes presented there. An account of Saint Louis' dinner on a *maigre* or "fast day" in 1248 lists fresh fish, crayfish, crabs, new beans cooked in milk, eel pies, rice with almonds and powdered cinnamon, and finally junket, tarts, and fruits. A formal dinner in the following century (according to the royal chef Taillevent) might begin with a first course of capons with cinnamon broth, chickens with herbs, and venison, followed by a second course of roast beef, peacocks, capon pies, et cetera, with a third course of partridges, stewed pigeons, venison pâté, sugared tarts, and so on. The banquet celebrating the marriage of Henry IV of England and Joan of Navarre in 1403 was of a still higher order, and was served in successive courses—three of meat followed by three of fish, including also young pigs, woodcocks, plover, rabbits, quails, snipe, sturgeon, shellfish, lampreys, and pike. Each course concluded with a "soteltie" of sugar and pastry, the final dessert fashioned in the form of a crowned eagle.

The "soteltie"—literally, a subtlety— was the showpiece of the medieval chef, and several might appear during the meal as distant reminders of Rome.

There were intricate sweetmeat confections representing such subjects as Saint George slaying the dragon, a stag at bay, the Trinity watching over the Virgin Mary, or a royal panther. There were also trick pies that opened to release flocks of birds ("four and twenty blackbirds, baked in a pie"). A peacock with

Public censure for a drunkard

gilded beak, symbol of nobility and incorruptibility of soul, or a swan, a symbol of satisfaction of desire, might also appear on the table, though both must have promised more delights than they delivered, the peacock being rather stringy and the swan oily.

At one of the most spectacular banquets toward the end of the Middle Ages, the "Feast of the Pheasant" given by Philip, the Duke of Burgundy, in Lille in 1454, the Knights of the Golden Fleece in their red velvet robes were treated to an immense pie which opened to the festive strains of twenty-eight musicians playing inside. The climax came when a giant in Saracen dress led in an elephant carrying a beauteous girl, who symbolized in her person the captivity of the church in the East. The girl implored the knights at their glittering tables to rise and rescue Constantinople, seized the year before by the Turkish infidels. Next, a pheasant decked out with jewels was borne in, and Philip and his knights vowed in its name, if not in the name of the "captive" girl, to take up the sword on a new crusade—which, however, they never did. The Renaissance, and the social and political changes it brought, saw to that.

Usually, at a high lord's table, there were not only "sotelties" between courses but also *entremets*—a word signifying in that day not lesser dishes but the jugglers, jesters, acrobats, dancers, and minstrels who entertained the company at intermissions. Important dishes—they might be *fylettys en galentyne* (an elaborate meat loaf) or roast swan in full plumage —were often announced by a flourish of trumpets, as in antiquity. And like Martial and Petronius long before, there was Rabelais, the satirist, to poke fun at excessive gormandizing, presenting on one occasion in *Gargantua and Pantagruel* a mock dinner to whose "regular menu" were added 16 oxen, 32 calves, 63 young kids, 300 milch cows soaked in sweet wine, 700 woodcocks, 6,000 pullets, and so on and on—all in the hands of the ravenous chefs Wolfsauce, Hotchpot, and Lickjuice, along with the stewards Jockbottle, Clearglass, and Guzzletun, who kept their own tankards "brimful with wine."

Indeed, the well-filled cup was ubiquitous in the age. While the early heroes had quaffed their viscous brew of mead made of fermented and spiced honey, and the English and Germans had vastly improved upon this with their superior malt ales, the culture and enjoyment of the grape survived the darkest days. Cultivators of the vine in England were especially protected by King Alfred, and the economic census known as the *Domesday Book*, assembled twenty years after William the Conqueror's arrival, lists thirty-nine productive vineyards there—several of them evidently pre-Norman. Some wine may have been made in Ireland in the earliest missionary days, and vineyards were established along the Moselle, Rhine, and Danube rivers in the eighth century, so successfully that German wine merchants were traveling to London in the early twelfth century and probably before. German grapes, however, were limited in that successful cultivation resulted almost exclusively in white wines, a rich and robust red growth eluding the vintners then as it has ever since. The wine of English vineyards, perhaps for reasons of climate, remained pale and thin; and with the shortage of labor due to the great fourteenth-century plague, and the consequent import of higher quality wines, its production eventually ceased.

The taste of the time ran to sweet and what we would call syrupy, or dessert, wines, among them the growths surreptitiously exported from the vineyards of Xeres (Jerez) where the Moslems were supposed to grow them, in accordance with the prohibitions of the Koran, for food rather than for wine. Also marketed abroad was the Portuguese wine known as Algarbe (an ancestor of port); such sweet types as the Trebbiano of Tuscany; and above all, what was known in England as Malmsey, a heavy drink which took its name from the Greek village Malmasia and was produced at its best in Crete.

It remained for France to build very gradually that culture of noble growths and vintages that one day were to be the accompaniment of the cuisine of a Vatel or a Brillat-Savarin; meanwhile, during the Middle Ages French wines were often drunk heavily sweetened and spiced, too. The monastery, again, played a part in improving and refining quality. Not only was a considerable amount of wine needed for sacramental purposes, as well as for refreshment at table for thirsty monks and those whom they entertained, but viticulture was a "cash crop," essential to the economy of their community. Large vineyards in Burgundy passed into the hands of clerical foundations. Several vineyards in Beaune, Vosne, and Gévrey were entrusted to the Abbey of Bèze by the Duke of Amalgaire in 630. Later, in 1275, the Gévrey vineyard was taken over by the Cluniacs; and shortly after, an enterprising peasant planted an adjacent vineyard, Le Champ de Bertin or Bertin's Field—source of Chambertin, the favored wine of Napoleon III. Pommard and Meursault wines in the Beaune district of the Côte d'Or can also be traced from the eleventh century and Cistercian husbandry. In the coastal valleys of the Gironde around Bordeaux, a somewhat lighter wine was developed (called *clairet*, or claret, for its clear color). Many of the estates there passed under English dominance following the accession of the duchy of Guyenne as part of Eleanor of Aquitaine's dowry in her marriage to Henry II. Perhaps one of the first Englishmen who had what we might consider an advanced taste in wine was King John Lackland, for in 1212 he had his bursar import eight casks of Anjou wine along with twenty-six of Auxerre for his table. Before the fifteenth century, a semiannual convoy of English ships was setting out for the Gironde, to bring home cargoes of the newest growths—fresh wines being generally preferred to those of a preceding year, until the craft and value of aging wine were understood. There were also vineyards in what is now the heart of Paris, a city today far more concerned with the consumption of wine than its growth: the vineyard of Clos Bruneau thrived on the site now occupied by the Théâtre de l'Odéon.

In A.D. 1234 we first hear of a vineyard in the Pauillac district in the Bordeaux region owned by one Gombaud de Lafite. What his wine tasted like, especially when drunk green and possibly sugared and spiced, we can only surmise. But it was one of the fifty or more wines of note—some Cyprian, some Spanish, some from the Moselle, but mostly French—cited in a thirteenth-century poem entitled the *Bataille des Vins*. One day it was to become the renowned Château Lafite, ultimately crowned at a summit meeting of wine experts at the Paris Exposition Universelle of 1855 as the first of the *grands crus classés*, or great classified properties, of Bordeaux, and thus in the judgment of many experts, the finest wine in all the world. Soon after, its 173 acres, at a price equivalent to $1,500,000 today, were to become the property of the Rothschild family of bankers, geniuses at imaginative and first-class investment.

THE
GROANING
BOARD

King Arthur and his knights at the fabled Round Table

Pigs and peasant gathering acorns in November

A warm hearth in February

Readying the fields in March

The Four Seasons

These early-fifteenth-century illuminations from the *Très Riches Heures* of the Duc de Berry depict the seasonal rhythms of life on a feudal estate. The first plowing and seeding took place in spring; vegetables were farmed in summer. With the arrival of fall, the peasant looked to his livestock and filled his larder for the approaching winter months. A minimum of thirty-six bushels of wheat was required to support the average peasant's family through one year on the manor, but according to Langland's *Piers the Ploughman*, "in winter they suffer much hunger and woe."

Grape harvest in September

The Common Market

Fairs and markets were the lighter side of the Dark Ages and focal points of the burgeoning international economy. Caravans of merchants, minstrels, and peasants met seasonally to display and sell products ranging from songs and salted meats to rare spices and silks. Most famous were the fairs of Champagne near Paris held in the twelfth and thirteenth centuries. They lasted anywhere from sixteen to fifty days.

At fairs, gingerbread was baked in the form of Saint Anthony's beloved pig, also commemorated in this stone church-stall carving.

The Bishop of Paris blesses a fair at the Abbey of St-Denis.

A poulterer clinches a sale in the market place.

Royal Rigors—and Rewards

Kings and knights may have had privileged positions at the medieval table, but they paid for them, and sometimes dearly. A seat above the salt more often depended on a man's military record in the field than on his virtue, social wit, or skill at a trencher—though the latter often proved helpful. If he drank too much, he risked being outmaneuvered by another guest for his liege's favor. If he ate too daintily, he might provoke rude comments among the servants, whose meals were often served just below the high table. Then, too, he could never be sure that the meat before him had not been poisoned by a jealous peer.

One of the duties that went with being noble was meting out alms to the poor, a chore engaging Saint Louis in the thirteenth-century manuscript drawing above. Opposite, Charlemagne observes the ceremony of assay—the tasting of food for poison. Below, an even more unappetizing ritual is undergone by a twelfth-century Irish king who, to win his crown, is taking a bath in horsemeat soup while he and his attendants eat blood sausages.

OVERLEAF: *The King of Portugal and his court entertain John of Gaunt.*

Fysshe Dayes

Grilling fish c. 1330, from the Holkham Bible

Fish was not only a popular and inexpensive dish in the medieval diet, but a fact of Christian life. Counting Fridays, Lent, and other fast days, meat was off limits for nearly half the year—to the profit of the fishmonger, left. Inland, many feudal estates like the German manor, right, stocked their moats with carp, trout, and other varieties of fresh-water fish to insure a weekly supply for the lord and his villeins. Some charged their tenants stiff rates for fishing rights, and though harsh punishment was meted out to trespassers caught with "angleroddes," poaching was widespread. Of coastal fish, herring was by far the most important. As an Englishman put it, "A red herring is . . . most precious merchandise, because it can be carried through all Europe. . . . The poorer sort make it three parts of their sustenance. It is every man's money, from the king to the peasant. . . . A red herring drawn on the ground will lead hounds a false scent. A broiled herring is good for the rheumatism. The fishery is a great nursery for seamen, and brings more ships to Yarmouth than assembled at Troy to fetch back Helen."

102

Camouflaged more for ceremony than for deception, huntsmen confront a buck, above. Clattering forth in a square-wheeled cart, below, they give their prey a better than sporting chance.

Good Form in the Forest

As in all noble pursuits, the sports of venery and hawking were attended by a complicated set of rules prescribing what to wear, how to handle weapons, and how to carve up the quarry afterward. The miniatures shown on these pages come from a fourteenth-century treatise by the French courtier Gaston Phoebus. Above, hunters dawdle over lunch spread in a clearing. A tablecloth was evidently *de rigueur*.

Of the poorly prepared artisan:
"He makes broth in a basket."

Of the imprudent husbandman:
"He eats his grain in the blade."

"Measure Is A Merry Mean"

While a select few could indulge in Rabelaisian repasts, the humbler folk of the later Middle Ages were of necessity more temperate in behavior. Just as the upper classes had their manuals of hunting etiquette, the *petite bourgeoisie* likewise had their guides for leading the correct life. Books of proverbs were both didactic and moral in purpose: through the combined force of word and picture, the reader was cautioned to follow the golden mean in his day-to-day activities. The *Proverbes en Rimes*, opposite, from a manuscript c. 1490, were written in the vernacular and were accompanied by illustrations literally interpreting the maxims, serving as models for those engaged in middle-class pursuits.

Of a slothful baker: "In the oven
of a lazy cook the dough freezes."

Of small-town gossipmongers: "An oven and mill are nurseries of news."

Of the glutton: "He grabs with both hands, chews with both jaws."

Of a Jack-of-all-trades: "He who makes crosetz makes lasaigne."

Of a clever manager: "He can pick new spoons out of an old house."

On a sense of measure: "The knife is chosen according to the meat."

On shopping: "Of a little take a little, of a mickle take a mickle."

Of a complaisant scullion: "He who turns the spit never tastes a bit."

Of a wanton wench: "There's many a slip between mouth and spoon."

Of the foolish spendthrift: "He winnows his corn in the wind."

A Flemish merchant samples the wine, while a human treadmill loads casks in the town square.

An ornamented drinking
horn of medieval Denmark
NATIONAL MUSEUM, COPENHAGEN

Good Cheer

One of the chief producers of wine was
the church, which maintained its own
vineyards. Part of the vintage went to
the brothers, part to the service of the
Mass; the remainder was sold to thirsty
travelers or was marketed in cities. The
cost of transporting it made wine more
often the rich man's tipple; beer, cider,
perry, and mead were the poor man's
cheer. Regulations were supposed to
keep tavern fare up to standard, and instances of doctored drink were dealt with
summarily. In 1364 one John Penrose of
England was given a penalty to suit his
crime: he had to drink his own brew.

OVERLEAF: *Honey collecting was hazardous*
duty—a race between the keepers and bees.

VATICAN LIBRARY, ROME

PIERPONT MORGAN LIBRARY, NEW YORK

Students carousing in a Strasbourg tavern

To the Manor Born

Women performed many tasks on the feudal manor. Here they pick spinach.

Taking a midday break in the shade

Digging truffles with a crude hoe

Agriculture in the Middle Ages was centered in the feudal estate, where a tenant serf led the dawn-to-dusk routine portrayed in these illustrations from *Tacuinum Sanitatus*, a fifteenth-century Italian herbal. The serf was literally rooted to the soil; he passed with the lands when the manor changed ownership. In exchange for his labor, he was given a small plot, providing him with a simple fare of cereals and vegetables.

Baking white bread in a wall oven

Depending on the vows of the order and the monastery's proximity to centers of commerce, a community might be secluded or very worldly indeed. Prosperity threatened to interrupt the contemplative life, particularly as agricultural surpluses were becoming sought on the open market; and overindulgence at table was a subject of numerous tracts by church reformers. Such sanctions did not discourage the brother at left, who is nipping at the cellar wine supply while filling the abbot's pitcher.

Peace or Prosperity

Kitchen work is interrupted by the arrival of the devil, above. Meals among the "Poor Clares" were not so diverting; opposite, they sup during a reading of the scriptures.

The festive "Marriage at Cana," transplanted to Renaissance Venice, by Veronese

RENAISSANCE
OF
THE TABLE

The year 1533 saw a trio of extraordinarily brilliant monarchs—the Tudor Henry VIII, the Hapsburg Charles V, and the Valois Francis I—seated on the leading thrones of Europe, each at the height of his prowess and display. It also saw a Florentine girl of fourteen arriving in France to marry a prince. Before long she would become the leader of a revolution in tastes of the table.

At Windsor Castle and Hampton Court, hearty Henry was stuffing in huge gobbets of food and disporting with Anne Boleyn, whom he was to wed that year in defiance of Pope Clement VII's refusal to grant him a divorce from Catherine of Aragon. On the Continent the austere Charles, heir to his family's domains in central Europe along with the crown of Spain, and since 1519 Holy Roman Emperor, was shuttling between his far-flung capitals at Madrid and Vienna, with little thought of comfort or pleasure. The year before, in 1532, he had thrown back the Turks along the Danube and had patched up a truce with

Luther's and Zwingli's rebellious Protestants at Nuremberg. Meanwhile, at Blois and his other châteaux in the French countryside, the prodigal, dashing Francis, devotee of arts and luxuries as well as of mistresses, was hard at work advancing his fortunes against the overweening Hapsburgs by means of alliances, marital and otherwise. His young son, aged fourteen, was that year to be the instrument of Francis' policy; and in casting about for a mate for the boy, the king shrewdly chose an heiress of the richest and proudest family in ducal and divided Italy. So it was that Catherine, daughter of Lorenzo de' Medici, landed in Marseilles in October to become there the child bride of the boy who was one day to succeed Francis as Henry II.

The match was arranged through the good offices of the girl's uncle, Pope Clement. Giulio de' Medici, as he was otherwise known, was a great lover of political machination and the arts. He had in fact been Catherine's guardian since the death of her father and her elder uncle Giovanni de' Medici, the munificent Pope Leo X, and thus held her as a pawn in international chess. Advantages would accrue to both sides in the match; for the Papacy, a political alliance with France; for Francis, a handsome Medici dowry and papal support. Young Catherine came bearing gifts of a more lasting sort, too. Trained at the papal court, she brought the elegant manners of Florence and a small army of Italian chefs. These *maîtres queux*, as the French called them, introduced to noble tables of France such refinements as artichoke hearts, sweetbreads, truffles, grated Parmesan, liver *crépinettes*, along

with *quenelles* of poultry, and a taste for veal (thitherto unappreciated north of the Alps). Predictably, Italian cooks became fashionable in households of rank.

More was to come with Catherine and her entourage, or in their wake. Among new confections were delicate macaroons, zabaglione, custard cakes, "iced cream" (Florentine cooks prepared a different flavor for each day of her wedding festivities), and frangipane tarts, an invention of Count Cesare Frangipani, who made them for her before she left for France. Melons, which had been introduced from the East by way of Italy sometime before, now enjoyed new popularity, spurred perhaps by Jacques

Saddle with pockets for food and drink

Pons, professor of medicine, whose *Sommaire Traité des Melons* suggested fifty different ways of serving them. Imported for the French table were fine works of Venetian glassware, faience from Urbino, embroidered napery, and table silver wrought by artists such as Benvenuto Cellini. Also from Italy came that new tool of the cultivated, the *fuscina*, or fork, though its use north and west of the Alps remained rare until the seventeenth century. Catherine herself may never have used one; we do know, however, that the implement was to travel as far as England by 1582, when Queen Elizabeth received as a New Year's present a coral-handled fork. How esoteric it was to the English, even after the turn of the century, is apparent in the chronicle of the voyager Thomas Coryate, who wrote of his discovery following his venture into Italy: "I observed a custome in all those Italian cities and townes through which I passed, that is not used in any other country that I saw in my travels. . . . The Italians . . . do alwaies at their meates use a little forke when they cut their meat . . . their forkes being for most of yron or steels, and some silver. . . . The reason of their curiosity is, because the Italian cannot by any means indure to have his dish touched with fingers, seeing that all men's fingers are not alike cleane." Such fastidiousness was long regarded by Englishmen as an affectation of "fops and jackanapes."

Queen Catherine was both a precocious gourmet and a glutton. She loved her *tournedos* (another Florentine specialty), veal dishes, kidneys, and cocks' combs, sometimes to the point of excess particularly as she grew older: one observer at a round of royal feasts in 1576 remarked that she "ate so much that she almost burst and was terribly ill with diarrhea." She did, however, insist on great ceremony at board. Late in the fifteenth century, ladies of the French court had taken to absenting themselves from their lords' hearty, often boisterous tables, to dine in the privacy of their own chambers. A particular notion of delicacy had persuaded them that it would be unseemly for them to be seen eating in public, since mastication of food supposedly distorted the contours of their face and detracted from their beauty. Catherine changed all that. If eating had any effect on beauty, it was to enlarge the body, not deform the face. Imperious, unconcerned with her figure, and as vigorous in personality as her husband Henry was dull, she ordered the ladies of the court to attend stately banquets which, in form and protocol, were to be both the models of Elizabeth's dinner rites across the Channel a few decades later and the precursors of the splendors of Versailles.

Catherine de' Medici—the most influential, worldly, womanly presence and maker of taste since Eleanor of Aquitaine—was an embodiment and transmitter of that revival of classical manners and modes that had arisen in Italy several generations before her birth. Her native Tuscany was not only urban, in contrast to the isolated feudal estates and monastic communities of northern Europe, but urbane in its extensive life of commerce with East and West, its wealth of finance, and its resulting leisure time for self-improvement. The enterprising, rich, and cultured merchant of the Tuscan town of Prato, Francesco di Marco Datini, lived before 1400 in a prandial style very different from that of the Gothic north. His dinners began, not with a heaping of crude slabs of meat or bowls of stew, but with a *minestra*, or soup, that was often sprinkled with Parmesan, or a dish of *lasagne* or *ravioli*. Datini's chef also favored garlic and mushrooms—especially the small, delicate *prugnoli*—to lend savor to the cutlets that followed. His doctor expressly recommended veal: "Place it in your belly, in every way you can, for you can have no more wholesome victuals." The

La Dolce Vita

*E*ven among the pleasure-loving Tuscans, the people of Florence were renowned for their lusty appetites. It was commonly charged that they made better use of their glasses than their plates, and a contemporary estimated that the annual consumption of wine was more than five barrels for every man, woman, and child in the city. A month rarely passed without some excuse for an uninhibited *convivio*—like the pre-Lenten carnival procession pictured below, or the star-crossed feast of Calendimaggio (May Day) that introduced

the young Dante and Beatrice. For some, even a public disaster could be a sociable affair, as Giovanni Boccaccio records in the *Decameron*, a collection of tales told by a fictional group of men and women who have retreated to a villa outside Florence to escape the great plague of 1348. For ten days they outdo each other with stories of the cupidity and pretentiousness of their fellow men. Florentines, it seems, are so greedy that they are easy marks for con men and pranksters. On the eighth day of exile, one of the party tells the story of a foolish painter who sets out for a fabulous "Nomansland" where, he is told, they tie up the grape vines with sausages and a goose and gosling cost but a cent, and there is "a mountain of grated Parmesan cheese, inhabited by people who [do] nothing but make macaroni and ravioli . . . [and] a stream of white wine, the best ever drunk. . . ." Several tales later, one of the listeners tops them all with a story of a Florentine doctor who is duped into providing lavish board for two men on their promise to introduce him at an imaginary social club. Describing the hall where the club meets, one of the pretenders gives an exaggerated picture of the elegant entertainments which Renaissance aristocrats did, in truth, know. "It is a marvel to see the hangings . . . and the tables royally spread, and the quantity of handsome servants . . . and the basins and jugs and flasks and cups and other gold and silver vessels from which we eat and drink, and the many varied dishes of food according to each man's desire which are set before us. I could never describe . . . the sweet sounds of infinite musical instruments and the songs full of melody . . . nor all the wax candles which are burned . . . nor the quantity of sweetmeats consumed nor . . . the wines. . . ." Upon hearing that the con men dumped the doctor onto a manure pile en route to a club dinner, the listeners agreed he got his just deserts.

merchant also prized the tender beans growing in his garden.

In nearby Urbino in the next generation, Federigo da Montefeltro—the ruler of the duchy—was known for the high style of his table: among his five hundred household servitors there were five "readers aloud at meals." Later, the Duke of Milan commissioned Leonardo da Vinci to organize spectacular festivals. Under Lorenzo the Magnificent, there were Florentine carnivals with processions representing old Roman triumphs; and his son Giovanni de' Medici, the future Pope Leo X, even as a cardinal, rarely dined without the musical accompaniment of Italy's leading chamber musicians. In Venice there were water-borne dinner parties and regattas: one year at the Festival of the *Sempiterni*, a corporation of nobles, a splendid ball was literally launched in the Grand Canal.

About this time printed books of etiquette and cookery began appearing in numbers second only to Bibles. The first of these, Platina's *De Honesta Voluptate* of 1475, provided some sound advice on the value of avoiding disputes at table: "The stomach needs natural warmth, little motion and little mental agitation; otherwise it becomes weak and unable to produce its digestive juices." It also offered some novel recipes for advanced tastes—fish in aspic and a tart of chestnuts and cheese that may have prefigured the *quiche* of French cuisine. There was an Italian volume of 1480, *The Fifty Courtesies of the Table*, which cautioned its readers, "Do not stuff too large mouthfuls in both cheeks. Do not keep your hand too long in the platter and put it in only when the other has withdrawn his hand from the dish"—a presentiment, perhaps, of the fork. But far more important was the discovery of eight books by Apicius found in manuscript by the traveling Italian scholar Poggio Bracciolini at the library of the Fulda monastery in central Germany. Eventually these classical recipe texts, no doubt reworked by monastic scholars, were to be brought to the Vatican library and published in Milan just before 1500. The interest in them was such that the edition was pirated almost at once by Venetian printers.

Polished behavior and courtly dining also absorbed the Florentine-born prelate Giovanni della Casa, who published his own guide to good manners, *Il Galateo*. Della Casa inveighed against expressing one's self with gestures of the fork and emphasized the ceremonious presentation of an orderly sequence of dishes, some served from the *credenza*, or sideboard, decorated with the family silver, others carried in from the kitchen and pantries.

Perhaps the most influential of Italian Renaissance books concerning the table was Bartolomeo Scappi's *Cooking Secrets of Pope Pius V*, published in 1570, which presented menus that began with Neapolitan spicecakes and marzipan balls and proceeded through *prosciutto* cooked in wine and served with capers and strained grapes, "songbirds roasted on the spit, served cold, with tongues sliced over them," legs of goat, a soup of pigeons and almond paste, "stuffed fat geese, boiled in Lombard style. . . ." Scappi prescribed a change of napery, water for washing the hands, and toothpicks as a fitting close to a proper meal.

121

There were, to be sure, occasional dark rumors about the nefarious uses to which such elaborate foods could sometimes be put, particularly in the hands of a Cesare Borgia and his sister Lucrezia, supposed experts at hidden poisons early in the sixteenth century. One such was a white powder, *cantarella,* sugary and of a pleasing taste when added to a dish, but deadly. Alexandre Dumas in

Chicken dinner in a Renaissance household

his *Crimes Célèbres* described how the Borgias obtained a particularly virulent poison. The concoction was made, says Dumas, by forcing a bear to swallow a strong dose of arsenic. As the poison took effect, the beast was suspended by his hind legs, and a stream of foam poured from its mouth; this foam was collected on a silver plate and bottled by someone in the Vatican in expectation of some future mischief.

The taster of food and drink, who sampled dishes for evidence of foul play in the presence of his lord and lady before they dined, would remain a functionary immediately attached to the royal or high ducal table in many courts until the nineteenth century. Elizabeth of England, for instance, insisted on one (as for that matter did Adolf Hitler centuries

later). To dispense with "the proof of the test," as Henry IV of France did on one occasion when he was the guest of Madame de Montpensier, was a sign of special confidence. Then there were nasty little devices, mentioned in an Italian book on magic and potions, for making an unwelcome guest sick at table by mixing his wine with the filth of a dog's ear; or for driving him away by cutting up harp strings and strewing the small bits on hot meat, causing them to writhe like worms.

But such meannesses, accompanied by violence and occasional death, could not prevent Italian taste and style from becoming the exuberant toast of fashion-seeking western Europe. True, there were elements among the French *bourgeoisie* and the prospering English yeomanry in particular that scoffed at this southern incursion, and cooks were to be heard denouncing the foreign fork itself as a possible poisoner of food. The urbane essayist Montaigne, a leading interpreter of the Renaissance spirit in later sixteenth-century France, was to poke fun in one of his liveliest passages at the pretentiousness and self-importance of Italian *maîtres queux* as they flocked with their new dishes into France. In an essay entitled "Of the Vanity of Words," he wrote of a conversation he had with "an Italian who was in the service of the late Cardinal Caraffa until his death, in the capacity of major-domo. . . . He entertained me with a dissertation on the science of the gullet with the gravity and demeanour of a schoolmaster, as if he were discussing some important point in theology. He minutely explained that there was a difference in appetites: that which we have when fasting, that which comes after the second or third course; the means, now of simply gratifying it, now of arousing and stimulating it; the organization of sauces: firstly in general, then particularizing the qualities of the ingredients and their effects; the different salads according to the season, that which should be warmed, that which requires to be served cold, the manner of adorning and embellishing them to make them pleasing to the sight also."

Still, though a Montaigne might smile at its vanities, Europe was rapidly growing more stable under strong monarchs or at least uncontested dynasties; far wealthier and better schooled than before the spread of commerce and the growth of cities, men craved both pomp and polish. Perhaps the ultimate example of Italian opulence at table was reached at the regal banquet given in Mantua in 1581 to celebrate the marriage of that duchy's ruler. At the raised head table, under an immense *baldacchino*, or canopy, sat four cardinals, three dukes, and many other dignitaries. At the next table (to follow a contemporary description translated in Colin Clair's *Kitchen and Table*) there were "100 ladies beautiful beyond measure and most richly garbed." Four choirs in galleries at the four corners of the hall provided music. The finest Venetian glass crowded the sideboard; and the guests, "after having drunk, smashed the glasses they held in their hands as a sign of great joy." Richly embroidered tablecloths had been laid; "the napkins were marvellously folded in various manners with columns and arches, which presented a beautiful sight with innumera-

ble streamers of coloured cloth gilded with the arms of all the noble lords who were at table." The first "service" from the credenza consisted of "salads decked out with various fantasies such as animals made of citron, castles of turnips, high walls of lemons; and variegated with slices of ham, mullet roes, herrings, tunny, anchovies, capers, olives, caviar, together with candied flowers and other

Fish market during the busy Lenten season

preserves." The more serious eating began with "venison patties in the shape of gilded lions, pies in the form of upright black eagles, pasties of pheasant, which seemed alive, white peacocks adorned and re-clothed with their fanned-out tails, and decked with silken ribbons and divers colours, as well as long gilded confections which hung everywhere about the peacocks, which stood erect as in life, with a perfume emanating from the kindled wad in their beaks and an amorous epigram placed beneath their legs." And so on, to "three large statues in marzipan, each four hands high," representing famous mythological personages and events.

Imitation in France of such Italian delicacies and grandiosities, the novelist and gourmet Alexandre Dumas wrote in his *Dictionnaire de Cuisine*, was to reach a height under Catherine de' Medici's son Henry III, who reigned from 1574 to 1589 under the domination of the aging, obese queen mother. The Italian influence was to continue: *apéritifs*, sometimes iced, were introduced, and much later, indeed not until about 1660, ice creams and ices reached the Parisian public through the enterprise of a Sicilian named Francisco Procopio, who opened a shop on the Rue de l'Ancienne Comédie on the left bank.

The taste for new dishes and styles in France was by no means limited to the courtly and rich of Catherine's time. Everyday middle-class Paris was receptive to the dissemination of Italian ideas, though without the accompanying pomp. The type of glutton satirized by Rabelais (the first part of whose *Gargantua and Pantagruel* had appeared the year before Catherine's arrival) was disappearing, a remembrance of a rough, hungry age. The vice of drunkenness among the lower classes had indeed continued, to which Catherine's father-in-law Francis I had applied a corrective (after some disorders in Brittany caused by mobs under the influence of wine) in an edict that specified, "Any man convicted of being drunk will be condemned: on the first offense, to detention in prison on bread and water; on the second offense, to be whipped in the inner court of the prison; on the third offense, to be whipped publicly. . . . And on the fourth offense, he shall have both his ears cut off and be banished from the kingdom of France."

By mid-century, Paris, with its ample supplies of food, was becoming the seat of a well-ordered, varied life. Great sales were held there on Wednesdays and Saturdays, when as many as two thousand laden drays rolled in through the city gates to what was to evolve into Les Halles, the central Paris food mart that survived until this decade; and nothing left unsold on one market day was allowed to be held over to the next. Vegetables came in from all sides, particularly after Olivier de Serres, a native gourmet of the late sixteenth century, had popularized them. Serres, who remarked to the Duc de Sully that "ploughing and grazing are the two breasts of France," owned an experimental farm whose yields were the richest in the country. New foods from distant lands, such as the potato, first praised by Serres, and the turkey, also arrived about this time. Great casks of Burgundy lumbered in from the Hospices de Beaune (a charitable but highly profitable lay foundation that had been set up a century and a half before to administer the holdings in the Côte d'Or), along with wains bearing *crus* of Pauillac and the Médoc.

Rabelais in his exuberant fashion lists his favorite wines as being "the Falernian, Malvesian [the Englishman's Malmsey], the Muscadine, those of Taige, Beaune, Moirevaux, Orléans, Picardent, Arbois, Coussi, Anjou, Graves,

Four cookboys with lever raising a heavy cauldron

Corsica, Vierron, Nerac, and others."

Fresh butter and milk (including that of asses) also came on the general market. There were wild strawberries, or *fraises de bois*, from the Fontainebleau woods. Oysters and salmon were available in season, and a middle-class specialty was a pâté of carp. Some oddities persisted: whale meat was still prized, particularly whale tongue which could be roasted and served with orange sauce or cooked in a court bouillon. A bishop of Sens appointed by Francis I was an advocate of donkey meat. Garlic was in vogue as a protector against disease. In fact, the food supply of Paris as well as its provincial capitals was so varied as to arouse the admiration of a Venetian ambassador who reported in 1577, "Since France abounds in woods, pastures and grain, the livestock is numerous and fat. Of the animals the sheep is the most esteemed, having the most succulent flesh. The beef is good, but not as good as in England. Calves are so plentiful that they cost no more than sheep. . . . Paris has in abundance all that one can wish for, for the merchandise of every country flows into it." He was also surprised by the irregularity of a Frenchman's dining hours. "They eat three, four, or five times a day without keeping to any fixed times or rules."

There had long been present in France a guild of *cuisiniers* or cooks and purveyors of food, who—remarkably—appear to have shown no organized opposition to the incursion of Italian chefs. There were many specialists in the trade: *charcutiers*, or pork butchers and sausage vendors; *rôtisseurs*, or roasters of poultry, game, and large saddles of meat, which

they sold from their own cookshops; and *pâtissiers*, or pastry cooks and confectioners. There were also *tamisiers*, bread bakers, so named for the sieve

Crushing olives in an olive oil mill, c. 1570

which they used for their flour; and *vinaigriers* or *sauciers*, those who concocted sauces. Still another guild was the *maîtres queux cuisiniers et porte-chappes*, professional caterers, able to put together and deliver to a client's house a cooked meal—even a feast—almost on demand. An Italian marveled that "at less than an hour's notice . . . [they] can furnish a dinner for ten, twenty, or even a hundred persons."

At the same time a custom of dining out spread in Paris, Lyons, and other French cities with the growth of *cabarets* —establishments not to be confused with the night clubs of a much later Montmartre, but the precursors of that French invention, the restaurant. The medieval inn had been a gross and sometimes dangerous place, often offering no food (one brought his own), just drink, rough company, and stabling for horses. Chaucer's famous Tabard Inn at

Southwark, with its hospitality that started the Canterbury pilgrims on their way, had been advanced for its time. Late medieval Paris saw numerous *tavernes* and *auberges* arising outside its walls—rustic but welcome retreats amid trees or near vineyards and far from the dank, crowded alleys of the city. From these there developed in the city itself a type of hostelry that provided tables laid with cloth and cutlery and some food in addition to drink. The *rôtisseur,*

English silver tankard, 1602

already the owner of a cookshop, often became an eating-house keeper—a *cabaretier* or *traiteur.* Many jurisdictional squabbles arose, and under Henry III and Henry IV legislation had to be enacted to regulate the functions of those who sold wine, according to whether the wine was drunk on or off the premises.

At a good cabaret late in the sixteenth century one could get a substantial dish of chicken fricassee or stuffed gosling, roast partridge, or a carbonade of beef, and moreover possibly see celebrities at the next table. "Today," said a pamphlet of 1574 that described some of the leading French eating houses, "everyone goes to the More, or the Sanson, or the

Innocent, or the Havard, all of them nothing but ministers of luxury and extravagance." A stranger to Paris reported that "there are certain cabarets where one can dine at almost any price. . . . Princes of the blood and even the king himself patronize them on occasion." Henry IV was recorded as a visitor at the Trois Maures in the old Marais quarter. Moreover, many individual cabarets became the meeting places of poets and their intellectual friends. The Pomme de Pin, in the Rue de la Juiverie, was celebrated by Villon and Rabelais, and in a later day by Racine. La Fontaine, Boileau, and others patronized the Mouton Blanc in the Rue du Vieux-Colombier, later moving over to the Croix de Lorraine in the Place du Cimitière Saint-Jean. University students frequented La Corne, lawyers Le Petit Diable; and there were others of engaging names and sometimes of gamy reputations: L'Ecu d'Orléans, L'Epée Royale, Le Grand Cerf, La Fosse aux Lions, Le Sabot, the latter made famous by Ronsard. All were centers of lively talk and occasional entertainment; some appear to have been equipped with *chambres séparées* for intimate rendezvous.

Though not previously known for culinary genius, the inventive French showed an amazing aptitude for catching up with their Italian tutors of the table. On March 29, 1571, there took place in Paris a feast demanding extraordinary kitchen talents and a public levy of 300,000 livres; the city offered a banquet to receive Elizabeth of Austria, bride of Catherine's reigning son Charles IX, but the appointed day was a Friday. Since fast had to be observed, the din-

German coconut cup

ner was entirely without meat. The city's kitchens met the challenge handsomely. After Mass at Nôtre Dame, the royal party and its hundreds of courtiers were served with 2 barrels of oysters, 50 pounds of whale meat, 200 crayfish, 28 salmon, 10 turbot, 18 brill, 400 herring (half of them fresh, half salted), 50 carp, great platters of broiled lobster, steamed mussels, 18 trout, and 1,000 pairs of frogs' legs as well, the frog being regarded as fish food since it was aquatic. To stage such a banquet, with its innumerable variations in taste on one theme and without any recourse to meat, was a triumph of the art of the Parisian chef and his *sauciers*. By 1600 it was apparent that French *maîtres queux* were equal or superior to the *maestri di cucina* of Italy.

In England during these decades, the evolution of tastes and manners of the table generally proceeded at a much slower pace. Under the early Tudors the English people seemed to stand on an uncertain threshold between old and new—between their own roughhewn, baronial ways and the growing attraction of more polished and urbane living. No man embodied this time of transition more than the ravenous Henry VIII.

"The king ate enormously," one of his biographers writes, "stuffing the meat into his little mouth with his knife. As he munched, the meat and vegetables popping from cheek to cheek, his eyes shone with happiness. He jabbed his knife, greasy as it was, into the salt cellar, blew his nose on his napkin, spat into the washing bowl—he was the king. The meat was soaked with sauces of parsley, garlic, quince, pear, wine; there were great pastries, glittering with sugar, or hiding haunches of venison cooked to rags and powdered with ginger; there was veal boiled with sage and smeared with cinnamon, cloves, and saffron, stiffened with eggs, all buried under pastry dotted with dates. . . ." Yet this was the Henry who wrote occasional lyrics, composed airs for the lute, danced elegantly, patronized the painter Holbein, and fathered one of the most cultivated and regal women in the history of Europe.

Throughout the era the English held ambivalent attitudes toward the Continent. By the end of the sixteenth century, the Tudors had finally put an end to those marital alliances and military adventures that had brought their kingdom many victories across the Channel, but in the end little save grief. On one hand, England had turned away from the rest of Europe and back to its particular life at home ("This other Eden, demi-paradise; This fortress built by Nature for herself. . . ."), with royal ships cruising the Atlantic to ensure that this isolation would not be disturbed. But on the other hand, prospering, high-spirited, and ambitious—never more so than under the Virgin Queen—England was strongly attracted by Continental ways. The French were more suspect than ever in Tudor England, yet the Elizabethan chronicler Holinshed speaks of the presence of "musical-headed Frenchmen," favorite cooks of the English aristocracy. Italian intrigues, after Henry's schism with Rome over his divorce from Catherine of Aragon, were widely feared, and the activities of an Italian musician, David Rizzio, a favorite of Mary, Queen of Scots, confirmed many Englishmen in their prejudice; yet Venetian glass and napery were favorite imports, and Lombard Street in the City was named for the Lombard banking agents with whom Londoners traded there. Spain, after Henry's divorce, became an outright enemy. But Spain and its Canary Islands produced the Elizabethans' favorite wine, "sack" (a type of sherry). What could not conveniently be bought was seized. Francis Drake, out to "singe the beard" of King Philip at Cádiz in 1587, also captured 2,900 butts of the Spanish wine.

The English yeoman, whose status rose markedly in the Tudor age, was by nature resistant to the foreign influences that were working upon the aristocracy. Thomas Fuller, in his *Worthies*, writes with pride and the prejudice of his class that "at our yeoman's table you shall have . . . no meat disguised with strange sauces, no straggling joint of sheep in the midst of a pasture of grass beset with sallets [*sic*] on every side, but solid substantial food; no servitors (more nimble with their hands than the guests with their teeth) [who] take away meat before stomachs are taken away."

The yeoman's diet was certainly substantial. He began his day with "pottage" of boiled meat with vegetables and oatmeal, and a tankard of ale—the common breakfast beverages, tea and coffee, not yet having made their appearance. His main meal at midday might include either beef, mutton, lamb, veal, or "souse" (brawn of pork); he had also acquired a taste for cheese and took his "flapjacks, fritters [and] pancakes" with a goodly portion of butter, according to one man who praised his mother's cooking.

His ale was usually a home brew, made from malted barley without hops, the "pernicious weeds" used only in the "Dutchman's strong beere." But beer began to invade England during the sixteenth century, first made in London by "straungers, Flemyngis, Duchemen." Neither drink was served in upper-class households, for as Fynes Moryson wrote in his *Itinerary*, "Clownes and vulgar men only use large drinking of Beere or Ale . . . but Gentlemen garrawse onely in Wine, with which many mixe sugar." The English lower classes were equally partisan toward their brew: a song published in the mid-seventeenth century, but thought to be of popular origin in Elizabethan times, runs:

> *Submit, Bunch of Grapes,*
> *To the strong Barley ear;*
> *The weak wine no longer*
> *The laurel shall wear.*
> *Sack, and all drinks else,*
> *Desist from the strife:*
> *Ale's the only Aqua Vitae,*
> *And liquor of life.*

Amid these differences, a generally amicable life between classes in the Tudor age went on. There was never a

Francis Bacon

"*T*o be free-minded and cheerfully disposed at hours of meat and of sleep and of exercise is one of the best precepts of long lasting . . . avoid envy; anxious fears; anger fretting inwards; subtile and knotty inquisitions; joys and exhilarations in excess; sadness not communicated. Entertain hopes; mirth rather than joy; variety of delights, rather than surfeit of them; wonder and admiration, and therefore novelties. . . ." Such a regimen of health, wrote Sir Francis Bacon, will carry a man comfortably to a benign old age. The essayist was not notably successful in following his own advice. Politically ambitious, forever embroiled in Elizabethan and Jacobean court intrigues, a man of remarkable literary and scientific inventiveness, he lived anything but a life of moderation. The chronicler John Aubrey gossiped that at Bacon's Twickenham Lodge, it "seemed as if the court had been there, so nobly did he live. Every meal, according to the season of the yeare, he had his table strewed with sweet herbs and flowers, which he sayd did refresh his spirits and memorie." As for expense, King James himself remarked of his lord chancellor, "He and I shall both die beggars." Bacon protested in his essay on riches that money is only "the baggage of virtue," a sort of good man's burden. When Bacon was impeached for taking bribes and sent into retirement, his "baggage," including one of the finest wine cellars in all England, was quickly dispatched. Bacon returned to his thoughts and his essays: "Of Truth," "Of Envy," "Of Travel," "Of Gardens". . . . Never one to be daunted by lack of firsthand knowledge, Bacon even wrote an essay on intelligent husbandry in the New World. "[Notice] what kind of victual the country yields. . . . Then consider what victual or esculent things there are, which grow speedily, and within the year; as parsnips, carrots, turnips, onions, radish, artichokes of Hierusalem [*sic*], maize, and the like. For wheat, barley, and oats, they ask too much labour; but with peas and beans you may begin . . . because they serve for meat as well as for bread . . . and of rice likewise." He advised against uprooting the hired help, for people when "displanted" make it "rather an extirpation than a plantation." Bacon died, appropriately, searching for a way to preserve food: seized with the answer one wintry day, he bought a chicken, stuffed it with snow, and promptly contracted fatal pneumonia. His essay on death provided a fitting epitaph: "He that dies in an earnest pursuit . . . scarce feels the hurt."

lack of willing servitors of the great. Henry VIII once called upon four hundred to prepare a Christmas feast including a meat pie nine feet long, baked in a rectangle to symbolize the Christ Child's manger, and the traditional presentation of a boar's head, richly garnished. How amply servants and masters lived appears in the records of a middle-sized Tudor mansion, Ingatestone Hall, seat of Sir William Petre in Essex, where in the year 1552 the baronial family, their guests, and their twenty or so retainers managed to consume 20,000 loaves of bread, over a ton of cheese, 17 oxen, 14 steers, 4 cows, 29 calves, 129 sheep, 54 lambs, 2 boars, 9 "porks," 5 bacon hogs, 3 goats, 7 kids, 13 bucks, 5 does, and 1 stag.

Whether the Tudor English generally consumed more or less than their predecessors is a moot point. Certainly the preparation of what they ate and the way they ate it had changed conspicuously. The great Tudor country house itself provided an altered setting much akin to the new châteaux rising in the Ile-de-France and the Loire valley. The turrets, the battlements, the latticed, slit windows for defense, gave way to spacious, glazed windows overlooking great gardens and pleasances such as those of Hampton Court or Longleat. The ancestral moat became a decorative fishpond. The smoky, communal Great Hall of Yorkist and Lancastrian days with its imposing central hearth was gradually replaced by private dining chambers with side fireplaces; and nobility and retainers no longer necessarily took their meals together at ranked tables, though the custom of a dais for the first table

persisted. High tables became massive and ornamental pieces of furniture, as against the portable trestle tables common in the all-purpose hall. Chairs for lords and ladies superseded stools or benches, which were now restricted to children, lesser visitors, and servants.

As in France, silver and glassware gradually replaced pewter and earthenware in the houses of the rich, and they were proudly exhibited on sideboards in the dining halls. The yeomanry advanced from wooden spoons and cups of leather and earthenware to pewter spoons and tableware, and the time was not far ahead when a prosperous farmer named

Crest of the Fishmongers' Company

Giles Heard could list in his inventory eleven pewter dishes, nine porringers, six spoons, and two pewter "salts." Some yeomen even reached the stature of possessing silver.

Tudor royalty, for their part, had gone considerably beyond silver and had acquired a taste for gold wine goblets and enameled "standing cups." A good deal of gilded ware had come into the hands of Henry VIII through his dissolution and despoliation of monasteries, and foreign princes and ambassadors made lavish gifts of both silver and gold to Elizabeth, whose love of pomp and finery was well known throughout Europe.

Still, new-found elegance and traditional ways continued to mix, even at the royal level. At Nonsuch Palace, the presence chamber for Queen Elizabeth was hung with tapestries and laid with rugs where she was to tread, but the rest of the chamber was simply carpeted with straw, as were most great ducal houses. The gentry wore hats at table, doffing them only for the occasion of a toast—a custom that was to persist through much of the following century.

Meals still were a confusion of old and new. The commentator William Harrison speaks in 1577 of the heavy breakfast as falling into disfavor among many persons of taste, yet at Queen Elizabeth's court, poultry, rabbit, mutton, veal, and beef, along with wine and ale, were served to start the day. The gentry still took their dinner at about eleven, the merchants of the city advancing it toward noon. A proposed menu for a summer dinner for fifty, in a tract on table etiquette called *Two Bookes of Cookerie and Carving*, by John Murrel in about 1641, calls for a first course of twenty dishes including capons, pike, partridges, wild ducks, quails, "a Florentine of Puft-paste," a "forced boyld meate," a hash of venison, a swan, a "Fawne or Kid, with a pudding in his belly," a bustard, a chicken pie, a potato pie, and so on, even to a custard; a second course including kid, carp, heron, trout, a "Hartichoake Pie," a "sowst Pigge," a gull, more partridge and such, along with salmon, sturgeon, a "dried Neatestongue," and a cherry or gooseberry tart; this in turn to be followed by a

seafood course of crabs, prawns, anchovies, lobsters, and oysters.

Such gastronomic chaos suggests how far English taste makers lagged behind their Italian and French mentors. To be sure, it was understood that a guest of breeding would by no means take a plate of everything presented, but would select from each course, or service, that which he preferred: it might be a fish here, a breast of fowl or cut of meat pie there, with sweets intermixed. As in medieval days, what was not chosen was sent on to retainers—in effect, the "second sitting." But the art of some order of presentation—from introductory dishes to main dishes to desserts, as it had been known in Rome—was not yet understood in England.

Restraints on self-indulgence, meanwhile, were being imposed both by edict and by an advancing taste. One act restricted the number of courses at table to three, though it was easily circumvented by the proliferation of dishes per course. The Dutch physician Levine Lemnie, who appears to have frequented many tables of the English rich at the time, comments that "although they be very sumptuous and love to have good fare, yet neither use they to overcharge themselves with excess of drink, neither thereto greatly provoke and urge others." Perhaps he had noted the custom in many good houses of removing the emptied glass or cup from the table, to be refilled only on request.

The Elizabethan table in any case was far more varied than before. Shakespeare in his plays speaks of apricots, mulberries, pomegranates, quinces, figs, gooseberries, and seems to have had a

131

particular interest in strawberries, then considered by many to possess some special health-giving qualities. In *Henry V* a courtier likens the emergence of the young king's virtues after a misspent youth to the strawberry thriving under the nettle. Indeed, the fascination with medicinal plants and herbs long survived: to Shakespeare, rhubarb was known as a "physicke" (which, to be sure, it is), and cowslips, lungwort, liverwort, pennyroyal, were respected for their special qualities along with the mysterious mandrake—celebrated in the second line of John Donne's lyric, "Get with child a mandrake root. . . ."

Melons, currants, foreign cheeses, arrived, along with oranges (first known in some London markets as "portyngales," having come from Portugal). And the appearance in England of the first yam from the New World in 1564 (the common potato coming some four decades later) and of tobacco in 1565 was to have far-reaching effects, the one on menu, the other on manners.

In the evolving Elizabethan style at table, nothing was more conspicuous than the passion for sweet dishes of every sort, often served at the outset of a meal as well as between courses and at the end. There were custards, marmalades, jellies, meringues, "suckets" (candied fruits), and other "comfits" in profusion, reminiscent of the "sotelties" of an earlier day. Describing these elaborate showpieces, sometimes whole castles of pastry, the playwright Thomas Dekker called them "sinful suburbs of cookery." There was a fad for "marchpane," a combination of pounded almonds and pistachio nuts, sugar, flour, and various

essences including vanilla, which made its first appearance in the confection prepared for Elizabeth. It was sometimes prized as an hors d'oeuvre (it survives today chiefly in central Europe, as *marzipan*, though as an accompaniment to the coffee hour or the close of dinner). In the numerous books of etiquette and cookery that began appearing in England, ladies were encouraged for instance to "gild" or glaze marchpane. They were given recipes telling how to "Candie Nutmegs or Ginger," to make "a sirup of Roses," or in Sir Hugh Plat's celebrated *Delightes for Ladies* of 1609, to create a "sugar plate" combining the colors and scents of flowers.

The "sack" that was widely drunk with meals was not "seke" or dry at all, but tasted perhaps somewhat like a modern sweet sherry. Some of the gentry preferred a still sweeter and richer drink called Hippocras, compounded of white wine, sherry, ginger, nutmeg, cloves, Jamaica pepper, and, again, sugar—a concoction that was to survive in later times as a Christmas or New Year's punch. Still others favored a very heavy wine known since medieval times as Bastard, after the Spanish Bastardo grape which was often used. Heavily sugared and perhaps fortified, it was no doubt the ancestor of the port wine that in the eighteenth century was thought to afflict so many English gentlemen with gout.

If the Elizabethans had an extraordinarily sweet tooth, no one surpassed the reigning queen herself, who constantly carried candies about with her in the folds of her gown, doted on fruit pies and on meringues, which became known as "kisses" because Elizabeth kissed the "faire cloth" of the table that held them. She consumed so many sweetmeats that her teeth eventually turned quite black. The intensity of the unmarried monarch's appetite for sweets is of interest to the psychologist. In other respects she was moderate at table. Unlike many other monarchs both before and after her time, she was not addicted to great and ostentatious feasting. On the contrary, she took many of her meals in the privacy of her chambers, surrounded only by the closest of her attendants, sometimes almost alone. The ceremony of utmost splendor that preceded this withdrawal served to emphasize the contrast. Her entrances, whether at Westminster, Windsor, Greenwich, or Hampton courts, or at one of the ducal mansions which she honored with a royal visit, or progress, were masterworks of stagecraft. Sometimes she did not deign to appear in person for a meal at all, and the elaborate ceremony went on without her. Thus, a German visitor who had the privilege of witnessing preparations for a royal dinner at Greenwich in 1598 wrote that while the queen was at prayer, noble gentlemen of the rod bore a saltcellar and other ornaments to the dining table and knelt before it; then came ladies of the court to "rub the plates with bread and salt, with as much awe as if the queen had been present"; they were followed in turn by yeomen of the guard "clothed in scarlet . . . bringing in at each turn a course of twenty-four dishes served in plate, most of it gilt." "Twelve trumpets and two kettledrums made the hall ring for half an hour" while each servant tasted the dish he carried for poison as the guests looked on (presumably the food grew cold). Then a group of court ladies bore selected viands to Elizabeth, seated all the while in her inner rooms.

Other Elizabethan women could not so absent themselves. Indeed, with its increasing refinement and complexity, the late Tudor household and that of the succeeding Stuart period fell very considerably into the hands of the ladies. There were gentlemen ushers, gentlemen of the horse, auditors of the revenue, chaplains, stewards, butlers, secretaries, carvers, yeomen of the cellar, brewmasters, maltsters, pantrymen, chamberlains,

English trencher, from a set made in 1600

dairymen, candlemakers, gardeners, and so on down to scullions and turnspits (and Sir Peter Legh even kept a jester in the reign of James I); but the management of estates, often served by two hundred to four hundred domestics of ever-increasing specialization, called for the superintendence of intelligent wives. Did they, perhaps, have some influence on the movement for diet restraint and reform that began on the eve of the seventeenth century?

That there was such a movement, we know from scattered records. Doctor

Thomas Muffet published before his death in 1604 a popular tract entitled *Healths Improvement*, calling for "temperancy," avoidance of "surfeiting," and a return to good, plain cooking. The writer Nicholas Breton, in his *Fantasticks* of 1626, proposed "a wholesome dyet that breeds good sanguine juyce," based primarily on poultry, beef, and "morning milk fasting from the cow." Robert Burton, author of the esteemed *Anatomy of Melancholy* (1621), believed that "all black wines, over-hot, compound, strong thick drinks" were "hurtful" and inclined to lead to "head melancholy." A peasant known as Old Parr of Shropshire observed a far more healthy regimen, remembered in the following lines:

> *That green cheese was most wholesome*
> *(with an onion)*
> *Coarse maslin bread; and for his daily*
> *swig,*
> *Milk, butter-milk and water, whey*
> *and whig,*
> *Sometimes metheglin, and by fortune*
> *happy,*
> *He sometimes sipped a cup of ale most*
> *nappy.*

His contemporaries were all the more impressed because he had been convicted of fornication at the age of 105 and died at 152.

The seventeenth century brought numerous changes in the form and content of European eating and drinking. Many were handsome advances; others represented retreats. In France at the outset of the new era, Henry IV, a ruler of high polish, appointed the master *cuisinier*, La Varenne, to be a minister of state;

then came Louis XIII, whose tastes in food were gross, and Louis XIV, whose appetites were Gargantuan. England experienced in James I an alcoholic who made drunkenness fashionable at his court, and then in Charles I a king whose lofty fastidiousness contributed to his fatal unpopularity. In disordered Germany the age witnessed the hunger and bestiality of the Thirty Years' War. Vatel arose at Chantilly as creator of a cuisine far more subtle than that of the old Florentines, and new foods and tastes arrived from around the globe. In England the Puritans frowned on pleasures of the table, and a Roundhead like Colonel Hutchinson fined his soldiers for drinking on the Sabbath.

The seventeenth century brought, among other institutions of taste, the rise of the English coffeehouse and the French café. They were improvements, to be sure, on the old French cabaret and the English tavern or alehouse patronized by Ben Jonson and his company of talkers, players, feasters, pipe-smokers, wenchers, and other dubious characters who enjoyed "a pure cup of rich Canary wine." Nostalgically, the poet Robert Herrick, who outlived that good company, was to write:

> *Ah, Ben!*
> *Say how, or when,*
> *Shall we thy guests,*
> *Meet at those lyric feasts*
> *Made at the Sun,*
> *The Dog, the Triple Tun?*
> *Where we such clusters had,*
> *As made us nobly wild, not mad;*
> *And yet each Verse of thine*
> *Out-did the meat, out-did the wine.*

THE
PERPETUAL
PARTY

A pleasant exchange with the fruit and vegetable girl in a Paris market, c. 1630

Rich Bride, Poor Bride

Gift cup for a new bride

Weddings were often boisterous and opulent occasions of banqueting and merrymaking that might last overnight or as long as ten days, depending on the capacities of the guests and the host's grip on his purse strings. One Elizabethan ascetic accused them of making a "brothel house of a bride house." In Italy the wedding of the Duke of Mantua was more refined if no less grand. Guests were entertained at a three-hour banquet by four choirs, and gifts of glass defied "competition from all the warehouses of Murano." Below, a panel painting from a cassone—a dowry chest—shows the typical Florentine wedding banquet of the times.

For couples who could not afford the luxury of a banquet hall, there was always the street. Workers' weddings, left, were festive despite meagre dowries. What the rich spent on their entertainment and feasts would have lasted the poor through a lifetime.

The Way to a Woman's Heart

Botticelli's banquet, laid midst a surrealistic landscape of Renaissance arcades, was inspired by a tale from the Decameron, *in which the rejected suitor wins another hearing with his lady by inviting the whole family to dinner. After a fine meal and a scarifying lesson about the eternal damnation of cruel women, she willingly capitulates.*

To Set before a King

Much that glittered on the Renaissance table was indeed gold, or some other precious material. The decorative arts enjoyed almost as much attention as did painting and sculpture, and many an artist began his career as a metalsmith, shuttling between princely courts to keep their sideboards filled. Italy was the fount of all these industries: Venice exported glass of almost magical delicacy; the towns of central Italy produced brilliantly glazed earthenware including the fine majolica above; and Florence supplied superb goldsmiths, none more urgently sought than Benvenuto Cellini, who was enticed to the court of Francis I with the promise, "I will choke you with gold."

Cellini's enameled gold figures above, executed in 1543 for Francis I, represent Land and Sea, allegorical sources of the precious pepper and salt contained within. The potte below, which belonged to a chamberlain of Henry VIII, combines striped Venetian glass with a silver-gilt mounting of English workmanship, hallmarked 1546.

"Happy, Happy Burgundy"

So wrote Erasmus in 1532, when he praised the wine from the fruitful region where the grape harvest in the tapestry below takes place, stating that Burgundy "deserves to be called the mother of man, since she gives [him] such good milk from her breast."

Saint Jude tops one of a set of English apostle spoons.

A Sign of Breeding

If the dish be pleasant, either fleshe or fishe,
Ten hands at once swarm in the dishe;
And if it be fleshe ten knives shalt thou see,
Mangling the flesh, and in the platter flee.
To put there thy handes, in peril without fail
Without a gauntlet, or else a glove of mail.

As polite society took up the fork, the hand-to-mouth dining described in this Elizabethan ditty ceased. Many early examples of Renaissance cutlery were hinged for carrying in the pocket—a gentleman could not be too sure of his host's social graces—but as time passed even the most modest baron began to accumulate chests full of finely wrought pewter, silver, and sometimes gold. When the novelty of forks wore off, craftsmen turned to more specialized tools—from mulberry forks to apostle spoons: a set of twelve was a traditional gift at genteel baptisms.

Left: Bird bills serve as tines for an Italian fork.

The cleaver at top is a miniature of an early battle-axe; the ivory-handled knife beneath it is scored with the words and music of the "Benedicite." Below are seven of a set of fourteen knives whose handles carry likenesses of English sovereigns from Edward V to James I.

With a more liberal code of behavior, men and women began to appreciate each other openly and extravagantly. In Italy, where the orgy was as much art as entertainment, even the Papal Palace had its social season. For rest and recuperation, there were bathhouses which cleansed the body but did little to dampen the passions. Scented waters, companionable tub mates, and a proper meal constituted the "cure." A traveler wrote of the baths at Baden-Baden, "I think this must be the place where the first man was created, which the Hebrews call the garden of pleasure."

Good, Clean Fun

When courtesans came to dinner at the Hôtel Nesle, the fine French manor above, no one cared if dinner got cold. A gentleman could always get into hot water at the public bath (left) later.

OPERA DI
BARTOLOMEO
SCAPPI,

M. DELL'ARTE DEL CVCINARE,

con laquale si può ammaestrare qual si voglia Cuoco,
Scalco, Trinciante, o Mastro di Casa:

DIVISA IN SEI LIBRI.

NEL
Primo Libro si intende il ragionamento che fa l'Autore con Giouanni suo discepolo.
Secondo si tratta di diuerse viuande di carne, si di quadrupedi, come di volatili.
Terzo si parla della statura, e stagione de' pesci.
Quarto si mostrano le liste del presentar le viuande in tauola, così di grasso, come di magro.
Quinto si contiene l'ordine di far diuerse sorti di paste, & altri lauori.
Scsto, & vltimo si ragiona de' conualescenti, e molte altre sorti di viuande per gli infermi.

Con le Figure che fanno di bisogno nella Cucina.

Aggiontoui nuouamente il Trinciante, & il Mastro di Casa.

DEDICATE AL MAG. M. MATTEO BARBINI
Cuoco, e Scalco celeberrimo della Città di Venetia.

IN VENETIA, M. DC. X.
PRESSO ALESSANDRO VECCHI.

The Cook's Companion

One of the earliest printed cookbooks to appear in Italy was written by Bartolomeo Scappi, chef to Pope Pius V. Scappi's *Opera*, dated 1570, covered gastronomy from menus and recipes to diet and decorum. Like other Renaissance innovators, Scappi seems to have had a particular penchant for mechanical contrivances, including the clockwork turnspit on the title page opposite. In the woodcut below, he instructs the *maestro di cucina* in kitchen planning and layout of equipment (note the bristling knife rack to the right of the fire).

padella p fare oui frittolate

diuersi caldari

nauicella có piastrelle et quarro piedi

Conserua grande

Scappi's recommendations for the well-appointed kitchen include an assortment of pots and pans: from top to bottom, a pan for fritters; divers cauldrons; a four-legged steamer; a roasting pan; a frying pan; a "Dutch oven."

padella ouata   *stufaroro*

Nobilis.hinc.pater.et.hinc.est.o
Circumfufa.feder.digna.paren
falis.erat.quondam.patriarchae
Menfa.fuit.Iobo: sic.cumulata.
Fac.Deus.ut.matres.haec.gignat.
Gennner.ut.Iobi.ftirps.renoua.
Fercula.praeclaro.donafti.laeta
Haec.habeant.longos.gaudia.ra
Aῆ dδ 156.

Æta 6

Ætatis svæ 5 ce

Æta 1

2

Seen
But
Not
Heard

Although children were permitted to join their parents at the family table, the "seen but not heard" dictum was strictly observed. Il Galateo, a popular book on etiquette by Giovanni della Casa in the sixteenth century, admonished children: "not to eat too quickly, not to put one's elbows on the table, not to pick one's teeth, [and] not to spit as far as possible." The rules appear to be well enforced at the Elizabethan table, left, shown in a portrait of Lord Cobham and his brood.

Separate Tables

When Alexander VII gave a banquet in 1655 in honor of Sweden's Queen Christina, it was only the third time in history a pope had dined with a woman. To grace the occasion, leading artists fashioned trionfi, *the elaborate table decorations made from sugar, right. But honor or not, protocol required that Christina be seated at a table which was considerably lower—and quite apart—from that of her host.*

a La Reyne de Suede, a monte cauallo
lan 1667.

West meets East in seventeenth-century India and finds that parties are the same everywhere.

IN
QUEST
OF
SPICES

Shortly before his death in 1481, the Florentine physician and amateur geographer Paolo Toscanelli addressed a letter to a young seafarer who was then in Lisbon trying to win support for an extraordinary expedition to Asia. The letter began, "To Cristóbal Columbo . . . greeting: I observe thy great and noble ambition to pass over to where the spices grow. . . ." Toscanelli was one of the few who shared Columbus' belief that a westward voyage across unknown waters would lead more readily to the riches of Asia than the difficult passages then being explored around the huge land mass of Africa. But he was only one of many Europeans who were fired by the urge to reach Asia directly by sea. By the second half of the fifteenth century, extension of Turkish and Arab power had made travel overland and through the Middle Eastern gulfs forbidding to the West. The need for Eastern spices directly served to open the age of exploration, of colonial empires, and of the winning of the Americas.

The traditional course of a spice cargo to Europe involved in succession Chinese junks, Indian luggers, Arab dhows, pack camels, and Venetian freight galleys. Chinese traders from remote Canton would pick up a load in the East Indies—particularly the Moluccas, or Spice Islands, an archipelago bound on the north by the Philippines, on the west by Borneo and Java, and on the east by New Guinea—and transport it to the great Oriental mart of Malacca, on the Malay Peninsula. From there Malayan, Arab, or Indian shippers would carry the spice cargo on the monsoon winds across the Bay of Bengal to one of the ports on western India's Malabar

Eastern flora, by a Flemish artist, c. 1600

Coast—Calicut or Cochin or Goa—or possibly to Colombo in Ceylon. Next it would be borne across the western reaches of the Indian Ocean, to a harbor on the Persian Gulf—perhaps wealthy, strategic Hormuz—to be carried overland to Constantinople, or via the Red Sea to Mecca, then to Alexandria or a Syrian port. In these ports Venetian traders and shippers were on hand in numbers to buy for the European market.

But by 1453 the great Eastern Christian citadel of Constantinople had fallen to the Ottoman Turks, whose spreading empire soon commanded the littoral and overland routes of Asia Minor and Egypt. At Alexandria the price of pepper climbed 60 per cent when in 1428 a sultan created a state export monopoly and demanded higher tribute from traders. Imperialist Arabs were on the way to establishing a monopoly on sea trade between the vast Arabian peninsula and India and the islands beyond.

The West could still buy Eastern spices, but only at enormous cost. Some spices, by the time they reached Europe, were worth their weight in gold. Venice, so long the chief purveyor of Eastern goods to the Continent, was particularly threatened economically, trapped in a sea which Turks now virtually controlled, while Arab sway extended all along the North African coast to Gibraltar. There was, among kingdoms that fronted on the Atlantic, an opportunity as well as an impulse to escape the Mediterranean trap.

The Renaissance inspired the spirit of adventure. Learned Arabs, who had studied Ptolemy's celestial treatise the *Almagest* at Alexandria, along with the work of early Indian astronomers, added a wealth of mathematical and nautical studies which were brought to Europe and translated by Portuguese and Italian Jews. Arab sailors had long navigated by star sights; in the fifteenth century the astrolabe and the quadrant came into Western use to determine a ship's latitude (its position north and south) when out of sight of land. The more difficult problem of finding one's longitudinal (east-west) position remained elusive, sailors relying on dead reckoning—that is, observation of wind velocity, speed over the water, drift, and current—to determine their progress.

Moreover, fairly seaworthy vessels for deepwater work were being constructed in Europe, rigged with two or more masts and a combination of square and fore-and-aft sails that made them a great improvement over the traditional oared galleys of the Mediterranean or the lateen rigged ships of Arab skippers when it came to accomplishing long voyages or sailing close to the wind in heavy weather. Clumsy as these vessels may now seem, with their lofty poops or sterncastles, they could accommodate the compact but precious cargo from the East. In such ships Vasco da Gama, Columbus, and Magellan made their historic voyages, and Sir Francis Drake reconnoitered the East Indies for England.

The impulse to locate and tap the spice sources was also aided by scattered travel accounts that had come down over generations, some even from antiquity. The Egyptians, a millennium and a half before Christ, had used cinnamon as an aromatic, although the bark of the tree did not grow in their land, nor in Arabia either. Phoenician skippers—the most enterprising of ancient times—had sailed down the Red Sea and out into the Indian Ocean. Moreover, they had struck westward through the Mediterranean and past the Pillars of Hercules into the Atlantic, all the way down the West African bulge and around the Cape of Good Hope. Whether they actually reached the Eastern spice lands or merely bought their spices at some entrepôt such as Aden or Mecca on the great Arabian

peninsula has never been determined.

The Greek geographer Strabo in the first century B.C. wrote of southern Arabia as a center of spice production and trade, but ancient Arabs were secretive about the true source of those spices that were not native to their land. The Roman natural historian Pliny the Elder accused the Arab merchants of concealing the origin of their wares to keep their prices high. But soon Roman sailors and merchants came to know the west coast of India well, trading there for spices, perfumes, and luxurious textiles in exchange for Western gold coin, pottery, wine, and occasionally slave girls. Along with the pepper, ginger,

Radishes and peppers en route to market

cinnamon, and cardamom of the Malabar region, they imported a small amount of sugar from Indian cane fields and saffron, the flavoring made from the crocus of the Himalayan foothills.

Three centuries before, the Arabs had pushed farther on and established direct sea contact with China. They may have traded in the East Indies as well. Indians, after the decline of Rome, also turned to China and the islands for trade. They appear to have been skillful shipbuilders as well as navigators; one vessel of the fifth century A.D. carried two hundred crew and passengers. (Columbus' largest, the *Santa Maria*, carried only about forty.)

Though Western trade for Eastern delicacies was sporadic during the Middle Ages, the continuing contact between Christian and Moslem stimulated the European appetite for exotic flavors. Sugar, brought back from Syria by the Crusaders, is an instance. Its Arabic name *sukkar*, derived from the Sanskrit *sárkará*, or "pebble," passed almost unchanged into various European languages as *azucar*, *sucre*, or *Zucker*. With it came such sweet drinks of the Moslem world as aromatic rose water. The Arabs called it *julāb*—a term that evolved, according to the historian Philip K. Hitti, into the Western "julep." He also argues that the Western word "syrup" derives from the Arab term *sharāb*, a therapeutic solution of sugar in water, and that the

Brewing a physic, from a 1222 Arabic herbal

word "soda" as we know it (as in Scotch and soda, for example) in medieval Latin meant "headache," and meant "headache remedy" in the form *sodanum*, which derived from the Arabic *sudā*, meaning a "splitting pain in the head."

From the Arabs the Crusaders also learned the pleasures of sherbet, mel-

ons, and asparagus, while the Moors implanted in Spain a love of saffron flavored rice dishes (the *pilaf* of the Middle East, the *paella* of Iberia). Meanwhile, citrus fruits, which probably originated in Malaysia and spread from there to India, were gradually making their way to Europe. The very name "orange" comes from the Sanskrit *nāranga*—which with slight phonetic variations came into Western languages almost intact, save that the Germans were oddly to call the costly fruit *Apfelsine*. The lemon was the Arabic *laymūn*, which in turn derived from the Persian *līmūn*.

In the Middle East the strongholds of the Crusaders on the Levant coast soon fell to the Moslems. But Venetian traders, such as the clan that reared Marco Polo in the latter part of the thirteenth century, reached out undismayed beyond Constantinople to the Crimea on the Black Sea and as far as Bokhara. They found western Asian gardens flourishing with almonds, basil, pomegranates, peaches, apricots, plums, eggplants, and watermelons, the last exported all the way to Baghdad packed in ice. At the same time, Christian missionaries were reaching even farther, venturing into inner India and to the Himalayas, and sending back astonishing reports. One traveler, the Franciscan friar Oderic, wrote of his Eastern travels from 1318 to 1330 that "While I was in the province of Mancy [in India], I passed by the palace of a certain famous man, who hath fifty virgin damsels continually attending upon him, feeding him every meal as a bird feeds her young ones. Also he hath sundry kinds of meat served at his table, and three dishes of each kind; and when the said virgins feed him, they sing most sweetly." The bemused friar also told of a "mount" near the wall of the palace, "wrought with gold and silver, whereupon stand turrets and steeples and other delectable things for the solace and recreation of

Jeweled sweetmeat box, India

the great man." Oderic added that he had traveled as far as "a certain kingdom called Tebek [Tibet]," where the women "have two teeth in their mouths as long as the tusks of a boar" and "wherein I think there is more plenty of bread and wine than in any other part of the world." He was wildly exaggerating and distorting, since mountainous Tibet has been throughout history one of man's leanest and loneliest places.

Even the description he gave of India was highly colored. Most of India was existing on a vegetarian diet, induced partly by religion and partly by sheer poverty: vegetable curries, boiled or fried rice, or flat cakes of flour, the modern chapatis, fried in ghee (clarified butter) or vegetable oil. For sweets, the Indian chewed a slightly narcotic mixture of betel nuts and lime.

Europeans of discernment could discount the tales of Oderic, but there was detailed truth in the travel reports of Marco Polo, who at the age of seventeen set out in 1271 with his brothers for eastern Asia and the court of Kublai Khan. On his way he passed through the city of Mosul on the Tigris to find great spice shipments coming in. ("The merchants transport their goods to and from the Sea of India," he wrote, "the distance being computed at seventeen days' navigation. . . .") From there he pushed overland through the wild, robber infested Kurdish lands of northern Persia to reach the port of Hormuz at the mouth of the Gulf. Then his route led across Afghanistan, the Pamir highlands, and the Gobi Desert to the Yellow River, to take him in 1275 to the summer court of the Great Khan. He brought back reports of the glittering wealth of Peking; of ginger under cultivation in Shansi and Shensi provinces; of an island kingdom of Cipangu (Japan) off the Great Khan's coast; of islands in the China Sea lush with aromatic trees; and of distant Java to the south, an island that abounded in "pepper, nutmegs . . . cloves, and all other valuable spices and drugs . . . which occasion it to be visited by many ships laden with merchandise that yields to the owners considerable profit. . . ."

His observations, circulated in manuscript and by word of mouth, aroused European imagination as well as cupidity. Yet, like those of Friar Oderic, the stories of Marco Polo were also widely doubted. He was asked, when on his deathbed in 1324, to recant some of his more grandiose descriptions of the East, only to respond, "I have not told half of what I saw."

Amid much rumor and misinformation, tentative knowledge of the East gradually spread. Genoese merchants

A Scurvy Life

The epic voyages undertaken in quest of the spice treasures of Cathay were fraught with dangers, real and imagined. An explorer never knew when a sea serpent might rise from the inky depths to swallow his ship and crew, and navigators kept a wary eye on the horizon for fear they might sail off the edge of the world. But there was nothing mythical about the shortage of food supplies during long voyages. Slow starvation at sea was a common occurrence. Although historians have concluded from early manifests of ships' stores that a mariner's diet comprised thirty-five hundred calories daily, this was true only under ideal conditions. A short three months' sail from port could find the crew left with nothing more than stagnant water and soured hardtack which was shared with rats and weevils. During Magellan's trans-Pacific ordeal, his crew was reduced to gnawing oxhide thongs and jerkins, and many of the men literally rotted from scurvy—a disease resulting from a deficiency of Vitamin C. On the long runs from Portugal to India, scurvy claimed the lives of one out of every five seamen. The Portuguese were among the first to discover that citrus fruits prevented the disease, and they established plantations of oranges and limes on St. Helena, an island convenient to the caravels en route to India's Malabar Coast. English ships later became popularly known as "lime-juicers" because of an admiralty order requiring the distribution of lime juice rations to all hands. But the 190 sailors who shipped on the vessel carrying the provisions below did not enjoy such solicitous care—neither fresh fruits nor vegetables were in the hold:

11,400 POUNDS OF SALTED MEATS AND FISH

A FEW BEEF TONGUES

20,000 BISCUITS

30 BUSHELS OF OATMEAL

40 BUSHELS OF DRIED PEAS

1 1/2 BUSHELS OF MUSTARD SEED

1 BARREL OF SALT

100 POUNDS OF SUET

1 BARREL OF FLOUR

11 FIRKINS OF BUTTER

1 HOGSHEAD OF VINEGAR

10,500 GALLONS OF BEER

3,500 GALLONS OF WATER

2 HOGSHEADS OF CIDER

were in at least indirect contact with India and China via Arabia during the first half of the fourteenth century, and before the middle of the next the Venetian merchant adventurer Niccolò de' Conti returned overland from twenty-five years in India and southeast Asia with extraordinary and explicit news. He had seen the cinnamon trees of Ceylon. He had traveled up the Ganges and encountered both elephants and wealthy cities along its shores. He had gone as far as Burma, Malaya, Sumatra, and Java, observing religious rites there and partaking of their foods. What was most important, in a time before there was any accurate cartography of the East, he postulated that the waters about India and the islands were an open ocean. It followed that these areas could be reached by ship directly from Europe, thus avoiding the dangerous overland trek through Arabia.

The greatest collecting point of all such information was the remarkable observatory established in 1418 at Sagres on the southernmost promontory of Portugal by Prince Henry the Navigator. This remarkable intellect, the third son of King John I of Portugal, was bent upon studies of the globe as well as the pursuit of African and possibly Eastern wealth, in a new crusade against the powerful Moslems. He set up, as the maritime historian Samuel Eliot Morison describes it, "the ancestor of every marine observatory and hydrographic office today." Geographers and astronomers were assembled at his retreat on the desolate cliffs above Cape St. Vincent, and from 1418 on, captains who had been briefed there set out on in-

creasingly distant voyages. The Canary Islands, the Madeira Islands, the Azores, were either located or rediscovered; the great western bulge of Africa was rounded, dispelling fears of a *mare tenebrosum*, or unmapped "green sea of gloom," to the south of it. Year after year Portuguese fleets brought home cargoes of western African pepper, elephant tusks, and slaves. Then in 1488 Lisbon—the most adventurous capital of the era—resounded with joy to the triumphal return of Bartholomeu Dias from his rounding of the Cape of Good Hope; the Genoese Christopher Columbus is said to have been at dockside to witness it.

While Dias was at sea, a Portuguese royal agent named Pedro de Covilhão was traveling to Calicut. Covilhão sent back secret intelligence to Lisbon on the location of thriving spice centers on the Malabar Coast and the prevailing winds of the Indian Ocean. Around 1493 the Genoese trader Girolamo da Santo Stefano, starting by an overland route, reached the eastern shore of India, Ceylon, Sumatra, and the Maldive Islands, bringing back more news of pepper and ginger. The Portuguese, attracted by reports of Eastern wealth and customs, promptly monopolized the trade. Upon learning that Columbus had failed to reach the Indies by a western route, the Portuguese determined to mount an expedition that would push on from the point Dias had reached and strike on to India by sea. The outcome was Vasco da Gama's arrival in the port city of Calicut in 1498, prompting the King of Portugal to proudly inform his royal neighbors at Madrid, "We learn that

161

they did reach and discover India and other kingdomes and lordships bordering upon it; that they entered and navigated its sea, finding large cities, large edifaces and rivers, and great populations, among whom is carried on all the trade in spices and precious stones. . . . Of these they have brought a quantity, including cinnamon, cloves, ginger, nutmeg, together with the boughs and leaves of the same; also many fine stones of all sorts, such as rubies and others."

For the moment, the Portuguese had won a vast advantage—over Spain, over Venice, over the Arabs as well, and it now became their intention to establish not just trading posts but permanent strongholds from which to drive out the Moslems, subdue the Hindus, and rule as much of the East as they could reach. A view of the Indian world which they were entering is contained in a curious

Jade green ceramic mug, Persia

description by the Italian traveler Lodovico di Varthema, who visited the court of Calicut at just about the time the Portuguese were arriving:

"When the King of Calicut wishes to eat he uses the following customs . . . four of the principal Brahmans take the food which the king is to eat and carry it to the devil, and first they worship him in this manner: they raise their clasped hands over his head, and then draw their hands toward them, still clasped together, and the thumb raised upward, and then they present to him the food which is to be given to the king, and stand in this manner as long as a person would require to eat it; and then the said Brahmans carry that food to the king. . . . This food is in a wooden vessel, in which there is a very large leaf of a tree, and upon this leaf is placed the said food, which consists of rice and other things. The king eats on the ground without any other thing. And when he eats, the Brahmans stand around, three or four paces distant from him, with great reverence, and remain bowed down with their hands before their mouths. . . . When the king has finished his meal, the said Brahmans take that food which the king did not require and carry it into a courtyard and place it on the ground. And the said Brahmans clap their hands three times, and at this clapping a very great number of black crows come to this said food and eat it."

What was of far more interest to Vasco da Gama was his discovery that pepper could be bought directly at Calicut for as little as three ducats per hundredweight—and this at a time when it was selling through middlemen in Venice for as much as eighty. It is estimated that on his second expedition to India, which comprised an armada of twenty-five ships, twelve of them sent by the king in a display of military might and the rest belonging to Portuguese merchants, he brought home a cargo worth sixty times the cost of outfitting it. Within ten years of setting up bases at

Hormuz on the Persian Gulf and at Goa on the Malabar Coast, the Portuguese seized control of Malacca in Malaya and in 1513 sailed across the South China Sea to bring a ship into Canton—the first recorded European visit to the lands of the Great Khan since Marco Polo. At nearby Macao they established a permanent foothold, while from their vantage point on the Malacca Strait they also set sail for the Spice Islands. There they established an overlordship ruled from headquarters at Goa.

A small island just off the Indian shore, Goa was a colorful crossroads of Eastern trade. A Portuguese account describes the island as "very beautiful and luxuriant with numerous and tall groves of palm trees that give much wine, oil, vinegar, and jaggery [a coarse brown sugar made from palm sap], that almost tastes like sugar. It also has areca . . . with which betel is eaten. All this makes them much money, and now many Portuguese have large incomes from it. [The inhabitants] have also many gardens in which they grow numerous and very singular fruits of the earth. . . . They have a large amount of sesame from which they make excellent oil."

Peaceable as this sounds, a major struggle for spice and empire was in the making. Having all but swept the Arabs off the Eastern sea lanes and having found Indian and Malaysian peoples submissive, the Portuguese were to be confronted in turn by a jealous Spain, an ambitious England, and the enterprising Dutch. Within a hundred years their vast, new-found dominion was all but shattered.

The storm center was the Moluccas,

especially rich in cloves. Spain's rulers, smarting over Columbus' failure to find spices, had heard enough about the islands to regard them as a prime objective and claimed them as their own under an earlier demarcation treaty, in

Kublai Khan's brother sipping a bowl of milk

which the Pope had portioned out the world between Spain and Portugal. A century later the Protestant English and then the Dutch, not party to this presumptuous agreement, would have none of it. They would make sail for the Spice Islands too, with shotted guns.

Portugal's first major setback came with the defection of one of its most experienced sailors, Ferdinand Magellan, who, after being removed from command for alleged trading with the Arab enemy, entered the rival Spanish service and there accomplished another of history's great naval feats—the circumnavigation of the globe. Bravely sailing down to far southern latitudes to round unknown, storm-tossed Patagonia and driving on across the Pacific, he not only vindicated Columbus' belief in a western passage but opened the spice trade of the Indies to Spain—though he himself was to die in the Philippines as the result of a chieftain's treachery.

Magellan had aboard his ship an Italian chronicler, one Antonio Pigafetta of Vicenza, who survived to tell much of this great voyage and of what he saw, gathered, and incidentally ate. Thus when anchored in 1521 off a small island in the Philippines, Magellan and his

Pot and drinking tube for maté, Paraguay tea

captains were invited to a banquet with the local chief: "Each bite of meat," as the historian Donald F. Lach transcribes Pigafetta's account, "was accompanied by ceremonial [palm] wine drinking. Before the chief took the cup, he raised his fist toward the sky and brandished it at his companions. After he had taken the cup to drink, he flung out his left fist so sharply and abruptly that Pigafetta thought for a moment that the chief meant to strike him. When the European came to realize that the chief was merely offering a friendly toast, he replied in kind. . . . After a supper of pork and rice, the Europeans were taken to the chief's abode. . . ." There, squatting on bamboo mats, under torches "made from tree gum wrapped in palm and banana leaves," they were offered a concoction of fish and ginger.

Pigafetta and his companions saw much else in the Philippines—bananas, described as "long, delicious figs," breadfruit, and sago palms. But their goal was the Moluccas, where the survivors landed late in 1521. There they found precious clove trees and ginger roots (along with pygmies, cannibals, and a small colony of Moorish traders complete with its own harem). The Spanish and Portuguese now contended for control of these treasure islands; in 1529 the Portuguese king John III paid Spain a royal ransom of 350,000 gold ducats to abandon any further claims. Prophetically, the Portuguese traveler João de Barros wrote shortly after mid-century that "Evil and strife are endemic to the Moluccas, for the clove, though a creation of God, is actually an apple of discord and responsible for more afflictions than gold."

About this time the English also went to sea in force. In Magellan's wake Francis Drake circumnavigated the globe in 1577–80 and explored the Moluccas. Thomas Cavendish followed him in 1586. The defeat of the Spanish Armada in the English Channel in 1588 had further repercussions on the opposite side of the globe. Victorious Englishmen were soon to rival expansionist Spaniards in the Far East as Spaniards had rivaled Portuguese, and as the Portuguese had overtaken the Arabs before them. Shortly before her death, Queen Elizabeth, after a meeting of London merchants, chartered a monopoly of traders to be known as the East India Company, with percentages due the Crown. Their first spice fleet sailed in 1601. Meanwhile, the Dutch, who had also been scouting the Eastern promised land, aided chiefly by a skillful observer in the Portuguese service, one Jan van Linschoten, arrived on the scene with a fleet in 1595. They befriended local rulers anxious for deliverance from the Portuguese and soon formed their own East India Company as a national merchant combine chartered to exploit anything it could lay hands on between Magellan's Strait and the Cape of Good Hope. It could establish bases, make war, coin its own money—a potential imperium on a hemispheric scale. Investors' money streamed into these rival ventures. A Cologne representative of the Fugger family of Continental bankers, busy selling shares for the Dutch, wrote his clients in 1601 that "We are advised that the profits of the East Indian vessels recently arrived are to be distributed to shareholders. Each one is to receive 50

Indian scepter: a cocoa whisk

per cent." A merchant adventurer, it was said, could ship six spice cargoes from the East, lose five to pirates or shipwreck, and still make a handsome return. The third expedition of the London East India Company earned 230 per cent profit. The Spanish-Portuguese entanglement in the East now diminished as a greater division of the spoils engaged England in India and the Dutch in the East Indies.

Most of the Eastern products for the table were familiar to Europe from times past—though now they could be had far more readily and cheaply. The coconut, the mango, and the banana made their first appearance on the tables of the rich, but the great source of new foods that were to enlarge the diet of the European common man lay elsewhere—just halfway around the globe.

On December 13, 1492, two months after his first landing, Columbus sent a party of men ashore on Española (Haiti), where they were well received by the Indians. The chronicle of the voyage records that "as soon as the natives had cast off their fear, they all went to the houses and each one brought what he had to eat, consisting of yams, which are roots like large radishes, which they sow and cultivate in all their lands, and is their staple food. They make bread of it, and roast it. . . ." This offering of yams was perhaps European man's first important encounter with the fare of the New World. But it was the white potato that was destined to be a staple of Europe's diet; cultivated in South America, the potato was discovered in the areas that were to become Peru and Bolivia by Spanish explorers searching for gold. Just how fast the potato's cultivation spread through Europe is a topic of continuing controversy. Some studies have held that it long remained a rich man's speciality; others, that it became familiar to everyday Spanish households as early as the 1570's. A traveler along the coast southeast of Lima wrote in 1586, "In the heights . . . are sown and gathered the seeds of the potato, which like cold ground. These are one of the best provisions which the Indians have in the said province, they are like truffles: and if we were to cultivate them in Spain in the manner they do there it would be a great help in years of famine. . . ." The likening of the sturdy potato to the delicate truffle is somewhat astonishing; one can only conclude that its finders considered it another delicacy. One of the first botanical studies of the potato called it *taratoufli*, Latin for "little truffle," a designation which survives in the German word for potato, *Kartoffel*. The potato was to serve Europe well—both in times of famine and good harvest.

On his second voyage, Columbus brought back the pineapple, known to the natives as *ananas*—the name it still bears in much of Continental Europe. It was a rare and costly import, the plant itself taking no hold even in the warm Mediterranean zone. (By contrast, on his outward passage, Columbus took with him the seeds of the first citrus trees to reach the New World.)

To the Spaniard Hernando Cortes and his men, a particularly pleasing discovery in Mexico was chocolate, which they may have first savored as guests of Montezuma. His table, as the expedition's chronicler Bernal Díaz del Castillo describes it, was both magnificent and barbarous. "For each meal," he writes, "over thirty different dishes were prepared by his cooks. . . . I have heard it said that they were wont to cook for him the flesh of young boys, but as he had such a variety of dishes, made of

so many things, we could not succeed in seeing if they were of human flesh or of other things, for they daily cooked fowls, turkeys, pheasants, native partridges, quail, tame and wild ducks, venison, wild boar, reed birds, pigeons, hares and rabbits, and many sorts of birds and other things which are bred in this country. . . ." But, Díaz adds, "I know for certain that after our Captain censured the sacrifice of human beings, and the eating of their flesh, [Montezuma] ordered that such food should not be prepared for him thenceforth." There was also an abundance of fruits and of tortilla cakes, made of corn meal and eggs. This was accompanied by a drink Díaz called *cacao*, served to him "all frothed up . . . in cup-shaped vessels of pure gold."

In his classic history of the conquest of Mexico, William Prescott elaborates, "The Emperor took no other beverage than chocolatl [*sic*], a potation of chocolate, flavored with vanilla and other spices, and so prepared as to be reduced to a froth of the consistency of honey, which gradually disolved in the mouth. . . . The Emperor was exceedingly fond of it, to judge from the quantity—no less than fifty jars or pitchers being prepared for his own daily consumption!" The Aztecs' drink was soon to become the rage in Europe, where it was served hot and topped with cream.

The conquistadors and others also encountered new varieties of beans in the Americas. The Lima bean, so called no doubt from the place where the Spanish may have first tasted it, proved hardy in transit and was a distinct addition to everyday European fare. Though Europe

Hafiz the Poet

*A*lthough the Persians were passionate defenders of Islam, they honored Mohammed's strictures on wine mainly in the breach; they not only lusted after the fruit of the vine, but as one visitor noted, drank "with freedom openly and with excess." Indeed, wine had been the sine qua non of Persians since ancient times—playing no small role in highlighting their sumptuous feasts, civilizing the barbarians that periodically conquered them, and stimulating their poetic instincts. By the fifteenth century they had a rich repertory of bibulous and erotic poetry, including the works of Omar Khayyám, Sadi, and above all Hafiz. Fate was especially kind to Hafiz, for he was born c. 1325 in Shiraz, at that time a haven for poets, philosophers, and artists, as well as the wine capital of Persia (the name Shiraz possibly coming from the Persian word for grape, *Sherab*). As a dervish Hafiz had earned his name by memorizing the Koran, but he soon decided that a loaf of bread was tasteless without a jug of wine to wash it down. He embarked on a new career, composing and singing amatory odes. In the lyrics below, Hafiz courts his monarch, Shah Shuja, ending with a note of self-praise common in Persian poetry.

The *"Pain of Love,"* one story,
  Is told us o'er and o'er;
Yet, strange to say, by no one
  Tis worded as before. . . .

From fumes of wine grown heady,
  My friend gave hope—last eve—
But what today the promise,
  What will that head conceive?

How strange a branch of candy,
  HAFIZ, thy reed has grown,
That honey and pure sugar
  No fruit so luscious own!

Potations and paeans could not, however, bolster the shah's crumbling kingdom. Shortly before Hafiz' death in 1389, Tamerlane's Mongol armies invaded Persia. At a time of civil strife and anarchy, Hafiz' poetry exalting the fleeting pleasures of the senses provided an opiate for the world-weary citizens of Shiraz. The poems, interwoven with many themes like the patterns of a Persian carpet, permitted the reader to extract his own meanings, and profit thereby.

had broad beans from ancient times, *haricots*—the generic term that came into use in France to describe the species—appears to be a corruption of the Old Mexican word for bean, *ayacotl*. North America also provided several new types of beans, including the kidney, pinto, navy, and pea beans, all of which eventually found their way into European peasant cooking.

Indian corn, or maize, except that transplanted to northern Italy, had little effect on the European diet, but the root crop variously known to tropical American Indians as *manioc* or *cassava*, found acceptance. Manioc, when properly ground and prepared, is the source of tapioca, as well as other foods, all of which Europe welcomed. More important still was the American tomato and the pimento, introduced chiefly by the Portuguese and Spanish, and destined to have a great effect on the cuisine of southern Europe. The plants (both tomatoes and pimentos are classified generically as fruits) were successfully cultivated in the western Mediterranean. Northern Europe, however, did not take to them, and there was a long-lasting, obscure prejudice in Puritan England against tomatoes as injurious "love apples." (The Austrians, not averse to love fruits of any sort, named them *Paradeis*.)

New England provided other new food experiences for colonists. Thus Francis Higginson, in his promotional description *New England's Plantation*, published in 1630, wrote that "This country aboundeth naturally with store of roots of great variety and good to eat. Our turnips, parsnips and carrots are here both bigger and sweeter than is ordi-

narily to be found in England. Here are also store of pumpions [pumpkins], cowcumbers, and other things of that nature which I know not."

Above all, of course, there was the turkey. A seventeenth-century book on heraldry records that three centuries earlier a certain William Yoo of Devonshire emblazoned his coat of arms with "three Turkey-cocks in their pride proper." This would seem to indicate that the turkey was known in Europe long before the discovery of America and the Plymouth settlers' first Thanksgiving dinner. But, as the American historian of the turkey, A. W. Schorger, points out, the word "turkey" was used in England long before the bird we know ever arrived there. The name was taken

A British-run sugar mill in Barbados, 1667

from the land of the Turks, which since the Middle Ages had been the route if not the source of strange new flavors and foods. "Turkey" thus became the generic term for any large, edible, unfamiliar fowl. What William Yoo and others of his time were relishing were probably peacocks and peahens, domesticated or wild. According to Schorger, the actual turkey was probably seen by Spaniards during their early forays among the Indians of Mexico, perhaps during

Francisco de Córdoba's 1517 expedition to Yucatán. The historian of the expedition, Bartolomé de Las Casas, speaks of Córdoba's men being presented by the Indians with large, roasted *gallinas*; they were, he said, as large as peafowls, with a distinctive dewlap, and better in taste. The bird was brought back alive to Spain as early as 1511. It appears next to have been transported to Rome, where the naturalist Gyllius named it *gallo peregrino*, "wandering chicken," and confirmed that it had been brought from the New World. By 1538 it turned up in France as *poule d'Inde* (later shortened to *dinde*). The late eighteenth-century French gastronome and pioneer historian of taste, Brillat-Savarin, explains the French word derivation: "Superlatively knowing persons," he wrote with irony in his *Physiologie du Goût*, "maintain that the *Romans* were addicted to the turkey, that it was served at *Charlemagne's* wedding feast. . . . The French name of the bird, which, being *coq d'Inde*, clearly betrays its origin; for at first *America* was always known as the *Western Indies*."

Now the European table, enriched with great spice cargoes from the East and new foods from the Americas, was on its way to greater variety and flourish than had been known before. Another major innovation was to come in the seventeenth century—coffee.

The source of the coffee bean and the drink that was brewed from it appears to have been Ethiopia. From there it had spread through the Arab world, aided particularly by Mohammed's strictures against the consumption of wine: coffee was to be known as "the wine of Islam." Avicenna, famed eleventh century Arab physician and philosopher in remote Bokhara, was familiar with the drink (known to him as *k'hawah* and thought to have medicinal qualities).

The social life of the Middle East—then as later—revolved around the consumption of coffee at all hours of the

A Turk and his coffee in 1685

day, at home or in the bazaars. The Italian man of letters Pietro della Valle in his *Viaggi in Turchia, Persia ed India* tells of the Turks imbibing a "black beverage"; "During the summer they drink it to refresh and cool themselves, whereas in winter they find it warming; yet it is the same drink in both cases, similarly prepared. They take long draughts of it, extremely hot, but not during mealtimes, since this would remove their inclination to eat any more. It is consumed after the meal, as a dainty. It also promotes fellowship and conversation. . . . It is also said that when drunk after supper, it prevents those who consume it from feeling sleepy. For that reason, students who wish to read into the late hours are fond of it."

Throughout the Middle East there was a considerable similarity of diet, with regional variations. Lamb or mutton—spitted as *kabāb*—was eaten everywhere except among the very poor. Sweet cakes and pastries, usually flavored with honey and often almonds, were also ubiquitous. Arabs had a particular fondness for date palm hearts and sugared fruits; Syrians, for baked eggplant and yoghurt; Persians, for melons and sherbets. But everywhere there was coffee, taken strong and sweet. Perhaps the first sample was brought back from the Levant in a ship that landed at Marseilles in 1634; but acquaintance with coffee in the West appears to have been limited until the Turks themselves brought it in—in one instance by diplomacy, in another by invasion.

In 1669 the Sublime Porte, then busy extending its power through the Balkans and toward the Danube, thought it might be wise to enter diplomatic relations with the court of Louis XIV of France as a possible ally against the Germanic peoples it was about to attack. That year an Ottoman emissary was received at Versailles in the person of Suleiman Aga, who brought with him large quantities of coffee in an equipage that also included an array of Turkish hangings, rugs, cushions, and other finery large enough to convert a mansion he had rented into an Oriental pleasure dome. Elegant, inquisitive Parisians flocked to his showplace, savored his strong brew, and—though some nobles resisted initially—soon became enraptured. The word of coffee spread downward from the aristocracy, and in 1672 an Armenian named Pascal opened the first Parisian coffeehouse.

Although Europeans had become used to the additions of new and exotic foods with each territory they conquered, coffee entered Vienna in 1683 in the baggage of Ottoman aggressors. The Turks by now had overrun all eastern Europe and were besieging the Hapsburg capital with a vast army. What happened next is related by Heinrich Jacob, author of the definitive history of coffee. An interpreter in the Austrian service, Georg Kolshitsky, who knew the Turkish language perfectly, managed to pass through the Ottoman lines in Eastern dress and get news of Vienna's plight to a relieving force headed by the Polish king John Sobieski. The relief was made, the siege was lifted, and the Turks retreating in disarray left behind vast spoils—perhaps the least of which were five hundred sacks of an unfamiliar bean of agreeable smell. While some wanted to throw the beans into the river or feed them to the animals, a few of the troops began to burn the sacks, but an extraordinary aroma rose to their nostrils. Kolshitsky, who knew good coffee when he smelled it, salvaged what was left. Before long, Vienna had learned to love coffee, especially when sugar and milk or cream were added. The city in its time was to become the great European entrepôt of coffee, developing no less than twenty ways of preparing it, from light to dark, from milky *eine Schaale Gold* to heavy *Mocha* and the murky Turkish brew topped with a mound of whipped cream. Thus, from the Danube, which the Turks had almost but not quite won, coffee traveled throughout Europe and then to the Americas. Needless to say, the proprietor of the first coffeehouse in Vienna was the enterprising Kolshitsky.

MORE
PRECIOUS
THAN
GOLD

Tropical fruits, the New World's gift to Europe, being sampled in an Ecuadorian market

Arab traders like the one above preferred buffeting sands to battering seas. Camel caravans brought spices overland from the Gulf of Suez to the markets at Cairo and Constantinople.

To Market, to Market

"The pepper business is profitable indeed; when the Lord God grants by His Mercy that none of the ships take damage either in coming or going, then the merchants wax rich." So ran the January, 1580, newsletter of the Fugger banking family, one of the principal investors in the spice trade. Pepper, being picked by natives in India, above, was the spice of life for most merchants, but ginger, nutmeg, and cinnamon also brought high prices on European markets. One shipment of cloves purchased in 1606 for £2,948 in the Spice Islands fetched no less than £36,287 in England. Opposite, a sixteenth-century map of Java and the Moluccas shows Europeans collecting and bartering for spices—while one wanders off to bag a deer. The boat at top has taken on cargo and is sailing for home.

EST

MOLVQVES

GRANDE-IAVE

PETITE-IAVE

MER DE L'INDE ORIENTALE

OVEST

Artists like Théodore de Bry were not daunted by a lack of firsthand information in their depictions of faraway places. Though he rarely ventured beyond Frankfort, De Bry confidently interpreted the botanical, zoological, and social curiosities of the West and East Indies. The unrealistically well-ordered native market below is his conception of Bantam, Java, c. 1601.

A *typical Arab coffeehouse in Constantinople*

The Wines of Islam

Although the Koran frowned upon Mohammedans who indulged in wine, once out of sight of Mecca the rule was not strictly observed. Sometimes the fondness for drink was turned to imaginative ends, as in the mechanical man above, who the author explained, "drinks wine left by the king." As the right arm raises the cup, the other arm waves a blue lotus blossom, possibly to distract the pious. Like the vessel opposite, it originally appeared in a thirteenth-century book of wonders called the *Automata* and was created by the Arab inventor al-Jazarī for the amusement of his patron. But most true believers drank coffee, according to Persian legend first served to a sleepy Mohammed by the angel Gabriel. Prohibitionists seeking to rid Islam of the evils of alcohol called it "Islam's Wine."

When this cup was filled with wine, so its inventor claimed, the bird would turn and whistle.

Pleasant Dreams

When Jahangir of India dreamed of making peace with his enemy, Shah Abbas I of Persia, the imaginary encounter took place not over a ten-course banquet before an audience of hundreds, but intimately, over a light repast of fruit, nuts, and wine. The seventeenth-century miniature opposite, depicting the occasion, reveals both the high degree of refinement which European spice traders met in their Eastern travels and the crosscurrents of products and ideas that resulted. Decorative arts of Mogul India, like the cloisonné and gold water jug above, were often exchanged for such European *objets* as the Italian ewer and wine glass on Jahangir's table. The gilded stag on wheels, held by an attendant, right, is of German design, though it was inspired by the *Automata*

of al-Jazarī. Filled with wine, it will be set in motion, and when its mechanism has run down, the potentate nearest will empty it. Well-intentioned as Jahangir's dream of brotherhood was, the mercurial shah, kneeling, right, probably would have found such entertainment rather pallid. A visitor to his capital at Isfahan recorded that Abbas loved nothing more than to wander through the Maidan, "as spacious, as pleasant and aromatick a Market as any in the Universe," where he would shop among the stalls for wines and sweetmeats and rough companions. Though Occidentals as a rule did not find the curries and chapatis of Jahangir's India much to their liking, Abbas' Persian markets, redolent with fruits, raw vegetables, and roasting coffee, were the wonder and envy of all Europe.

OVERLEAF: *An eternal youth and a large-eyed maiden share much wine, many promises, and perhaps a Persian melon (bowl, left) in a scene that once decorated a wall of the shah's palace.*

The Gardens of Paradise

It was written in the Koran that on the day of judgment deserving Moslems would be served "wine, fruits, and flesh of fowl" in the gardens of Paradise. Meanwhile, Persians and Indians alike contemplated the pleasures of their earth-bound existence amongst shaded groves and gardens. Above, Persian cooks pre-pare an outdoor feast in a palace courtyard. In the Mogul miniature opposite, the treetop musings of a poet are interrupted by the arrival of lunch. While one servant prepares to climb the ladder with more wine, another fans the fire.

A New World

"Sail by the west into the east where spices grow," was the cry raised by explorers who groped for new and shorter passages to the Spice Islands and Cathay. Though the route ultimately proved too long and costly to be profitable, the early voyages of Columbus, Cabot, and Magellan had revealed a veritable horn of plenty—the Americas. The New World held many surprises, some pleasant, like the banquet shared with friendly natives, above. But other tribes were somewhat less cordial; mariners were aghast to learn that certain Indians preferred a sailor's well-tanned flesh to the salt beef of the ship's stores.

Europeans found that Indians were already exploiting the rich soil and lush climate of the New World; techniques were often crude, but crops were varied and plentiful. The scenes on this page, drawn by native artists, show (clockwise from top left) maize being planted, an early Mexican produce market, Indians picking corn, and two pages from an Inca calendar, with natives first spading the earth and then harvesting the potato crop.

Pineapple—Cuba

Maize jar—Peru

Cacao bean—Ecuador

Potato jug—Peru

Riches of El Dorado

"The abundant increase of corn proves this country to be a wonderment. Thirty, forty, fifty, sixty fold are ordinary here. Yea, Joseph's increase in Egypt is outstripped here with us." Maize, thus described in 1630 by Francis Higginson in his book *New England's Plantation*, was first known as "Turkey wheat" by the earliest settlers in the Americas. Though corn was never to become popular in Europe, many New World foods were soon to change Western menus and tastes. South American potatoes and yams became staple food for both rich and poor. Mexican chocolate and vanilla and a variety of beans and squashes were also imported. But few of the new foods caught the fancy of the homeland as did the turkey. The bird first reached European shores in 1511, after the Bishop of Valencia ordered Miguel de Passamonte to return from the Americas with ten "well-guarded" turkeys in the holds of his ships. Turkey raising quickly spread through Europe and by the early seventeenth century became so common that, according to Cardinal Jacques Davy Du Perron, farmers were "driving them from Languedoc to Spain in flocks like sheep." Through the good offices of the Portuguese, the bird also reached Goa, whence it was introduced to the Middle East.

Emperor Jahangir of India was so impressed by the turkey that in 1612 he commissioned the portrait opposite.

TOP TO BOTTOM: OVIEDO, *Coronica de las Indias*, 1547, N.Y. PUBLIC LIBRARY, RARE BOOK DIVISION; MUSEUM OF THE AMERICAN INDIAN HEYE FOUNDATION, NEW YORK; DUFOUR, *Tractatus Novi De Potu caphe*, 1685, N.Y. PUBLIC LIBRARY, RARE BOOK DIVISION; SMITHSONIAN INSTITUTION, MUSEUM OF NATURAL HISTORY, ARCHAEOLOGY COLLECTION, WASHINGTON, D.C.

Rapt in transcendental thoughts, a Chinese poet gazes on his companionable bowl of wine.

FROM
THE
GOOD
EARTH

China, which produced the first civilization in the Far East, was from earliest times one of its greatest taste makers. In due course it was to exert its influence upon the West as well. In the thirteenth century Genghis Khan's rough Mongolian tribesmen broke through China's ancient walls and overran its heartland, only to take on in a generation the aristocratic manners of the Peking they had captured. The Japanese, emerging from the obscurity of their island realm, borrowed many traditions from Peking and cosmopolitan Hangchow. India, with which dynastic China had entered into close trade relations especially during the fifth and sixth centuries A.D., also absorbed Chinese influence. But ascetic Buddhism, followed by the incursion of fervid Mohammedanism, set India far apart from the land guided by the urbane precepts of Confucius and the mystical, romantic ideas of Lao-tse. The principalities of Indonesia and southeast Asia, despite their penetration by early Chinese traders, were equally resistant, remaining worlds unto themselves in social customs, religions, and culinary traditions.

A recent interpreter of China, Lin Yutang, wrote in *My Country and My People*, "If there is anything we are serious about, it is neither religion nor learning, but food." Coming from a man who was himself a scholar, the remark was no doubt intended as a whimsical exaggeration. He was, it would seem, out

Ancient ceremonial wine pitcher

to correct an impression held by some Westerners of a certain otherworldliness among highly educated Chinese of the past—as symbolized by the painting (see page 188) of the solitary scholar-poet gazing into his bowl of wine. China from its outset was a worldly civilization, craving not only food but very good food. In the time of its first flowering under the Chou dynasty, more than a millennium before Christ, it raised cookery to an art and dining to a ceremony beyond anything the Greeks had imagined.

Confucius himself (born in or about 551 B.C.) was not only an apostle of virtuous living but a gourmet and a stickler for excellence and ceremony at table. He set forth numerous rules for correct preparation and presentation of viands. As Lee Su Jan writes in *The Fine*

Art of Chinese Cooking, "His rice had to be polished white; his meat had to be finely minced, properly marinated, and served with the right sauce." If food was incorrectly combined, or if the table was not set to perfection as he saw it, he would not eat. It was from such influences as Confucius that there developed in China what has been called one of the world's two great cuisines—the other being the French.

But the preoccupation of the Chinese with their food, and their unique ways of preparing it, rest on many factors. Besides the classical Confucian ideal of gentleman-scholar-gourmet and of the meal as an expression of inner harmony through the ritual of friendship, there was the quite different Taoist school. It derived from the teachings of Lao-tse, a contemporary of Confucius, and emphasized simplicity, frugality, and a return to nature. This pursuit, apart from calisthenics, breathing, and certain sexual exercises, involved also a search for hygienic foods—particularly "life-giving" young and tender plants to be eaten raw or only half-cooked. From the former school there came much of the elegance and ceremony of Chinese cuisine; from the latter, its pleasure in very light, fresh, low-fat substances.

As in all other cultures, what was eaten was dictated by available resources —in China's case, an extraordinary mixture of scarcity and variety. It has been estimated that less than 15 per cent of China's land is today arable. What portion was arable in the time before Christ must remain conjecture, but we know that millet was the first recorded crop under cultivation there, followed by the soybean. The latter was a most valuable boon to the Chinese diet as a legume with a very high protein content (38 per cent), adaptable also to the making of curds, mashes, vegetable oils, and sauces, and moreover useful as fodder. In addition, the roots of the soybean had the rewarding quality of returning fertilizing nitrogen to the soil as the plant grew. The legendary father of Chinese agriculture, the emperor Shen Nung ("Divine Husbandman"), said to have lived c. 2700 B.C., had his clerks classify the plants of his realm, and listed the soybean as one of the five principal and sacred crops of China, the other four being rice, millet, wheat, and barley.

Still, despite intensive cultivation, recurrent famines and a tradition of undernourishment persisted in the land, and anything and everything that was edible had to be found and used, and nothing

Bronze cooking vessel, Han dynasty

wasted. This explains the inclusion in the Chinese diet of many foods that the Westerner finds forbidding if not repulsive. Locusts, silkworms, grubs, grasshoppers, snakes, and "thousand-year eggs" (actually only a few weeks old but preserved and ripened in a packing

of mud) were consumed. So were horses, mules, camels, rats, and alley cats. A chef in the imperial court of the khans around the time of Marco Polo's arrival wrote a three-volume cookbook which describes dishes using the meat of tigers, wolves, and monkeys. In the sixteenth century the Portuguese traveler Fernám Mendes Pinto wrote of food boats coming into Chinese harbors with otters, adders, and lizards for the market. He also saw compounds, or "parks" as he called them, where dogs were raised for the butcher's knife, and commented that dried orange peels were boiled up with dogs' flesh in victualing houses "to take away the rank savor and humidity" of the meat. And one Chinese tells of instances of cannibalism early in the twelfth century, when wars, invasion, and starvation had disrupted the empire. He reports that there were restaurants in Hangchow that served human meat under the name of "two-legged mutton." If this is true, it should be recalled that it occurred at the height of the Sung dynasty, renowned for its painters, mathematicians, inventors, and students of architecture and horticulture—a period when Chinese civilization was by all accounts the most advanced in the world.

Out of this background of need there developed an extraordinary, even playful, imagination in the seeking out of unusual foods. The roots of water lilies were enjoyed, along with pickled fir cones, seaweed, and kelp. A favorite dish was sharks' fins, soaked, marinated, and then simmered with ham or chicken, all of which took several days. Another was the famous "bird's-nest soup"—the nest being that of a particular species of offshore petrel that subsisted on certain types of seaweed to produce in its spittle an alkaline fluid with which it bound together its fragile roost. The resulting flavor, the Chinese found, was delectable, and immense care was taken in collecting, cleansing, and preparing broth from them. There was also a soup made of lotus seeds and a cake made of wisteria blossoms. There were even stranger dishes. A group of eighth-century A.D. poets, led by the renowned and alcoholic Li Po and calling themselves "the Eight Immortals of the Wine Cup," gave an annual banquet that included monkeys' lips, bears' paws, and something called dragon's liver—whatever that was.

Chinese cuisine was also affected by a persistent shortage of an essential element—firewood. Timber in the plains and valleys of the old provinces was extremely sparse, and stands in the remote highlands were all but inaccessible. Since fuel had to be used sparingly, it followed that cooking had better be quick rather than protracted, except where very low heat was used. Brief cooking time, as against the Western practice of slow-roasting large cuts of meat, required a great deal of preparation; foods had to be reduced to small pieces (sliced, diced, shredded, or minced) that would convert rapidly in thin, round-bottomed *woks*, or skillets. Moreover, the Chinese method was also economical in that brisk sautéing or "cook-stirring" kept down shrinkage and loss of precious juices and food values and preserved the tenderness and crispness of fresh vegetables as the Taoists had recommended.

But while scarcity or the threat of famine was ever-present, China by reason of its extensive land area—from the cold Manchurian north to the subtropical south—knew an extraordinary variety of foodstuffs. This, together with the foods that entered through conquest or foreign trade, gave China a range of diet far exceeding that of medieval Europe and in turn helped shape the diet of the West.

A court agricultural inventory made under the Han dynasty and covering the period from about the third century B.C. to A.D. 124, lists a total of 365 edible plants; not all of them can be identified

Informal lunch at a Chinese stall, c. 1300

from their ancient names. The modern writer Peh der Chen, more modest in his estimate, speaks of some 150 different types of vegetables as traditionally present and of Chinese pride in their variety. In the coastal region of Hangchow, it is reported that eighteen different kinds of beans were cultivated, along with nine varieties of rice, eleven of apricots, and eight of pears.

The Han period was one of particular luxury and expansion. Under the warrior emperor Wu Ti, who shortly before 100 B.C. extended his dominion westward toward Persia and southward beyond the Yangtze as far as Canton, oranges, grapes, pomegranates, walnuts, litchi nuts, and other novelties were introduced. (The period was also that in which glazed pottery appeared in China, along with the first experiments with porcelain—from which delicate and almost transparent bowls were to develop.) Han dynasty merchants grew rich traveling throughout the empire selling fine sauces, dried fish, dates, chestnuts, relishes, and such specialties as stuffed sheep's stomachs. Beginning in about the sixth century A.D., still more variety was introduced, reflecting Chinese contacts with Indochina, India, and the Middle East—pepper, sugar, almonds, figs, sesame, coriander, chives, onions, lettuce, garden peas, cucumbers, and probably olives. Later, carrots, kidney beans, and pistachio nuts appeared on the Chinese table, and there are records of Arab traders introducing the art of refining sugar to the Chinese.

Still later, in another instance of the transmigration that marks the history of the world's foods, maize, the sweet potato, and the peanut reached China: the corn, it is supposed, came via central Asia and the Moslem traders who got it from the Moors in Spain; the others came from Spanish traders in the Philippines. (On the other hand middle European sauerkraut can be traced to Chinese "sour cabbage"—that is, cabbage soaked in rice wine to preserve it over the winter. It is said to have been a favorite dish of Genghis Khan's invaders, who substituted salt brine for the rice wine and carried the recipe westward.) In the seventeenth and eighteenth centuries as foreign trade expanded, the pineapple and the white, or "Irish," potato appeared, as did squash and still more varieties of beans. Somewhat earlier, cultivation of the opium poppy, introduced from India, also took hold, with results at first pleasant when the seeds were used in cooking, but destined to be tragic for China when its consumers turned to the opium pipe.

The cumulative effect of all this (leaving aside the opium poppy) was a remarkable proliferation of dishes in China north and south. The common people, to be sure, subsisted primarily on a diet of rice, the soybean and its derivatives, fish, and various domestic animals and their intestines, supplemented by an occasional platter of pork. China's vast size and the range of its resources promoted numerous regional schools of cookery, each drawing on favorite and indigenous foods. The northern school of ancient Honan along the Yellow River leaned to sweet-sour dishes, using for instance the river's famous carp and the valley's delicate mushrooms. The more robust cuisine of inland southwestern Szechwan ran to highly spiced combinations, often including pimento; that of Canton on the southeastern coast, to rich sea food.

Peking, China's capital since the twelfth century, drew chefs from many provinces and developed a mixed style that at its most elegant and courtly was to be known under the Manchus as "imperial food." But perhaps the greatest variety existed at Hangchow, in effect a refugee center of Chinese gentry who emigrated down the Yangtze from northern Honan during the Mongol invasions. Hangchow boasted fresh-water fish from lakes and streams, game from nearby hills, catches from the sea, and local geese and ducks raised in huge hatcheries —some holding as many as ten thousand ducklings at once. Numerous restaurants dedicated to one or another speciality arose there. One thirteenth-century establishment offered only iced foods; another in the Mixed Wares Market concentrated on sweet soy soup; one specialized in pig cooked in ashes in front of the Longevity-and-Compassion Palace; Mother Sung's establishment outside the Cash-reserve Gate featured fish soup; still another in front of the Five-span Pavilion sold honey fritters.

Yet, however widely Chinese cooking varied from province to province and from class to class, it was governed by a general body of principles. Chinese precepts, reflecting a people of strong aesthetic and sensory bent, called for food that first must gratify all the senses —those of sight, touch, hearing, and smell no less than that of taste. Furthermore, dishes should strive for harmony coupled with contrast and accent, and always for a subtle blending of tastes. Innumerable elements entered into this scheme. Lin Yutang has explained, "We eat food for its *texture*, the elastic or crisp effect it has on our teeth, as well as for fragrance, flavor and color," and he adds that "a great part of the popularity of bamboo shoots is due to the fine resistance the young shoots give our teeth." (The use of water chestnuts, almost without taste themselves, but added to many dishes, whose flavor they absorb, is another instance of this fondness for texture; Lee Su Jan speaks of their "pleasing crunch.")

The pure whiteness of the polished rice on which Confucius insisted provided a background for the brilliant effects of color sought—the light emerald of very young vegetables, the golden brown of the swiftly sautéed morsels of duck, pork, or fish, the red of pimento. Clear, transparent broths were often graced with flower petals of a contrasting or subtly related hue: thus the light yellow chrysanthemum petals strewn in a bowl of amber chicken soup. The very bowls in which such dishes were served were works of remarkable artistry, sometimes richly colored, sometimes elegant in their sheer fragility, and were thought of as an essential ingredient to full enjoyment. An Arab merchant who visited China in the mid-ninth century, when the art of porcelain was developing, wrote that "there is in China a clay of superior quality from which are made cups (or bowls) as thin as bottles of glass; by reason of their transparency one may behold the liquid they contain."

The Chinese theme of harmony in foods was also subject to countless variations, harmony itself meaning both accord and diversity. The great eighteenth-century gastronome Yüan Mei—often referred to as the Brillat-Savarin of China—was to write, "Cookery is like matrimony. Two things served together should match. Clear should go with clear, thick with thick, hard with hard, and soft with soft." In a tone of revulsion he added, "I have known people to mix grated lobster with birds' nests, and mint with chicken or pork!" Yet he did not mean by this that all foods in the mating process should be alike. There should simply be an agreeable blend of foodstuffs on good terms with each

The Great Khan

Shortly after Kublai Khan consolidated his Tartar domain in China, he relinquished warfare in favor of less strenuous pastimes. When Marco Polo arrived at Khanbalik (Peking), he was greeted by a sinocized sovereign who wore the robes of a Chinese emperor, lived in a palace adorned with gilt dragons and lacquered ceilings, and like his new subjects, had a marked propensity for eating and drinking. Visitors from all parts of the empire came to the enormous hall where the khan held court. Before they could pay their respects and render tribute, they had to lower their voices, don white leather slippers, and equip themselves with lidded spittoons. Inside, Tibetan lamas reportedly performed such sorcery as sending goblets of koumiss (a Mongolian brew of fermented mare's milk) flying through the air to Kublai's mouth, and when empty, whisking them back with equal mystery. One banquet attended by as many as twenty thousand nobles is described by Marco Polo in splendid but probably accurate terms. Only about six thousand can be seated at tables; the others sit on carpets. "The tables are arranged . . . [so] that the Great Khan . . . on his elevated throne, can overlook the whole." Near the khan is a buffet, "hollow within, for . . . receiving a capacious vase, of pure gold, calculated to hold many gallons. On each of its four sides stands a smaller vessel . . . one filled with mare's milk, another with that of the camel." Gilt flagons, such as those in an illustration of Marco Polo's visit opposite, are each shared by two guests. "Stewards are continually . . . inquiring . . . whether any of them wish for wine, milk, meat, or other articles, in which case it is immediately brought. . . . At each door . . . stand two officers of a gigantic figure" armed with staves to prevent "persons from touching the threshold with their feet [a bad omen]." If anyone is guilty, "these janitors take . . . his garment, which he must redeem for money; or . . . they inflict on him [a] number of blows. . . . As some . . . may be affected by the liquor, it is impossible to guard against the accident, and the order is not then strictly enforced." Kublai's waiters must "cover their noses and mouths . . . that his victuals or his wine may not be affected by their breath." Whenever he drinks, all servants and guests lie prostrate, and music plays until he has finished. Later, "tumblers and jugglers . . . exhibit their skill . . . to the . . . gratification of all."

other. He also recognized five primary flavors: sweet, bitter, sour, pungent, and salty, each with its complement.

Thus Yüan Mei: "Let salt fish come first, and afterwards food of more negative flavor. Let the heavy precede the light. Let dry dishes precede those with gravy. . . . Salt flavors must be relieved by bitter or hot tasting foods, in order to restore the palate. Too much wine will make the stomach dull. Sour or sweet food will be required to rouse it again into vigor. . . . Don't make your thick sauces greasy nor your clear ones tasteless. Those who want grease can eat fat pork, while a drink of water is better than something which tastes of nothing at all. . . . Don't over-salt your soups; for salt can be added to taste, but can never be taken away. *Don't eat with your ears*; by which I mean do not aim at having extraordinary out-of-the-way foods, just to astonish your guests. . . . *Don't eat with your eyes*; by which I mean do not cover the table with innumerable dishes and multiply courses indefinitely."

Yet it is erroneous to speak in terms of separate "courses" at all. More correctly, no two dishes offered must be alike. The Western scheme of a series of dishes ending on desserts or sweetmeats was unknown in China. Sweets appeared in the middle or even at the beginning of a meal. Guests were invited to sample from numerous platters or communal bowls what most appealed to them, and in the order they preferred, always having in front of them their personal bowl of rice. There was, furthermore, a division of foods in three main orders: those that called for just a touch of garlic or soy or other sauce to bring out their

natural flavors; those that involved what Lee Su Jan calls a whole "alchemy of condiments" enhancing one main ingredient; and still others comprised of two or more main ingredients and several condiments so that in the final dish the elements had undergone complete

Chinese porcelain water bucket

transfiguration. The result might be a "breakfast" such as the one served the emperor Ch'ien Lung in 1754, the eighteenth year of his festive reign.

The emperor rose at about four o'clock in the morning in the Imperial Palace at Peking, bathed, and was waited upon by a court eunuch with a dish of crystal sugar and swallows' nests. Afterward, he was carried to the audience hall in a palanquin to hear his courtiers, then returned to his chambers to rest a while. At about nine o'clock he was regaled by the following: a dish of fat chicken, pot-boiled duck, and bean curd, cooked by the master Chang Erh; a dish of swallows' nests and a julienne of smoked duck, cooked by the same; a dish of salted duck and pork, prepared by Jung Kuei; a dish of smoked chicken and Chinese cabbage; a bowl of clear soup; a dish of bamboo-stuffed steamed dumplings; another of rice cakes with honey; and the following, "served in a ceramic container patterned with hollyhock flowers": pickled cabbage, cucumbers in soy, pickled eggplant—and so on.

This was only the first of three meals of comparable magnitude during the day—though no doubt the emperor, following the custom, took only bits and pieces here and there with his porcelain soup spoon or his chopsticks. (The use of chopsticks—pidgin English for *faai jee* meaning "quick little boys"—was a sign of cultivation, in contrast to using one's fingers or the "barbaric" foreign fork. In polite society the table knife was also unheard-of, cutting in all its forms being the task of the chefs and servants, and never done at meals.)

A formal banquet would, of course, offer a far greater variety. There might be as many as fifty dishes, representing every category of food from land, sea, and air; a dinner of the empress dowager Tzu Hsi is reported to have included over a hundred. One Chinese book of dining goes further and mentions more than two hundred dishes that might be served at a very grand affair, including 41 of fish, shrimps, snails, pork, goose, duck, mutton, et cetera; 42 concocted from fruits and sweetmeats; along with 17 liquid refreshments, ranging from wine to pawpaw juice, litchi juice, and honey and ginger drinks. Since a basic principle of Chinese high cuisine was to offer only what was most fresh and to serve it immediately, the sheer logistical problems of assembling so many foods in prime condition for a given banquet must have been immense.

Another problem confronting the chef and his assistants was the selection of a site for such complex meals; in winter indoors, but in warmer seasons in some harmonious grove or pavilion or beside a lake or stream—the place was very much a part of the Chinese aesthetic. A banquet might be served on a terrace such as that of the ancient Han emperor Wu Ti where "amid the perfumed cassia trees, peacocks flocked together, monkeys screamed, kingfishers gathered, and phoenixes flew about," or in accompanying gardens lit by multi-colored lanterns. Or the court might decide to pick a remote spot for what the French call a *fête champêtre*. Banquets might also be served in pleasure barges. An eighth-century poet of the T'ang dynasty tells of such an evening in a brief fragment:

Forthwith we steered our boat in changèd course.
A meeting with the Muse we fain would seek.
We dressed our table with fresh food and wines.
All lights gone out were lit up once again. . . .

The custom had not changed by the eighteenth century. Of the later emperor Ch'ien Lung, a recent historian Lucille Su Chung Davis writes, "The greatest difficulty in serving the emperor came from the fact that there was no regular place for him to eat. The imperial cuisine was required to serve meals whenever and wherever the emperor demanded. For example, when the emperor was taking a walk, men of the refreshment division had to follow him with two round bamboo baskets containing plenty of refreshments, tea, and a small stove so that food might be ready within minutes after it was ordered." Not only the portable stove, but iron cooking pots and pans, silver bowls, and fine porcelain cups had to be transported. This was "cook-stir" cuisine at perhaps its most demanding.

Dining and ceremony were inseparable. The greatest annual festival, that of *Sun Neen* (New Year's), involved special rituals concerning the god of the kitchen, who was supposed to ascend to Heaven to report on the virtues and vices of the family. A week before the New Year, the family gathered before his picture hung on the kitchen chimney to send him on his way: his lips were smeared with sticky sweets to prevent them from uttering evil, and then the image was taken down, set upon a straw or paper horse outside the house, and burned. On the last day of the year, his triumphal return to the kitchen was observed with fireworks and banqueting, and a new picture was placed upon the chimney.

Among the gentry not only banquets but even an everyday dinner with friends was governed by elaborate forms of reception, courtesy, and protocol of seating as well as of conversation. For more formal gatherings invitations were sent out—perhaps on red paper with gold inscription—to ten or a dozen guests, usually not more, mentioning the names of the others who had been invited, and thus giving each recipient a convenient way of excusing himself if he preferred not to join the particular company. (The West has not yet learned this subtle touch of "harmony.") The ultimate ceremonial, the state banquet, is described by Tien-Hsi Cheng, former member of the Chinese diplomatic corps, in his *Musings of a Chinese Gourmet*:

"1. The host stands on the west side of the hall a few yards from the dinner table. 2. The "Master of Ceremony" bows to the guest of honor and conducts him to a place on the east side of the hall not far from but opposite to where the host is standing. 3. The host bows to the guest, who bows in return. 4. The host ascends the hall up to the dinner table and bows to the empty chair on which the guest is to sit. The guest, now facing the host, bows in return. 5. The host walks to the chair and, with both sleeves, touches the cushion of the chair as a symbol of dusting it. After this, he bows to the chair and the guest bows in return. 6. The host, with a bow, raises the pair of chopsticks to be used by the guest, who bows in return. 7. The host, with a bow, raises the wine cup to be used by the guest, who bows in return. 8. The host returns to the place where he stood and bows to the guest, who bows in return. 9. The guest leaves and is conducted to his seat."

"Solemn but cheerful music" was frequently played at such festivities. The table was usually round, both to encourage general conversation and to provide all guests with equal access to the various dishes placed in the center, as against the European custom of a long table where one could converse comfortably only with his immediate neighbors and where food was served by footmen. The order of seating also ran counter to the European forms: the host, after mutual obeisances, sat opposite the guest of honor, who was placed nearest the family altar or farthest from the door. To be seated at the left hand of the host was thought to be a higher honor than to be at his right. In polite houses there was a rule against religious, political, or other disputatious talk at table, which might disturb the friendship or conviviality of those present. One discussed art, philosophy, and no doubt one's neighbors—and above all, the food itself.

One also played table games at intervals during the meal. A chief purpose of these games was, clearly, to encourage drinking—the Chinese, with his elaborate sense of formality, evidently needed some "urging" to toss off another cup. Many responded to the urging quite

Mandarin banquet in an orchard, Ming dynasty

readily. There is ample evidence that from early times alcohol was consumed in quantity. Confucius himself admitted that he was sometimes "overcome by wine." A Chinese proverb claims, "No wine, no conversation; no conversation, no company." Poets told of the transcendental pleasures of becoming drunk. Li Po, one of China's greatest lyricists, wrote, "The rapture of drinking, and wine's dizzy joy, No man who is sober deserves." He is said to have drowned after falling overboard while in a state of drunken exultation, trying to seize the moon's reflection in a lotus pool.

By wine, however, the Chinese did not generally mean that made from grapes. The earliest sources of wine were fermented grains and a variety of fruits. An old tale has it that the drink originated in China when a palace cook placed some rice in a crock to soak and then forgot it. Several days later he returned to the crock wondering if the rice had spoiled. Not only was the rice delicious but the water had been transformed into something wonderful. He continued to sample the liquid, singing a happy song all the while.

The early yellow rice wine tasted, perhaps, somewhat like sherry. As Marco Polo observed on returning from thirteenth century Peking, the beverage the Chinese preferred was "a liquor which they brew of rice with a quantity of excellent spice in such fashion that it makes better drink than any other kind of wine; it is not only good, but clear and pleasant to the eye. And being very hot stuff, it makes one drunk sooner than any other wine." He was describing something similar to Japanese *sake*. There was also a stronger grain concoction resembling vodka; and rose petals, pears, oranges, and quinces were sometimes used. Wine made from grapes may have entered China in the second century before Christ, as a result of Han dynasty contacts with Persia. An envoy brought back seeds of *Vitis vinifera*, but for more than a millennium and a half grape wine remained an unfamiliar, imported luxury.

In early T'ang times, wine was apparently taken only after the meal, each guest awaiting his turn to raise his cup. In later centuries it was served through-

Games People Played

*I*n Chinese society playing games during the meal was not only good manners, it was almost *de rigueur*. Games kept the conversation flowing and discouraged discussion of sensitive subjects which had a way of souring the stomach. Since the Chinese also observed that the road to conviviality was paved with empty wine cups, most contests were designed to encourage drinking. One of the more popular mealtime entertainments was a Cantonese game called Guess the Unknown, which demanded stratagem, ruse, and digital dexterity. It involved two players, each of whom threw out on signal a hand showing one or more fingers extended, simultaneously calling out the total number of fingers between them. After each round, the loser—and often the winner—was consoled with wine. Another contest that probed the minds and capacities of guests was the "Wine Command." It relied not on guesswork but on erudition and was a favorite among the mandarins, the scholarly ruling class whose com-

petitive wits were well-honed at all times. Initially, the host chose a word, using it in a quotation from a literary classic. Depending on the position of the key word within the sentence, the player that many places to the left of the reciter then had to offer another sentence from the same work, using the chosen word. The "punishment" for failing to produce a quotation on cue was another

cup of rice wine, a handicap that one with a faltering memory could ill afford. The diner's attainments as a muse might also be tested in a poetry contest—a theme was proposed by the host, and guests were expected to compose spontaneously a few lines. Whether born of the sheer joy of creation or the heat of competition, many of these poems have become classics. Tiring of such exercises and while waiting for a new siege of dishes, the assembly might debate the virtues of their favorite recipes for shark fin soup or the most refined blend of tea, each speaker trying to outdo his companions in evocative language. All these games presupposed an extraordinary degree of intelligence on the part of host and guests alike. Anyone planning a party among dullards could always resort to paid entertainers, highly specialized professionals such as riddle makers, tellers of obscene stories, imitators, slight-of-hand artists, and singers of songs. As European travelers visiting China for the first time discovered, capacities of mind as well as of stomach were required of the successful guest.

out the meal, still in cups and, as always, warmed. The warming served to overcome its "green" or harsh flavor, since it was consumed soon after fermentation. One thirteenth-century report, discussing Hangchow restaurants, taverns, and households, speaks of fifty-four different kinds of rice wines available. Evidently a quite remarkable selectivity of tastes had come into being by then. In the eighteenth century the fastidious Yüan Mei wrote with perception, "I am not much of a wine drinker, but this makes me all the more particular. Wine is like scholarship: it ripens with age; and it is best from a fresh-opened jar. The top of the wine jar, the bottom of the teapot, as the saying has it."

When the Chinese—and the Japanese who followed in their culinary wake— were not enjoying food or wine, their primary refreshment was of course tea, of which they made not only a ceremony but a cult. Tea, the national drink of China, was drunk at all hours and on all occasions—from breakfast at home to midnight and beyond at the many classes of teahouses. Business was (and is today) conducted over it. The first act of a host on receiving a visitor at his home or place of business was to offer a steaming drink, perhaps accompanied by almond cakes. Caravans, coaches, and then railroad trains stopped repeatedly at way stations to obtain boiling water from local purveyors for brewing the tea that individual passengers carried with them. The use of boiled water as a basis for refreshment, it might be remarked, in a land in which so many rivers and canals were polluted, had distinct advantages. Although one legend attributes the

discovery of tea to the emperor Shen Nung, another popular myth credits the founder of Zen Buddhism in India, Bodhidharma, with its origin. The saint, on a mission to China, decided to spend nine years in a sanctuary contemplating a wall, but exhaustion finally overcame him, and he fell asleep. As penance, he cut off his eyelids and threw them to the ground, where a strange bush sprang up. After tasting the leaves, Bodhidharma found that his drowsiness had passed, and he was able to continue his meditations without further interruption. Actually, it appears that the tea plant was indigenous to India where it thrived on steep slopes in poor acidic soil otherwise incapable of supporting crops. It may have entered China in about the third century A.D., after the Han empire had reached out to the subtropical regions south of the Yangtze valley. We know that tea was widely used in the eighth century, if only from a record of taxes imposed on it. Also about that time, a poet named Lu Yu is said to have traveled the countryside with cooking pots and a water tank to demonstrate methods of brewing the beverage.

Before long, an extraordinary proliferation of varieties of tea occurred in China, involving perhaps more subtleties of taste than exist among the wines of France. Since all tea comes from the same type of plant, its quality depends on the altitude; the month the leaves are harvested; whether or not the leaves are broken in handling; and whether the leaves are picked high (for better quality teas) or low on the bush. In the curing process certain teas are chemically altered by oxidation before they are dried, producing black teas; others are dried directly, hence green teas. Today, green teas are limited mainly to China. Most black teas come from Ceylon and India. Romantic and inviting labels are given to them: "Dragon's Whiskers," a delicate green growth of Shantung; "Water Nymph," "Eyebrows of Longevity," and "Clear Distance" of Kwantung; "White Clouds" and "Forest of Fragrance" of the region of Hangchow. Two extra-fine blends of dessert teas, known as *Tit-koon-yum* and *Tit-lo-hon*, of northern China were at last report still picked by monkeys trained to scale the heights and retrieve basketfuls of their tiny leaves. In early days, ginger, orange, or onion was used to add savor to the tea; in later times, jasmine blossoms or those of roses or crysanthemums or camellias added fragrance.

The ritual of tea prescribed that it be brewed not in the kitchen but in the presence of the guests themselves, usually in the individual cups they were to use; the Chinese as a rule used the pot for hot water only. Each cup was fitted with a lid, and when the cup was raised to the lips, its lid was lifted just enough to let the liquid flow but to hold back the leaves. A second or third cup brewed with the same leaves was generally thought to be an improvement on the

Embroidered covers on tea caddies, Japan, 1600's

first, and each pouring involved more ceremony and more compliments (the host, needless to say, denigrating the quality of his tea, though it might be the finest money could buy). A particularly graceful form of tea service took place as part of the marriage ceremony, when the bride presented tea in red (signifying joy) lacquer cups to her blood relatives and in-laws and the friends of both families, in order of precedence.

But if the offering of tea in China was a rite, in Japan it approached the status of a religion. It is said that the first Japanese ruler to taste the brew was the emperor Shomū, who accepted a cup from a party of visiting Buddhist priests in the year 729. He bestowed his approval, and soon the plant was being raised on the slopes of Mount Hiei; but it was not until much later that tea was taken for other than its medicinal properties or that the ritual of "teaism" developed. Out of the contemplative qualities of Zen Buddhism, the formalities of their own Shintoism, and their native aesthetic predilections, the Japanese developed during the sixteenth century the idea of the teahouse or tearoom attached to the house as a place to worship and to learn harmony, tranquillity, unselfishness, and dignity. Tea—not the clear, amber tea which was drunk with meals but a kind of soup whipped up from tea powder into a froth—became the substance and symbol of communion.

The classic "tea ceremony," *cha-no-yu*, of Japan was conceived far more in terms of symbols than substance. One came to a friend's teahouse not to enjoy a number of warming cups of *o cha* ("honorable tea") and conversation so much as to engage in a complex ritual. Following the teachings of the famed "tea master" Rikyu and successor *chajins*, even the tea-ceremony rooms were constructed according to precise specifications—a subtle play of assymetric proportions that were said to give full range to the imagination of the communicants. The ritual began with the invitation of the guests, usually four, after which each would call to express his *zenrei*, or polite thanks. Then, on the following day the guests would arrive, wearing properly muted kimonos and carrying their personal tea cloths and fans. After gathering in the waiting room, the group walked to the teahouse, preceded by the host or his gardener, who carried a bronze swordlike instrument which he brandished about as if to lop off branches that might obstruct the guests or snag their garments, this to symbolize the host's desire to give his guests every comfort. Before entering the chamber, everyone stopped for a ceremonious washing of face and hands and removal of sandals. Then, as Okakura-Kakuzo's classic *Book of Tea* records, "The guest will silently approach the sanctuary, and, if a samurai, will leave his sword on the rack beneath the eaves, the tearoom being pre-eminently the house of peace. Then he will bend low and creep into the room through a small door. . . . This proceeding [is] incumbent on all guests, high and low alike, and is intended to inculcate humility. The order of precedence having been mutually agreed upon . . . the guests one by one will enter noiselessly and take their seats, first making obeisance to the picture or flower arrangement on the *tokonoma* [a niche designed especially for their display]. The host will not enter the room until all the guests have seated themselves and quiet reigns with nothing to break the silence save the note of the boiling water in the iron kettle. . . ."

The rest of the ceremony went on in like ritual fashion, a sequence of precise movements being prescribed for the elevation of the cup to one's lips, as well as a practice, if a communal bowl was

Japanese invention for suspending kettle

used, of passing it around the table when emptied to be admired by the guests as a work of art. After each guest had made sucking sounds to signify his pleasure at his last sip, and the host his profound obeisances, the company departed through the same door by which they had entered.

When eating or drinking normally, the Japanese were not subject to such excruciating practices. Their basic diet (almost unchanged to this day) was akin to that of the coastal Chinese, both in foodstuffs and preparation, though there were many differences. Rice and soy were their staples, along with local seafood. The Japanese rice was served both steamed and in the form of rice cakes, or *moshi;* it was, in fact, so important to the diet that the word for rice, *gohan*, was also used to describe a whole meal. Soybeans appeared at table as bean paste and curd, vegetable oil, sauce, and as a fermented preservative for other foods. Fast or "instant" cookery of cut-up foods, also learned from China, was the rule. The Japanese also shared the Chinese' fondness for rice wine. A Chinese historian of the third century remarked that the Japanese "are given much to strong drink"; by the tenth century the amount of drinking had become formidable. The only time it was considered improper to drink was while eating rice.

Differences between Japanese and Chinese cuisine were due chiefly to the period of Japanese seclusion and Buddhist ascendancy beginning in the tenth century when Buddhist prohibitions against the killing of animals limited the orthodox to a vegetarian diet supplemented by fish. The meat of cattle, though Jesuit missionaries recommended it highly during the brief period of their access to Japan in the sixteenth century, continued to be despised as unfit for human consumption, and the real or imagined smell that accompanied meat eaters was deemed most disagreeable. But the nineteenth century was to see a turnabout, when Japanese came into close contact with carnivorous Americans and Europeans, and young intellectuals propounded the theory that red meat was advantageous to mind and body. In 1872 the emperor gave the signal by going over to beef himself; thereupon all Japan took to it, and beef eating, according to one Japanese historian, "was regarded as a sign of [an] advanced state of civilization." One result of this

revolution is the dish most familiar to Westerners, the beef-and-vegetable *sukiyaki*, though Japanese gourmets look down upon it as untraditional and of peasant origin.

Like China, Japan from early times enjoyed its annual court festivals, all involving food and drink. Thus there was the ceremony of "The Medicinal Offerings and the Tooth Hardening," which an old court calendar describes as follows: "Various types of spiced wine are prepared by the Palace Medicinal Office and, after being tasted by specially appointed virgins, are offered to His Majesty as an elixir of long life. Radishes, mirror-shaped rice cakes, melons, and similar auspicious foods are presented to the Emperor in order to 'harden his teeth' [to ensure his good health] during the coming year." And for the "Festival of the Young Herbs," officials of the Imperial Storehouse went out to pluck the "seven lucky herbs" to mix with rice and make a gruel for the emperor; the same seven-herb gruel was also prepared in private households to ward off evil spirits and to protect the family from any dangers ahead. Another annual event was the exquisite chrysanthemum celebration in which the emperor and his court, after inspecting the blossoms in the royal garden, sat down to drink wine in which the petals had been steeped, to dine on white trout and compose poetry.

Such food ceremonies have long since disappeared. But China and Japan, despite their overwhelming changes in the last half century, remain profoundly attached to their traditions, and a meal is never really a meal without a bowl of good white rice and a cup of tea beside it.

LANDS
OF THE
LOTUS-EATERS

Kublai Khan and wife at a Mongolian cookout, from a contemporary Persian history

The Flowery Kingdom

According to Taoists, by observing the cyclic rhythms of nature, man could learn to live in harmony with the universe and even discover the secret of long life. Perhaps because Buddha (under a mango tree opposite) first attained perfect wisdom contemplating a Bo or wild fig tree, fruit trees such as the peach were particularly sacred. Chinese artists were inspired to capture the fragrance of pomegranate blossoms and the sweetness of the ripening fruit, above, or to convey the fragility of arbutus berries, below, with their brushes. A poet advised: "fruit trees should be painted in the chill of the evening. Then they lose their wildness. . . . Those who do not care for flowers need not look."

Cultivating the paddy

Sowing in floodtime

The Hard-won Crop

Reaping the harvest

Bringing in the sheaves

Sifting

Winnowing

Preparing to transplant

Planting the seedlings

Rice was as basic to the Oriental diet as bread was to the European meal, but its cultivation was a far more demanding task. The good grace with which these Chinese peasants bend to their labors is purely imaginary, the romantic conception of the eighteenth-century Englishman who engraved the series. Except at harvest time, there was little joy in the rice paddy, and even the most bountiful yield, when polished to a properly Confucian white, provided little real nourishment.

OVERLEAF: *A British painter in Canton c. 1835 traces the progress of tea from its growth in the highlands, upper left, to its packing, sale, and shipment on the wharves, below.*

THE GALLERY OF MODERN ART, INCLUDING THE HUNTINGTON HARTFORD COLLECTION, NEW YORK

Threshing

Breaking the husks

Grinding

Offering thanks

Travel kit of eating and cooking tools, Korea, 1700's

Wine vessel, ancient China

The Perfect Setting

Porcelain dish, China, c. 1630

At the Oriental meal, form was as important as content. The distinctive diet of the East required tableware often very different from that of the West, and no dish or utensil was too insignificant to have its own standards of perfection. Above, a picnic set provided everything a nobleman needed for a cook-stir meal, including tongs for the fire, a marrow pick, and tiny cups for sipping a particularly refined brew of tea buds. Traditional drinking vessels in the shapes of animals are represented here in a bronze owl jar for sacramental wine, c. 1000 B.C., and in a seventeenth-century porcelain

Lacquered kettle, Japan, 1500's

CREDITS FOR PHOTOGRAPHS ABOVE, CLOCKWISE FROM TOP: CHARLES R. GRACIE AND SONS, INC.; THE MINNEAPOLIS INSTITUTE OF ARTS, ALFRED F. PILLSBURY BEQUEST; M. H. DE YOUNG MEMORIAL MUSEUM, ROY LEVENTRITT COLLECTION, SAN FRANCISCO; COURTESY OF DR. AND MRS. PAUL VIGNOS, JR.

Ginger jar, China, c. 1700

Rhino horn cup, China, 1600's

Covered soup bowl, Japan

elephant bottle for table use. The cup carved from rhino horn in the shape of a lotus leaf combined the symbolism of a highly touted aphrodisiac and a dream-inducing plant. The ginger jar, in the cobalt blue and white perfected under the Ming dynasty, held sweetmeats sent to friends on the New Year. Chinese porcelain was also designed to suit foreign tastes —the dish in the shape of Mount Fuji was marketed for the Japan trade. Tableware created by the Japanese was often of a simpler, more robust design, like the kettle and the soup bowl, whose cover, when inverted, became a second dish.

Elephant bottle, China, c. 1600

The Floating World

CHARLES R. GRACIE AND SONS, INC.

"Living only for the moment, turning our full attention to the pleasures of the moon, the snow, the cherry blossoms and the maple leaves, singing songs, drinking wine, and diverting ourselves just in floating, floating . . ." was the not so elusive ideal of the newly risen feudal lords of sixteenth and seventeenth century Japan. The delicate Buddhist-inspired sensibilities of their predecessors were overthrown in favor of worldly diversions. Among these, the picnic held an especially favored place. The stylish couples opposite, depicted by the genre painter Shunsho, have taken to the countryside with a *samisen* (a three-stringed banjo) and a lacquer picnic box, wrapped in a cloth, but presumably like the four-tiered carrier above.

On the Road

Between the Imperial city of Kyoto and the shogunate in Tokyo, the traffic of Japanese pilgrims, bureaucrats, and feudal lords never slowed. For their protection, in 1601 the government established fifty-three way stations along the 305-mile Tokaido Road and ruled that no traveler could stay even a single night in a house other than a public inn. Though notable guests might appear for dinner and lodging at any time, innkeepers were in a special state of readiness every spring when a retinue of two hundred men set out from Tokyo for Uji, there to refill the Shogun's "precious tea canisters" and assorted lesser containers with the finest tea leaves of the country. On the return trip, messengers preceded the party to alert innkeepers, supervise the sweeping of the roadway, and halt all burning of fires or other activities which might flavor the tea. During these days, the usually attentive service to other clients might, understandably, suffer.

Opposite: The number of "waitresses" permitted by law was two; some proprietors gladly paid the fine.

Chop Chop in the Kitchen

For all the subtleties of Oriental cookery, the traditional kitchen was a rudimentary affair, uncluttered by batteries of utensils, ovens, and cutlery so dear to Western chefs. Below and opposite, the preparation of a samurai's meal, painted by an anonymous fourteenth-century artist, is divided among five men: two carving masters, cross-legged behind their low work tables, address a cormorant and a carp, the fish held upright between two chopsticks for filleting. Their companions attend to the vegetables in round-bottomed pans over the fire pit, and ladle soup with a spoon fashioned from a scallop shell. The woman-run kitchen above has a more relaxed atmosphere, as drawn by the eighteenth-century artist Utamaro: left, one servant chats with the baby and gives a bowl a peremptory wipe, while another peels vegetables, washing them in the bucket at her side; right, they tend the fire, blowing on it through a pipe.

ABOVE AND OPPOSITE: OKURA SHUKOKAN MUSEUM, TOKYO; BRADLEY SMITH, NEW YORK

Both in China and in Japan, vendors of specialty foods called regularly at the kitchen door. The Chinese sweetmeat peddler at right carries a variety of preserved fruits—winter melon, kumquats, orange rinds—along with ginger and dried litchi. In season he also sells mosquito repellent. The Japanese boy below scurries through the streets with buckets of pure well water, a tray of cups, and a canister of tea leaves.

亞墨利加人
遊行酒盛

The Open Door And The Butter Stinkers

The young man at left, who has already equipped himself with a foreign pocket watch and an umbrella, is about to break one of old Japan's most sacred dietary taboos by eating meat. Not only did such acts of defiance raise conservative eyebrows, they also wrinkled noses. Westerners and their imitators were said to give off a strong odor of animal fats and were known as *bata-kusai*, or butter stinkers. Within three decades of Commodore Perry's arrival, trading ports boasted numerous Western-style restaurants: Rokumeikan, or the "Club of the Deer's Call," was Eastern in name only, recalling an ancient Chinese ode about hospitality. Inside, Oriental gentlemen in frock coats and trousers dined with ladies wearing the latest Paris fashions.

At the banquet above, tables are adapted for American comfort, but the raw fish is uncompromised. Opposite, a tar copes more manfully with a bottle of sake and a geisha robed in stars and stripes.

At a luncheon of French aristocrats, c. 1740, oysters take precedence over etiquette.

THE
TRIUMPH
OF
FRENCH TASTE

On a sultry August afternoon in 1661, young King Louis XIV climbed into his state coach at his château at the edge of the forest of Fontainebleau and, accompanied by the queen mother and a splendid cavalcade of princes of the blood, dukes, courtiers, *gardes du corps*, and pages, all in their richest array, bounced over thirty kilometers of rutted roads to attend one of the greatest festivities ever seen in France. The visit was to have unexpected and momentous results.

The occasion was a fete to celebrate the completion of the vast country seat erected by the young monarch's chief minister, Nicolas Fouquet, on a handsome slope beside a bend of the upper Seine. Fouquet's showplace, called Vaux-le-Vicomte, was a dazzling sight. As the king passed through the forecourt gateway, he saw a majestic white edifice encrusted with decoration and topped by a cupola. The structure was surrounded by a moat flanked by spacious outbuildings and was set in an immense preserve of gardens, promenades, pools, grottoes, and some fifty fountains and cascades.

The most brilliant artists and designers of France had been enlisted to create it, along with an army of a thousand craftsmen. Le Vau was its architect, Le Nôtre its landscaper, and the painter Le Brun director in charge of its decor, from its ceiling frescoes to its tapestries and rugs. The entertainment for the king's evening was planned on the same

Faience platter depicting a rustic garden

splendid scale: the famed composer Lully would lead the orchestra; Molière would present a new play written for the occasion. Vatel, the rising *maître d'hôtel* of genius, would supervise the chefs in preparing for some five hundred people a banquet that included ortolan, pheasant, quail, partridge, and assorted bisques and ragouts, along with the best wines of Champagne and Beaune. An outdoor ballet under countless lanterns, a display of fireworks, and a salute of cannon were to be the climax of the day.

On hand was the poet La Fontaine, who wrote in a strophe, "Le ciel en fut jaloux." But not only the heavens grew jealous. Louis was not amused. His minister had gone too far; he had displayed a magnificence far greater than that of the Crown. With his ever-present cour-

tesy, Louis remarked of the dinner service: "What admirable plate." Fouquet, falling into a trap, explained: "Pardon, Sire, it is not plate, it is gold." Whereupon the king, reportedly—and ominously—answered: "We have nothing like this at the Louvre."

Indeed both the old Louvre, hemmed in by dank city streets, and Louis' ancestral Fontainebleau were warrens of unpremeditated plan, thrown up over centuries—no match for Fouquet's smashing new palace and pleasure dome. The king's decision was soon made. He already knew of Fouquet's huge profiteering as the realm's minister of finance. The end was near. Within three weeks the minister was arrested, tried, and jailed for embezzlement, his property was declared forfeit, and Louis, just twenty-three years old, set out to build for himself a palace that would surpass Vaux—taking into his service the same Le Vau, Le Nôtre, and Le Brun. The result was Versailles, for well over a century to be the seat of Europe's greatest court, the scene of Europe's most lavish entertainment, and the embodiment of French hegemony of taste.

Louis XIII, a somewhat unprepossessing person as Bourbon rulers went, had owned a pleasant hunting lodge on the site his son chose for Versailles, but it had never occurred to him to enlarge it. Frugal yet tasteful, he liked on occasion to prepare with his own hands the game he had shot, and his skill as a cook was esteemed. He was also interested in gardening, to the extent of personally supervising the raising of spring vegetables at the small château, seeking to bring them in earlier than other producers in the area—and he was par-simonious enough to sell some of his own harvest to his neighbor Seigneur de Montauron, who kept a table more ample than his own.

This way of life bore little resemblance to that of his imperious son. When building the new Versailles, Louis ordered that the *grands appartements* of the royal family be flanked by wings, one to accommodate his mistresses and illegitimate children, the other to house several hundred courtiers in continuous attendance. There were quarters for some fifteen hundred officers and servants of the household, as well. To feed this many mouths every day, along with his numerous guests, was itself a vast undertaking. Versailles, though still called a château, became in effect a city; its kitchens, presided over by a hierarchy of stewards and *maîtres queux*, were the largest yet constructed, and its many service

Designs for Louis XIV coffeepot and server

departments employed hundreds of men. Together, the bakery and wine cellars had fifty or more on duty. Mass feeding imposed its limits on cuisine.

In Louis XIII's time there had been, at fine houses such as Seigneur de Montauron's, a distinct effort at what might be called culinary reform—a search for a

better harmony and order of dishes to replace the riot of tastes inherited from the preceding century. That older disorder was satirized by Boileau, one of Louis XIV's leading court poets, when in the course of his *Festin Ridicule* he described a pyramid of meat:

> *On top of a hare flanked by six chicks*
> *Lay three rabbits, animals domestic,*
> *Who since their tender infancy in Paris*
>   *were bred,*
> *Smelt still of the cabbage on which they'd*
>   *been fed.*
> *Round this mass of meats piled high*
> *A long border of pressed larks did lie,*
> *And on the edge of the dish, six pigeons*
>   *went,*
> *Exposing their burnt skeletons as rein-*
>   *forcement.*

Among the chefs before mid-century, none was greater than Francois Pierre de La Varenne, who may have learned the art of cookery as a young man at the court of Henry IV (for whom he also ran numerous amatory errands). An artist of sauces as well as a logician of menu planning, he tried to do away with the heavy spices and heaped-up dishes of the past. Meats were served in their own reduced juices. Fish were similarly prepared in a *fumet*, or stock of their trimmings. A sauce thickener known as *roux* (a carefully heated mixture of butter and flour) was introduced as a binder of flavors. Marinades, pâtés, mushrooms and truffles used as subtle accents, were also elements of La Varenne's art.

Recipes for sauces, along with rules governing the sequence of courses, were set forth in his *Le Cuisinier Français* of 1651, a treatise that became the bible of the "new cuisine." Among the first sauces perfected after La Varenne's teachings was a particularly fine white sauce called *sauce Béchamel* after Louis' lord steward. It was produced by adding chicken or veal stock to fresh cream and *roux*, and was a great advance over the tart *verjus* of sixteenth-century fare.

The king, however, was less interested in the art of the *cuisinier* than in the sheer gratification of his appetites, which were as formidable at board as they were in bed. As Louis remarked, "One eats

Forces of Lent attacking . . .

well who works well." In 1656, when he was not yet eighteen, he was served a banquet at the château of Pontchartrain that embraced 16 hot hors d'oeuvres and 8 potted meats and vegetables; 8 "broths" and 16 entrees of fine meats; 8 roast dishes and 16 vegetables cooked in meat stock; several pâtés of cold meats, fish dishes, and assorted salads; and as the fifth course, 24 different kinds of pastries and fresh and preserved fruits for a grand total of 168 garnished dishes. Of course it was understood, as in times past, that the diner would be highly selective in picking from such an array.

The full achievements of French cuisine would have to await the eighteenth century. What Louis XIV did contribute to the table was a new grandeur and protocol. Le Roi Soleil made dining not only a ceremony but a spectacle, with himself as the principal actor. Once he was established at Versailles, his daily meals became rituals resembling tableaux, and they changed little from decade to decade. His day began with a *grand lever* at which a hundred or more courtiers with the right of entrance observed or assisted him in donning his first morning dress, after which he took a light breakfast of white bread, wine, and water. (Louis, it appears, though he lived on into a time when coffee, tea, and chocolate became fashionable, never consumed any of them; though in his later years, according to the court chronicler and gossip Saint-Simon, he enjoyed "an infusion of sage and veronica.") Then, after a morning of audiences with his ministers and Mass at 12:30, he took luncheon at one or two o'clock *au petit couvert*, dining alone or with his queen, the former Infanta Marie Thérèse of Spain, at a table beside the windows of his bedroom overlooking the central court of the palace.

Not that this was an informal or light meal. High officers of state, accompanied by an echelon of the king's guards, made ceremony of presenting it, marching through chamber after chamber of the palace crying, "the king's meat!" As the food passed, rapidly cooling in its long transit from distant kitchens, all the courtiers doffed their hats and bowed. Two archers followed by a gentleman usher and the lord chief steward, usually a prince of the blood, led the procession. Inside the apartments, the king's brother, Philippe, Duc d'Orléans ("Monsieur" in French court parlance), would sometimes be on hand to proffer a napkin and at the king's bidding might sit down but not eat; lesser nobles stood about in attendance. After the dishes were "tasted" by a gentleman in waiting, the king attacked his formidable lunch.

At ten o'clock the main meal was served *au grand couvert* in one of the state salons with the whole court in attendance, some of the nobles seated at the tables, the *petite noblesse* standing as spectators, along with such commoners as had been admitted. By this time Louis was again ravenous, and dinner began with a variety of soups, some very rich and thick, such as *soupe Colbert* topped with poached eggs and named after the finance minister who had succeeded Fouquet. Like many heavy eaters, Louis was but a light drinker, taking only a goblet or two of champagne. The champagne he drank, however, was not the bubbly drink we know today (the chemical invention of a Benedictine monk and cellarer named Pérignon in 1670); it was a still white wine of the province, mixed with water. Louis also favored the traditional syrupy "hippocras"—concocted of white or red wine, honey, and aromatics—and cordials, which, as Saint-Simon explained, were invented to provide "solace in his declining years."

Princess Palatine, Louis' sister-in-law, claimed to "have seen the King eat, and that very often, four plates of different soups, an entire pheasant, a partridge, a large plateful of salad, mutton cut up

in its juice with garlic, two good pieces of ham, a plateful of cakes, and fruits and jams." Madame de Maintenon, his final mistress *en titre*, who was also to become his second wife, is said to have remarked that if she ate half as much as he did she would be dead in a week. (It was discovered at his autopsy that his intestines were twice the length of an average man's.) His physician Fagon managed eventually to put him on something approaching a diet (this was the Fagon whom Molière satirized in

. . . Mardi Gras en garde

his comedy *Le Malade Imaginaire* as Doctor Paragon, the man who makes his king's life miserable by cutting off his favorite foods), and Saint-Simon was to go so far as to suggest in his memoirs that Fagon's regimen had contributed to the monarch's death. Saint-Simon particularly disapproved of the doctor's treatment for Louis' gout: the king was regularly sweated and fed iced, overripe fruit.

Louis' manners were impeccable, though from this distance it may seem odd that he firmly refused to use a fork, preferring to eat with his fingers, while

Ben Franklin

*A*s representative of the rough, simple, and egalitarian Americans, and more especially as a victim of the gout, Benjamin Franklin was not really in a position to become an epicure during his eight-year visit to France. In fact, he learned that most of French society found his rustic table habits absolutely charming. He picked up his asparagus and bit off the tops, and he cracked his eggs into a cup and messed them about with salt, pepper, and mustard, making a veritable "philosophical ragout . . . like the kind of savage he was," as one of his few detractors churlishly put it. The attention he was unable to give to food he turned to wine. Franklin assembled an excellent cellar—for

health reasons, of course. He found no more efficacious tonic for aching joints and dull wits than three or four glasses of fine wine which on occasion moved him to write vinous thoughts to his friend Abbé Morellet. (It was almost as if Franklin were trying to create a French alter ego for his puritanical and pious American Poor Richard.) "'*In vino veritas*,' said the sage. . . . Before Noah, men, having only water to drink, could not find the truth. Accordingly . . . they became abominably wicked, and they were justly exterminated by the water they loved to drink. This good man, Noah, having seen that all his contemporaries had perished by this unpleasant drink, took a dislike to it; and God, to relieve his dryness, created the vine and revealed to him the art of making *le vin*. By the aid of this liquid he unveiled more and more truth; and . . . since this time all the best things, even the gods, have been called *divine*. . . . He made the wine to cheer us. When you see your neighbor at table pour wine into his glass do not hasten to pour water into it. Why would you drown truth? . . . know that the apostle Paul advised Timothy very seriously to put wine into his water for his health; but that not one of the apostles, nor any of the holy fathers, ever [watered] wine. P.S. In order to still more confirm you in your piety and recognition of divine providence, reflect on the position God has given the elbow . . . by its present location shown in fig. 5 [the figures above were obligingly drawn by Franklin's grandson to illustrate his letter], we see it designed so that we can drink at our ease, the glass comes just to the mouth. Let us then adore, glass in hand, that wise benevolence; let us adore and drink."

his grandchildren were being trained in the use of the new utensil. He wore his hat at table, and was punctilious in doffing it to ladies or raising it in various degrees to salute princes and nobles, with the result that his hat brim became covered with the grease of what he had just consumed.

Moreover, his tastes, though robust, were unpredictable. He had a great taste for delicate fruit, and in the course of relieving Fouquet of some of his treasures at Vaux, he transplanted to Versailles over a thousand orange trees— then exotic and costly rarities—setting them in long rows outdoors and in silver tubs in the salons, creating that particularly French form of conservatory, the *orangerie.* For his adored granddaughter-in-law, twelve-year-old Marie Adélaïde, he gave a ball in 1697 in the Hall of Mirrors, graced by numerous orange trees bearing hundreds of fruits which had been coated with sugar. He was also an ardent lover of fine peaches and pears, and so admired the manager of his exquisite orchards and gardens, Monsieur de La Quintinie, that he both befriended and ennobled him.

In the summers of his immensely long reign there were usually military campaigns to be fought (it was neither practical nor *comme il faut* to undertake them in winter), but even in the field a style not unlike that of Versailles was observed. The king and his general officers, often accompanied by their ladies, went into large and luxurious encampment: sieges rather than wars of movement were the order of the day, and often the whole court would turn out to watch Louis assault a fortified town. The pro-

tocol could be magnificent. Thus when Louis was investing Lille in 1667, its defender, the Comte de Brouais, discovering that the king was without ice for his provisions, sent him a supply every morning. When the king sent an emissary to ask for more, Brouais answered courteously that he would like to oblige but that he must conserve his resources, since the siege was likely to be a long one.

If there was not an actual battle in progress, Louis loved nothing better than to simulate one; he staged a mock assault at Compiègne one summer with some sixty thousand troops for the delectation of all who might like to watch. "There was never a spectacle so brilliant, so astonishing," wrote Saint-Simon, though he added that he was somewhat frightened by its magnitude. "There were innumerable tables, always freshly laid and ready at all times for the entertainment of any officers, courtiers, or spectators who might drop in— the merest sightseer was made welcome and served with courteous promptitude. . . . There was every sort of drink, hot and cold, that you can think of—French wines, foreign wines, and the rarest liqueurs flowed in abundance. There was every sort of game and venison, and the most unusual seafood was brought from Normandy, Holland, England, Brittany, and the Mediterranean fresh several times a day by means of a prodigious number of couriers." And when not taking to the field in the pleasant months of the year, Louis relished making regal descents with his entourage upon the estates of his greatest courtiers, as he had upon the unfortunate Nicolas Fouquet.

His Bourbon relative Le Grand Condé had acquired the services of Vatel, late of Fouquet's household, to make his own table at Chantilly one of the finest in France. Vatel was not a working cook, but something much higher—an *officier de bouche*, a gentleman-master of cooks, service, and cuisine. To be sure, he knew every detail of the culinary arts and could write in courtly fashion about them. In an essay on carving he declared, "A carver should be well bred, inasmuch as he should maintain a first rank among the servants of his master. Pleasing, civil, amiable, and well disposed, he should present himself at table with his sword at his side, his mantle on his shoulder .... He should make his obeisance when approaching the table, proceed to carve the viands, and divide them understandingly according to the number of guests .... A carver should be very scrupulous in his deportment, his carriage should be grave and dignified, his appearance cheerful, his eye serene. . . ."

But Vatel's own serenity broke down when the king arrived at Chantilly in April, 1671, with a company evidently larger than had been expected. Various meats and fish that had been ordered did not arrive in time, and there was a shortage of food. Madame de Sévigné, one of France's great letter writers, hurried to write her daughter, Comtesse de Grignan, "I have just learned . . . of what passed at Chantilly with regard to poor Vatel. I wrote you last Friday, that he had stabbed himself; these are the particulars of the affair. The King arrived there on Thursday night; the walk, and the collation, which was served in a place set apart for the purpose, and

strewed with jonquils, were just as they should be. Supper was served, but there was no roast meat at one or two of the tables. . . . This affected [Vatel's] spirits, and he was heard to say several times, 'I have lost my fame! I cannot bear this

Expert directions on carving, 1647

disgrace!' " When, during the night, the fish ordered for the next day's lunch did not appear in adequate quantity either, it was too much: Vatel, like an old Roman, ran himself upon his sword.

The Olympian rounds continued. In 1715, when Louis at last reached his end, having outlived both his heir the dauphin, and the dauphin's own son and heir, the nobles and gentry breathed more freely. France felt young again. A new boy king, the patriarch's great-grandson Louis XV, was on the throne. A regent in the person of the boy's distant cousin, the second Philippe, Duc d'Orléans, set him an example of sybaritic gaiety, intimate pleasures, and gilded taste. Louis XV proved an apt and enthusiastic pupil.

In the years after 1715, elegance, not just grandeur, was the ideal. Exquisite porcelain, first imported at great cost from China, then from its adapters at Dresden, and finally in the reign of Louis XIV produced by France's own craftsmen at Sèvres, appeared in dining rooms and salons. The drinking of coffee, tea, and chocolate (the latter already promoted by the late Louis XIV's Spanish queen) became a late-afternoon social cult. The regent introduced the custom of the *petit souper*—an intimate supper at which a few noblemen and their ladies (usually their mistresses) could enjoy themselves without oppressive protocol. On such occasions the regent invited his male guests to join him and the cooks at preparing dinner.

Louis XV, when he came to his majority, enjoyed cooking, too. At the end of a hunting day, the new king particularly liked to gather around him a circle of lively spirits. Would-be guests put their names on a list from which the king might choose. One evening he invited the Prince de Beaufremont, the Ducs de Gontaut and de la Vallière, and the Marquis de Polignac to try their hand as *cuisiniers*, while he prepared the *poulets au basilic*. On another evening, according to the Prince de Cröy, "We were eighteen, squashed round the table, beginning at my right: Monsieur de Livry, Madame la Marquise de Pompadour, the King, the Comtesse d'Estrades, the Duc d'Ayen, the tall Madame de Brancas, the Comte de Noailles (governor of Versailles), Monsieur de la Suze, the Comte de Coigny, the Comtesse d'Egmont (the Duc de Richelieu's daughter), Monsieur de Croix, the Marquis de Renel, the Duc de FitzJames, the Duc de Broglie, the Prince de Turenne, Monsieur de Crillon. . . . The Maréchal de Saxe was there, but he never has supper so he walked about tasting bits of food, for he is very greedy. . . . We

were two hours at supper, all very free and easy but without any excess. Then the King went into the little salon, where he made the coffee and poured it out, there were no servants and we helped ourselves."

Sometimes Louis XV's *petits soupers* were a good deal more intimate. A scheme was devised for a disappearing table which dropped through an opening in the floor to be re-set below for the next course. Thus, one record has it, "Guests are not annoyed by the importunate glances of servants. They are freed of all embarrassment and need not blush on being caught unawares." On occasion, just two or three couples took part, the supper being planned as the

Brass and iron nutcracker, sixteenth century

prelude to other pleasures. The rakish Duc de Richelieu, a grandnephew of the illustrious cardinal, appears to have pursued this idea to the point of inviting a few couples to dine in the nude. His servants were models of discretion.

Almost everyone in France, it seems, was becoming concerned with fine cuisine, whether it led to *amour* or not. The Regency and the period of Louis XV were without doubt times of the most engaging invention in French dining. The era glorified the chef, for as the epicure Brillat-Savarin was to remark several decades later, "the discovery of a new dish confers more happiness on humanity than the discovery of a new star." Fresh discoveries were being made continually. Marin, the famed *maître d'hôtel* of the Prince de Soubise, wrote in his classic treatise *Les Dons de Comus* of 1739 that the "old cookery" had suffered from "an excess of spices. . . . [and] was very complicated and full of details; modern cookery is a sort of chemistry." Marin's own repertoire included a fluffy omelette made with cocks' combs and carps' roe which he invented for Louis XV.

Louis Sébastien Mercier, introducing his *Tableau de Paris* of 1781–82, echoed Marin's opinion: "The dishes of the present day are very light, and they have

Happy gourmand in an hour or two of ecstasy

a particular delicacy and perfume. The secret has been discovered of enabling us to eat more and to eat better, as also to digest more rapidly. . . . The new cookery is conducive to health, to good temper, and to long life. . . . Who could enumerate all the dishes of the new cuisine? It is an absolutely new idiom. I have tasted viands prepared in so many

ways and fashioned with such art that I could not imagine what they were."

One of the most spectacular demonstrations of the new cuisine was a *souper* given by the Duc de Richelieu (fully dressed) to a group of Hanoverian princes and princesses captured during a campaign of the Seven Years' War. Though his field supplies were reduced to a carcass of beef and some root vegetables, the enterprising duke, never at a loss, dictated the following elaborate directions: the table was to be decorated with his large *surtout*, a centerpiece adorned with the figures of great heroes of France. Then, a first course of beef consommé was to be served, followed by hors d'oeuvres of beef in various forms; then a rump of beef garnished with root vegetables; then such delicacies as oxtail with a purée of chestnuts, civet of beef tongue, *paupiettes* of beef *à l'estouffade* with pickled nasturtium buds, fillets of beef braised with celery, beef *rissoles* with hazelnut purée, beef marrow on toast, beef *à la mode* with pistachio nuts, fritters of beef brain steeped in Seville orange juice, and so on.

The Prince de Soubise took to the battlefield with a wagon train of complete kitchen equipment and table service. His campaigns were more distinguished for their dinners than for their victories: the Prussians overran his corps at Rossbach, but did not succeed in capturing his *batterie de cuisine*, his plate, or his chef, the renowned Marin.

Just how much the cuisine may actually have promoted health and longevity is an open question. It did promote refinements in cooking equipment: in wealthier households the days of cooking chiefly by spit or stewpot over the fire were past. A stove along with an array of copper or iron saucepans of various sizes and shapes accommodated the multitude of processes. New foods were constantly augmenting the diet

Wine taster made in Orléans, 1759

and challenging the chef. Lentils, long thought fit only as animal fodder, were made fashionable by Louis XV's queen, and the potato became the rage at court when an army pharmacist, Monsieur Parmentier, presented a bouquet of purple potato flowers to Louis XVI at a birthday reception. The king liked the blossoms so much that he placed one in his buttonhole and gave another to his queen Marie Antoinette; many courtiers followed suit, and the future of the *pomme de terre* was thenceforth assured.

The new and exciting dishes created were often named after members of the nobility, something a *maître queux* was only too happy to do in anticipation of reward. Thus there came into the French repertoire such creations as filet of sole *Pompadour* and chartreuse of partridge *à la Du Barry*, honoring Louis XV's chief mistresses. The most spirited ladies at court were not above devising dishes to seduce the king. Madame Du Barry arranged a *souper* that included such novelties as *coulis de faisan* (stewed pheasant), *salmis de bécassines* (ragout of young woodcock), *écrevisse* (crayfish) *au*

vin de Sauternes, and *fraises au marasquin* (strawberries in cherry liqueur); and the Marquise de Pompadour is credited with such diversions as *filets de volaille à la Bellevue* and *palais de boeuf* (palate of beef) *à la Pompadour*.

A few critics felt that preoccupation with good eating was going too far. In 1749 Voltaire warned his countrymen that their gluttony "would eventually numb the faculties of the mind." Though moderate at board, Voltaire was guilty of another form of self-indulgence: he was a slave to coffee, consuming as many as fifty cups a day. Madame du Châtelet, one of his closest friends before his exile, was noted for her intellectual dinners at which the conversation was brilliant but the food indifferent. (Like Voltaire, she took only one light meal a day.) Voltaire's secretary sniffed in disdain of her hospitality, "What wine! Burgundy made in Paris, and champagne of the same brand!"

But the *bonne table* rapidly became within reach of the middle classes, which were more interested in emulating the aristocracy than in following Voltaire. A typical bourgeois meal of about 1740 was recorded by Brillat-Savarin: first, beef bouillon; then an appetizer and an entree of veal cooked in its juices; then a turkey with vegetables and a salad; finally cheese, fruit, and preserves. In 1746 the gifted chef Menon produced for middle-class wives and their domestics his *Cuisinière Bourgeoise*, a book offering popular menus for those wishing only two or three dishes in a meal.

Brillat-Savarin, looking back, was able to sum up in his review of the latter part of the eighteenth century: "The ranks of every profession concerned with the preparation of food, including cooks, caterers, confectioners, pastry-cooks, provision-merchants, and the like, have multiplied in ever-increasing proportions. . . . Physics and chemistry have been called in to aid the alimentary art; the most eminent scientists have thought it not beneath them to apply their wisdom to the first of all our needs, and improvement has followed improvement, from the laborer's simple broth to transparent extracts that are never served but in vessels of crystal or of gold. . . . The wines of all countries have been cultivated or imported and make their appearance in regular order: Madeira to open up the way, French wines to accompany the main courses, and African and Spanish wines to crown the work. French cookery has annexed many dishes of foreign extraction, such as curry and the roast beef of England; relishes such as caviar and soy. . . . Coffee has come into general use, as a food in the morning, and after dinner as a tonic and exhilarating drink." The working man, for his part, especially enjoyed starting the morning with a bowl of *café au lait*, sold at street corners by women vendors from huge tureens.

And there were visitors to France who did not have to wait for Brillat-Savarin to proclaim the genius of new French cookery. Benjamin Franklin, American emissary to Paris, wrote home: "I have never dined so handsomely as at Madame de Courtances' table." An English traveler in 1790 was one of the first to deplore the difference between what was being served to his countrymen under the name of food and what the French were enjoying. "The variety given by

their cooks to the same thing is astonishing," he reported. "They dress a hundred dishes in a hundred different ways, and most of them excellent; and all sorts of vegetables have a savouriness and flavour, from rich sauces, that are absolutely wanted to our greens boiled in water. . . . The English dinner of a joint of meat and a pudding, as it is called, or *pot luck*, with a neighbor, is bad luck in England; the same fortune in France gives, by means of cookery only, at least four dishes to one among us and spreads a small table incomparably better."

The period just preceding the French Revolution also saw the emergence of a new institution—the restaurant. It was to rise to great influence particularly after the estates of the *ancien régime* were seized or broken up, and from then on was to remain the center of French culinary genius. The renowned *maître queux*, so long a princely retainer, went into business for himself.

A superior hostelry known as the Tour d'Argent had been founded in 1582 on the Quai de la Tournelle outside the walls of Paris. Many historians have bestowed on it the honor of being the first restaurant. King Henry IV, who frequented the place as did many other monarchs, awarded it a coat of arms, thus distinguishing it from the other taverns or cabarets of the time. The Tour d'Argent (whose prestige, along with its regal prices, continues to this day) did not in its early years depart materially from the traditional tavern scheme of offering a "dish of the day" from the host's table *(table d'hôte)*.

The well-to-do bourgeois of Paris, in search of a hearty fish stew, might so-

Best Behind Bars

To the hungry Parisians storming its walls on July 14, 1789, the Bastille symbolized the tyranny and corruption of the *ancien régime*. Ever since Louis XIV converted the medieval fortress into a state prison, rumors of dank dungeons, prisoners in rotting rags, and food "worse than would be given to a pig or a dog" were widely circulated. Though it was true that the inmates were held without trials, for indeterminate lengths of time, they were, nevertheless, "guests" of the king, and in this unique prison were treated as such. Jailers made sure that their wards had the amenities to which they had been accustomed, and politely catered to their whims, however eccentric. Nobles resided in spacious apartments equipped with fireplaces, into which they moved suites of furniture and a few retainers (before entering the Bastille a servant had to agree to remain until his master was freed). If a prisoner lacked the means, the king would foot the bill for his expenses, the amount varying according to his rank; three livres provided an adequate dinner for a common man; thirty-six for a *maréchal*. A morale-boosting meal might include green pea soup, a joint of fowl, sliced roast beef, meat pie garnished with sweet-breads, cocks' combs, asparagus, mushrooms and truffles, sheep's tongue *en ragoût*, biscuits, fruits, a bottle of Burgundy, and Mocha coffee. Occasionally complaints were voiced by such finicky eaters as the confidence man Danry, alias Vicomte Henri Masers de Latude. The prison commander noted that on fast days "He sends for us at eight . . . in the evening to tell us to send his turnkey to the market to buy fish . . . saying that he cannot eat eggs, artichokes or spinach. Danry is just as exacting on meat days. He swore like a trooper and said . . . 'when I'm given fowl, it should at least be well larded.'" Danry also collected silk shirts, and at one point possessed 162, from which the ingrate wove a ladder and escaped; he was soon apprehended. A prisoner was free to pass his time attending parties, singing in ensembles, bowling, or breeding cats and dogs. Pens and paper were provided, but Danry insisted on writing in blood on linen or on slices of bread. Only seven prisoners remained in 1789. One, in the three months before his liberation, consumed 12 bottles of brandy, 121 bottles of beer, and 167 bottles of wine. Though meat pies *garni*, however fine, do not equal freedom, the mobs were rescuing victims of a despotism far more benevolent than that reigning outside.

journ to such traditional inns as the popular Relais du Gros Caillou on the banks of the Seine near the Invalides. Gentlemen and ladies, often disguised or masked, went slumming at such rough-and-ready resorts as the Taverne Hospitalière de la Coquille, or at Le Grand Salon on the Rue Lamartine. Cafés, which originally had provided only a

Commoners toasting the Third Estate, c. 1789

cup of coffee, had proliferated to some six hundred by 1750, often offering light meals (at the celebrated Café Procope, one might find Diderot and his fellow *philosophes*); but those were not restaurants as we understand the term. That connotation may have originated with a Parisian named Boulanger who was not a restaurateur at all, but the owner of a streetside stall whose fare was soups sold under the label of *restaurants,* meaning restoratives, and whose signboard is said to have proclaimed in near-liturgical Latin, *"Venite omnes qui stomacho laboratis, et ego restaurato vos"* ("Come all ye that labor with your stomach, and I will restore you").

Semantics aside, the true restaurant probably appeared in 1782 when the masterful chef Beauvilliers, former steward of "Monsieur," the Comte de Provence (the later Louis XVIII), made the bold experiment of setting up for the elite a formal dining-out place where he offered a long list of dishes, individually prepared *(à la carte),* and in surroundings just short of palatial. This was his Grande Taverne de Londres on the Rue de Richelieu, and it was a model for generations to come.

Beauvilliers, a master of protocol, presided in courtly dress, including sword and frilled shirt. Accomplished in five languages and aware of every political nuance of the day, he knew precisely where to seat ambassadors and ministers, royalists and republicans. As Brillat-Savarin was to write admiringly, "Beauvilliers was for more than fifteen years the finest restaurateur in Paris. He was the first to combine the four essentials of an elegant room, smart waiters, a choice cellar, and superior cooking." The Londres was not to be outdone for generations. It survived all upheavals and in 1835 was catering to European aristocracy with a menu that included fifty different *entremets* and at least thirty vintage wines. Although French chefs were not usually attracted to English cooking, Beauvilliers made a point of presenting in his treatise *L'Art du Cuisinier,* published in 1814 not long before Waterloo, some English recipes, including what he called *Wouelche rabette* (Welsh rarebit), *bifteck, plumbuting* (plum pudding), *machpotetesse* (mashed potatoes), and *ket-chop,* a sauce first popularized across the Channel.

Among the rival establishments that opened soon after Beauvilliers, were such fashionable meeting places as the

Café Conti and the sumptuous restaurant of Monsieur Véry—the latter featuring some 12 soups, 24 hors d'oeuvres, 24 entrees of fish, 15 of beef, 30 of game, and so on. The Café Conti eventually evolved into the famed Restaurant Grand Véfour; still later it incorporated with Monsieur Véry's restaurant, and continues to this day to occupy some of the old premises under the long arcade of the Palais Royal.

Louis XVI, the heavy, dull man who ascended the throne upon the death of his grandfather in 1774, played little part in this evolution of French taste. He dutifully followed court ritual—the public dinner *au grand couvert,* particularly on Sundays, though his queen Marie Antoinette hated to be stared at when eating, and usually absented herself. The Revolutionary Directoire, in power until Bonaparte seized sole control, far from reducing lavishness at table often gave dinners as splendid as those of the Louis'. Napoleon, for all his longing to acquire some polish, was the very opposite of a gourmet. He ate "at military speed," often wolfing a whole meal in just fifteen minutes, and moreover at wholly unpredictable hours. As his chronicler Las Cases recorded, "Never did one manage to make him eat his dinner while it was hot, for once he had settled himself to work no one knew when he would leave it. Therefore, when dinner time arrived, chickens were placed on the spit for him at half hourly intervals, and I have personally seen dozens of them so roasted before coming to the one finally presented to him." Distracted one day, gluttonous the next, fearful of putting on weight but likely to call for a huge meal at two or three o'clock in the morning, his habits resulted in chronic indigestion and early obesity.

The great tables of the empire were those of his foreign minister Talleyrand and his archchancellor Cambacérès. Not that Napoleon objected: on the contrary, he often advised foreign dignitaries to go to one or the other of their houses for a great repast. The two households naturally fell into competition. Cambacérès gave twice-weekly dinners for fifty or more distinguished persons, serving sixteen or eighteen dishes. State messengers were placed in his service to bring fresh game from his estate at Livet, and Alexandre Dumas père recalled a particularly magnificent dinner at which the archchancellor directed his footmen to pretend to stumble and drop the *pièce de résistance,* a rare Caspian sturgeon weighing some 170 pounds. Then, while the guests were still gasping at their loss,

Fitted campaign kit for Napoleon's chef

the prodigal host called out, "serve the other sturgeon," and a second, still larger, fish was brought in.

Yet Talleyrand appears to have had the better of it, since he had recruited the great Antonin Carême (1784–1833), a man of genius. Born of humble parents and first trained as a *pâtissier,* he went on in the next ten years to study the art of roasting and of making sauces and cold dishes under the leading chefs of France. Carême was as intrigued with the visual delights of pastry as with its taste. At one point he went so far as to say, "The fine arts are five in number, to wit: painting, sculpture, poetry, music, architecture—whose main branch is confectionery." Talleyrand liked to spend an hour each morning discussing with Carême what might be created for the evening's dinner. The minister's own principles were elegant and simple: two things were essential in life—"to give good dinners and keep well with women." In describing life under his culinary mentor, Carême wrote, "Only the most sanitary and the finest products were employed. Everything was ability, order, splendor. Talent was happy there, and highly placed. The chef governed the stomach. . . . Forty-eight course dinners were given in the halls on the Rue de Varenne. I have designed them and I have seen them served. What great tableaux [were] created! Who has not seen them has seen nothing."

Carême, whose genius at survival was equaled only by that of Talleyrand, was to serve Czar Alexander, Lord Castlereagh, Baron Rothschild, England's prince regent (the future George IV), and Louis XVIII. With a staff of forty cooks, he provided a great birthday feast for Czar Alexander following a review of Russian troops after Napoleon's defeat. He shared in presenting an even greater dinner for twelve hundred guests in the halls of the Louvre in 1815, upon Louis XVIII's Restoration. For this huge undertaking, a fifty-foot-long range

was installed in the principal hall of the palace; Carême took charge of the *entrées froid* and the *entremets du sucre*. He also wrote essays on every aspect of cuisine, emphasizing "lightness," "grace," "order," and "perspicuity" in the preparation of food. His was the crowning effort in the revival of gastronomy after the convulsions of the Revolution.

The Restoration also saw the emergence of such literary epicures as Grimod de La Reynière, who was fired by the impulse to systematize and refine French cuisine. He launched his *Almanach des Gourmands*, a guide to the restaurants and food purveyors of Paris, and organized a *Jury Dégustateur*. He tossed out such aphorisms as "A well-made sauce will make even an elephant or a grandfather palatable." In Brillat-Savarin, originally a country doctor, later a rotund provincial magistrate, the era found its philosopher of the table. His *Physiologie du Goût*, published in 1825 when he was seventy, became the classic work of the arts and sciences of gastronomy—though Carême himself sniffed at Brillat-Savarin because of his habit of consuming two dozen oysters at breakfast. Later still, in 1870, Alexandre Dumas père was to provide in his *Grand Dictionnaire de Cuisine* a compendium of lore concerning *grande cuisine*. The matter of fine eating was to be taken most seriously. After a banquet held in the celebrated restaurant Le Rocher de Cancale in 1834, one of the company recalled, "I remember the chairman, I can see him now, hear him saying to [his guests] in his most solemn voice, 'I advise discretion, gentlemen. No distractions. Remember. I know the menu. We shall be at table for three hours.'"

RECIPE
FOR
REVOLUTION

A baker, his helpers, and an old woman selling brandy, portrayed by Jean Michelin, 1656

LE DINE DV ROY A L'HOTEL DE VILLE DE PARIS

CALENDRIER POUR L'ANNEE BISSEXTILE MDCLXXXVIII.

Chez Louis

What the French court gained in grandeur over the centuries, it lost in culinary amenities. Clever as the royal chefs were, they could not overcome the limitations of palace and protocol that made serving a hot meal impossible. The kitchens were often at great distances from the halls of state, and every dish was carried in solemn procession down long, drafty corridors, past ranks of admiring courtiers, tasters, and other functionaries, before it reached the royal consumer. Louis XIV did not balk at the system, but he added some light touches. He enjoyed pelting his guests with rolls; they were encouraged to return the fire. One lady in waiting, smarting from a well-aimed *pain*, volleyed with a salad. Under Louis XV state dinners became more elaborate than ever. Musical fanfares and complicated new rituals accompanied each dish. But, when his schedule allowed, the king enjoyed informal suppers, so *intime* that no servant entered the dining salon. Louis XVI, capitalizing on one of his few natural abilities, entertained his subjects by eating a spectacular meal in public every Sunday.

Opposite, Louis XIV and guests pause for a portrait during a dinner at the Hôtel de Ville. The menu at top was once served to Louis XV and Madame de Pompadour. Above, Louis XIII dines in splendor; below, Louis XVI eats crow in prison.

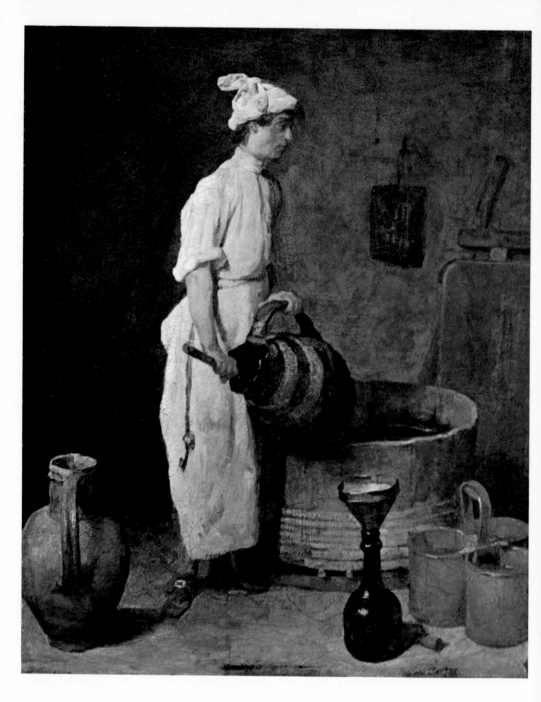

Life Belowstairs

The subjects of Chardin's paintings, above, perform their tasks in the depths of a *grande maison*. The poor scullery maid faces an endless succession of dirty pans, but the youth, while scrubbing out his wine pitchers, can at least dream of becoming head cook. Then he will exchange his rakish cap for a toque and

his modesty for the disposition of a martinet
—only the king himself could outdo the *chef
de cuisine* when it came to tyrannizing his
subjects. The great eighteenth-century cook
was, after all, an artiste of temperament so
fragile and taste so delicate that he often
had to be granted several days' rest and special diet to soothe his sensitive soul and ex-
hausted palate. If the cellar boy is a more
genial sort, he can aspire to become *maître
d'hôtel*, director of the dining staff, whose
brazen members, an American visitor complained, were "often observed in France inter-
mingling in the conversation of the table."

Fun for All

The favorite haunt of many a member of the Third Estate was his neighborhood tavern, where he could buy a carafe of wine and watch the entertainment, sometimes planned, more often impromptu. Taverns on the outskirts of Paris had the added advantages of a verdant setting—and untaxed liquors. The uproar of the good times in the country cabarets wafted all the way back to the salons of the great, who began to appear in droves to "join in the amusements of the people" by dancing with fishwives, drinking the good, cheap wine, and listening to slang "in all its native beauty."

Ramponneau, opposite, the proprietor of a tavern which could accommodate six hundred people, is portrayed with the symbols of his calling. Below is the sign of another cabaret. At right, top, customers purchase wine to take home, while others enjoy theirs on the premises. Below, patrons who tested their host's hospitality too far are shown the way out.

OVERLEAF: *Slumming was not the only outdoor recreation of the rich. Romanticized notions of the innocent pleasures of peasants had made gamboling about attired as swain or shepherdess a mandatory form of fun. Ollivier's painting of a picnic during the reign of Louis XVI illustrates another aspect of the noble back-to-nature movement. Before the guests gathered under the tent to eat, they undoubtedly had pushed one another on swings, played hide-and-seek, and trysted in the bushes. The fetes seemed less fun to the servants, who in planning and executing them had to make sure that none of the nature lovers lacked for any of the comforts of home.*

Habit de Cuisinier

Habit de Pescheur

Les Vendeurs

Habit de Poiſſonniere

Habit de Rôtisseur

Habit de Paticier

Habit de Fruitiere

During the eighteenth century, Parisians bought most of their food from wandering vendors whose raucous cries made a sizable contribution to the cacophony that filled the streets. The engravings by Nicolas de Larmessin reproduced here show vendors clothed in imaginative costumes appropriate to their specialties.

Habit de Vinaigrie

Habit de Cabaretier

The
Delicate
Art
of
Porcelain

A pierced spoon for powdered sugar, from Mennecy, specialists in small porcelain pieces

A mustard jar from Rouen, c. 1645   *A small jam pot from Sceaux, c. 1770*

The soup tureen, top opposite, made for Madame Du Barry, and the *solitaire* coffee service, above, are both products of Sèvres, after 1753 the *manufacture royale*. Support of the porcelain industry had in fact begun with Louis XIV, who ordered his subjects to melt down their silver and gold plate to refill the impoverished treasury; but Louis XV was the first to give official sanction to a French factory. To attract the finest artisans, he restricted the use of decorative gold to the royal works and regulated firms under other patronage. Louis even worried about balancing Sèvres' books—to stimulate trade he personally auctioned off the annual inventory of porcelain to courtiers eager to show their good taste at any cost.

Café Society

The ten years of slaughter that Marie Antoinette was supposed to have sparked with her naïve suggestion, "Let them eat cake," left the poor who made the Revolution worse off than before. There were bread riots in the provinces, and in Paris it was difficult to find vendors who would sell food in exchange for the nearly worthless new currency with which working men were paid. The *nouveaux riches*—the speculators, the profiteers, the grafters, and the merchants who catered to them—had replaced the aristocrats as the group that was eating well. The milieu for dining had changed, too; the Revolution indirectly gave France its first fine restaurants. With most of the gourmet aristocrats destitute, departed, or dead, chefs of the *ancien régime* were forced to perform their magic in public establishments.

The ladies opposite, caricatured in 1827, were members of the new fashionable set that gathered every day in Parisian cafés to gossip over ices and Mocha. Two water colors at left by Carle Vernet show that citizens of the working class, eating at traveling snack bars, did not fare so well. The soldier at top, who drinks a cup of cocoa, probably has tasteless rations to look forward to; the sausage speared for the demobilized hussar may constitute his only nourishment for the day.

OVERLEAF: Frascati's near the Opéra was one of the most popular of dozens of cafés that sprang up in post-Revolutionary Paris. People gathered there to eat ice cream, sip liqueurs, gamble, and flirt. In the background is the ballroom, which could accommodate some two thousand dancers.

The Amphitryons

Carême, the pâtissier known as the "cook of kings and king of cooks."
CAREME, L'Art de la Cuisine Française, 1854

Parmentier, who prophesied that potatoes would make starvation "impossible"
PHOTO BULLOZ

Dumas père, famed for his salads and his culinary dictionary of 1870
STUDIOS JOSSE-LALANCE

Brillat-Savarin, whose treatise separated gourmets from gluttons
PHOTO BULLOZ

Any gourmet wishing to keep his head and wits during the Revolution did well to follow the credo of Grimod de La Reynière: "Life is so brief that we should not glance either too far backwards or forwards. . . . therefore study how to fix our happiness in our glass and on our plate." In the aftermath, these amphitryons gave elegant dinners and formed such epicurean societies as the *Jury Dégustateur*. Its role as a supreme court of cookery was "to pass judgment on the quality of foodstuffs and their skill-

Grimod de La Reynière, *author of etiquette guides for parvenu hosts*
STUDIOS JOSSE-LALANCE

The Jury Dégustateur, *active from 1804 to 1812, assembled here to prove a pudding*
STUDIOS JOSSE-LALANCE

Cambacérès, *president of the* Jury, *although susceptible to meat balls*
BIBLIOTHEQUE NATIONALE, PARIS; SERVICE PHOTOGRAPHIQUE

Talleyrand, *a diplomat who chose dinner tables over conference tables*
BIBLIOTHEQUE NATIONALE, PARIS; SERVICE PHOTOGRAPHIQUE

ful preparation." Meeting weekly for five-hour séances at private homes or select restaurants, the jurors sampled food and drink donated by contributors who remained anonymous until every dish was voted on by secret ballot and an impartial verdict reached. The *Jury* awarded its certificate of *légitimation* charily. It could immortalize a talented *pâtissier*; conversely, it dealt out punishments fitting the crime, and a restaurateur living on his reputation might find the "truth" published all over Paris.

Plain and Fancy

Napoleon cared little for the niceties of *haute cuisine*. Not even a dinner for the czar and the King of Prussia, below, could change his habits noticeably. For the infrequent occasions when he entertained in the grand manner, the cupboards held a store of treasures worthy of an emperor: the Sèvres plate at right is one of a set depicting city views; the nef above, in which cutlery, napkins, goblets, and a poison tester were locked, was the gift of the city of Paris for Napoleon's coronation supper.

MALMAISON

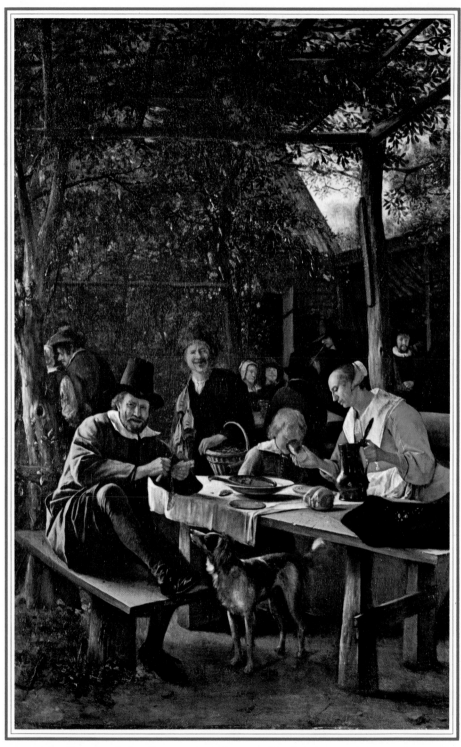

A family outing, by Jan Steen, seventeenth-century Dutch painter and tavern owner

THE
OTHER
EUROPE

From the reign of Louis XIV onward, French manners spread across Europe with astonishing speed. Following the king's revocation of the civil and religious rights of his Protestant subjects, Geneva became a center of French thought in exile, and of French cookery as well. Princelings in the gray flatlands of Schleswig and Pomerania vied for French tutors as well as *pâtissiers* to enhance their provincial courts. Young Czar Peter I of Russia, anxious to westernize and modernize his isolated domain, in 1697 set out from the Kremlin on an educational "grand tour" of the West that resulted in the building of a new, French-inspired capital and "window on Europe" at St. Petersburg. Frederick II of Prussia, a kingdom previously known chiefly for its production of turnips and stalwart grenadiers, responded to the French influence by entertaining in his new summer palace such men as Voltaire, conversing socially only in French, and making French cuisine *de rigueur* at the palace. The chefs of Empress Maria Theresa's table in

Vienna were either French or French trained. The university town of Leipzig became so taken up with French manners and cuisine, and with the Enlightenment radiating from the French capital, that a student who matriculated there in 1765, the poet Goethe, later bestowed on it the compliment *"ein klein Paris."*

Yet while the nobility fell under the French spell, there was another side of Europe that remained to a great extent untouched—the Europe become prosperous through heightened productivity, stability, and trade. The regional cuisines were not refined in the French sense: they were hearty and robust, varying from province to province in accordance with the produce most available, the commerce that was most profitable, and even the religious traditions of the people.

It was the world of the heavy Dutch stew called *hutsepot*, of the Belgian *hotchepot*, of German *Sauerbraten, Bierwurst*, and dumplings, of Scandinavian *smörgåsbord*

Danish bowl for Bishop's Cup

and herring pudding, of Austrian *Schnitzel*, of Hungarian *gulyás*, or goulash, of Polish and Russian *blini, pirozhki,* and cabbage soup. It was the world of coarse "black" bread, paprika, pickles, sour cream, and hot peppers; of such drinks as Dutch *genever*, or gin, German *Bier*,

Scandinavian *akvavit*, Bohemian *slivovitz*, and Russian *vodka* and *kvas*.

Solid bourgeois life perhaps flowered first in the urbanized Low Countries after the overthrow of Spanish rule. From the great Flemish and Dutch genre painters of the day, we get a general portrait of well-fed domesticity, of great attention to food and furnishings without ostentation, of a certain gravity coupled with a love of gatherings, processions, and joyous holiday feasts.

The center of the Dutch burgher's house of the seventeenth century was unquestionably the kitchen, often tiled with colored porcelain from Delft, and graced by a display of copper and pewter utensils gleaming fresh-scrubbed in their cupboards or above a marble sink. The middle-class Dutch obsession with cleanliness occasionally reached such lengths that only the boiling of water was permitted in the kitchen, with meals being prepared in the pantry and served in still another informal family room so as not to "dirty" the parlor and dining rooms. There was also usually a display of big, thick-stemmed wine goblets—for use on special occasions, since the everyday drink was beer, served in lidded mugs of pewter or porcelain.

Meals were formidable, as the resulting girth of many a stout *Stadtholder* or burgher painted by Rembrandt or Jan Steen indicates. Yet meals were perhaps more nourishing and varied than those of the time in other parts of Europe. Limited grazing area supported few beef cattle and little game, but the Low Countries were rich in vegetables, fruits, fish, and dairy cattle. Indeed, the use of butter in Dutch cooking gave dishes a lightness not common to cuisines dependent on vegetable oils, lard, and the like. At the main meal at midday, a prune and pea soup and a platter of herring or Rhine salmon might precede the *hutsepot* of stewed meat and vegetables, followed by an array of cheeses, puddings, fruits, and waffles. To tide the body over until supper, a midafternoon snack of bread and cheese, fruits and nuts, and beer or tea was also taken.

Prayers and readings from the Bible generally went before and after the domestic Dutch dinner. Yet the burgher and his wife, for all the composure and dignity they displayed to the portrait painter, enjoyed nothing better than a rousing good party. The Dutch of Rembrandt's time and after were addicted to banqueting—and the affairs were far from sedate. A French traveler recalled an engagement dinner in 1691, which he attended along with some highly respectable elderly couples and a number of local divines: eating and drinking continued for five hours, the guests "shouting out toasts, arm in arm, smashing glasses," and spilling Rhine wine on the table. To accommodate such celebrations, great inns and taverns arose. The Amsterdam police, observing in 1665 that as many as fifty different dishes were being served at such noisy festivities, clamped down on the number of courses and the size of the guest list in a token effort to quell disturbances.

There were also religious feasts, many carried over from Roman Catholic rite into the Protestant Church, and secularized. Martinmas, though Dutch Reformed ministers denounced it as a ceremony of Popery, continued to be observed on the eleventh of November. Saint Martin, the patron of wine growers, tavernkeepers, and reformed drunkards, was understandably a muchloved saint, and his day was celebrated with a traditional dinner of roast goose, perhaps in retribution for the cackling goose that once betrayed him. Twelfth Night and Shrove Tuesday were also retained. May Day, which derived from ancient pagan custom, was celebrated

Dutch butchers' escutcheon

with the erection of Maypoles, a procession of townspeople, and singing and dancing in the streets. But the climactic event of the year was the carnival known as the kermis, celebrating some special saintly patron or local tradition. After the Reformation, the kermis was secularized into an annual civic festival identified with liberty, political fraternity, and good cheer; it might continue for as long as three weeks, during which, as in the pre-Lenten Fasching or Mardi Gras in many Catholic areas, serious business was all but suspended.

Bakers, entertainers, wine and beer sellers, all had their stands at what was in effect a fair. Confectioners hawked special kermis cakes—griddle cakes with pink sugar icing and preserved fruit. As the historian Paul Zumthor writes in his account of the times, "The taverns were jammed. For many peasants the kermis in the neighbouring town was essentially an occasion to drink in unaccustomed surroundings. Long tables were placed out of doors, and people sat on benches, barrels or on the ground. The adults danced; the children yelled, chased each other and played the tambourine and penny whistle; fiddlers scraped away among the goods displayed in the stalls. Passers-by were sometimes seized by the scruff of the neck, and a glass of beer poured down their shirt, or their faces smeared with flour and wax. The kermis began to turn into an orgy. In some villages, a 'kermis ox' was solemnly paraded, wreathed with flowers, and then slaughtered in the market-place, roasted, and eaten by the population on payment of a contribution. . . . Everyone sang. Women's yells mingled with the creaking and groaning of the merry-go-rounds. The atmosphere [was] unbreathable. Ladies fainted."

So much for Dutch sobriety. Daily consumption of beer, among women as well as men, appears often to have begun quite early in the morning. In the following century, the young James Boswell, seeking out a quiet place to recuperate from his dissipated life in London, recorded in his journals the exuberance of the Dutch at table. He found them enjoying their potent geneva gin (a drink which is not to be ascribed to Geneva, but to *geneverbessenwater*, a distillation of grain flavored with juniper berries, whose discovery is attributed to a seventeenth-century professor of medicine in Leyden). Boswell indulged with

Distillery, c. 1580

Dutch students and on one occasion reproved himself, "Yesterday you recovered very well after your riot. . . . But remember how near you was to getting drunk and exposing yourself." A massive dinner at the house of his friend and tutor, Professor Trotz of Utrecht, was almost too much for him. He wrote:

Of learned Trotzius I have been the
    guest,
And with his heavy supper am
    oppressed.
Lazy and hot, most sensibly I feel
That I have eat roast rabbit and roast
    veal;
And though impatience goads my
    fretful brain,
Not one idea can I thence obtain.

The communities of neighboring Germany, meanwhile, were only in a few instances remotely describable as "a little Paris." The country, or rather the states, since German nationhood was not yet in sight, labored for generations under the memory of the ravages of the Thirty Years' War, in which in one principality alone some one thousand "witches and wizards" had been burned at the stake in the space of a year. Teutonic culture, after such horrors, was not

Oktoberfest

When Crown Prince Ludwig of Bavaria wed on October 12, 1810, forty thousand well-wishers gathered on the Theresienwiese, a Munich meadow, to stage a Bavarian bash worthy of the occasion. The party—if not the marriage—proved so successful that the day was promptly adopted as an annual affair.

Part of the original celebrations had been wagon races among teamsters from the local breweries. Later, competition took a more commercial turn, with tents set up to sell beer and the fried and roasted delicacies of fish and chicken called *Schmankerlen*—and the day stretched into the Oktoberfest disrupting life for two weeks in the early autumn. More than 125 years later, the American Monk Webber, a character in Thomas Wolfe's *The Web and the Rock,* was alternately delighted and appalled by the fun. Munich, he observed, was a kind of German heaven (the scene from a Bavarian stein, right, of a burgher bound for paradise astride a beer barrel bears this out). "It was an enchanted land of Cockaigne, where one ate and drank forever and where one was never filled. It was Scharaffenland—it made him think of Peter Breughel's picture of that name, which showed the little roast pigs trotting conveniently to serve your pleasure, with knives and forks stuck juicily in their tender, crackling hides, with pieces cut out of their hind quarters . . . and bottles dropping from the sky, and trees and bushes drooping down with growths of pastry and with fruits of food. . . ." In one *brauhaus* Webber saw "hundreds of tables with people sitting together devouring tons of flesh—ox flesh, great platters of sliced cold sausages, huge slabs of veal and pork—together with the great stone mugs that foamed with over a liter of the cold and strong October beer. There was a heavy and incessant rumble of voices full of food, an enormous and excessive clatter of heavy pottery and knives, that rose and fell in brittle waves." It seemed to Webber in his intoxicated condition that "In all the world there was nothing but Food—glorious Food. And Beer—October Beer. The world was one enormous Belly—there was no higher heaven than the Paradise of Cram and Gorge. . . . The doors of the great hall kept opening and shutting constantly as the incessant stream of beer drinkers pressed patiently in. From within Monk heard the shattering blare of a huge brass band and the roar of five thousand beer-drunk voices, rocking together in the rhythms of 'Trink, Trink, Brüderlein, Trink!'"

of a high level of refinement. Like the Dutch, the Germans leaned toward robust conviviality, and they developed a whole hierarchy of eating and drinking places. On the lowest level stood the ordinary *Wirtshaus*—the common man's rough tavern, virtually unchanged from the Middle Ages (and at whose tables, in some remote country districts, local people were to be seen even well into the twentieth century eating from a common stewpot, without plates of their own). Next was the *Gasthof*, a country inn which could be good, bad, or indifferent: in the eighteenth century, when German roads and travel amenities were far behind those west of the Rhine, a cross-country voyager of any class frequently had to put up with crude lodging and worse food. Boswell wrote during his "grand tour" in 1764:

> *Here am I, sitting in a German inn,*
> *Where I may penance do for many a*
>   *sin,*
> *For I am pester'd with a thousand*
>   *flies,*
> *Who flap and buzz about my nose and*
>   *eyes.*
> *A lumpish landlord has the easy chair;*
> *Hardly he speaks, but wildly does he*
>   *stare.*
> *In haste to get away, I did not dine,*
> *And now I've had cold beef and*
>   *cursed wine.*
> *And in five minutes, or a little more,*
> *I shall be stretch'd on musty straw to*
>   *snore.*

More rewarding and pleasant were the taverns—the *Keller*, the *Brauhaus*, and the outdoor terrace, which was often attached to or owned by a local brewery.

Along with the beer, hearty roasts and sausages were served, bands played, and huge salt-studded pretzels were provided at every table to promote thirst. The *Weinstube* was a similar establishment, specializing in wines. For the middle class the *Kaffee-Konditorei*, or combined café and confectionery, came into vogue, serving not only coffee but

German Easter egg

tea and hot chocolate as well, along with an array of heavy pastries. For the municipal dignitaries in the more prosperous German towns, there was the *Rathskeller*, which was located in the cellar of the town hall. There in the spacious vaults, the civic leaders assembled around the *Stammtisch*, or reserved main table, for their saddle of venison and red cabbage, their beakers of Rhenish wine, their puddings and cheeses, and probably a round or two of *Schnaps*—German spirits. Lastly, townsmen had their *Delikatessen*, a place selling delicacies, where they could buy prepared, sometimes imported, foods to take home.

The Germans were generally looked down upon by their English and French contemporaries for their supposedly boorish and unrestrained ways. A traditional *Schützenfeste*, or hunters' banquet, was prone to degenerate into a wild spree, ending with a memorable *Katzenjammer*, or hang-over, all around. One hostile report of the early seventeenth century had it that Germans, when traveling, often consumed only aquavit and gingerbread for breakfast. The ecclesiastical courts of Würzburg, Bamberg, and Fulda, cities in the German wine country, had a reputation for alcoholic overindulgence; and the lofty Lord Chesterfield, when making his own tour of Germany, called the diet "execrable." Boswell was somewhat more tolerant and fortunate, though he saw some things that astonished him. He went to a ball in Berlin at the house of Counsel of State Behmer, where he "saw the vivacity of German ladies and counts and captains and Herren. We had at ten o'clock a collation in the garden; three or four tables with cold meats and pastry and sweetmeats and fruits and wine of different sorts. Behmer was a big, gallant Allemand; his wife, hearty even to excess. . . . She had no cap, and her hair dangled about her head. While she ran from table to table, with bottles in her hand and health most florid in her face, she seemed quite a female Bacchanalian. I was just celebrating the *orgies*. Her daughter was little and lively and kind . . . . I eat [*sic*] much and drank much and found animal life of very great consequence. I danced a great deal, and was an easy man, without affectation."

The German diet was, to be sure, very limited in range. Unlike the Dutch, the Germans raised hardly any green vegetables commercially until well into the nineteenth century. Middle-class as well as lower-class families relied on their own garden patches and vineyards back of the kitchen or on the outskirts of town. Only staples such as rye, cabbage, wheat, and root crops were sold in the market place. The potato, destined to become indispensable to the Germans, was not generally cultivated until the 1770's, when Frederick the Great personally promoted it. The enlightened

Larder crown for hanging meats

ruler also assisted Prussian agriculture by draining some 300,000 acres of marshlands, distributing seed corn, and after the Seven Years' War, sending his army's horses to be used in his subjects' fields; but German agriculture remained backward until late in the century. On the Junker estates in Silesia, many of which were still worked by serfs bound to the land, the production of wheat acre for acre was only half that raised on comparable English soil. Herds of beef cattle were all but unknown, and most of the meat eaten was pork. Superior, thick-joweled hogs were raised in Westphalia, and local varieties of sausage abounded in every part of Germany. The principal fats used in cooking were lard and bacon fat. Except in Alsace, where French and German influences met to produce Strasbourg pâtés and delicate fish dishes, German cooking tended to be heavy and monotonous.

There was a considerable variety of soups, mandatory at almost every meal —lentil soup, cabbage soup, soup with liver dumplings, and the cucumber soup that Goethe favored. Thomas Mann, in his *Buddenbrooks*—the chronicle of a merchant family of Lübeck in the middle of the nineteenth century—describes a traditional local concoction known as bacon broth, "a bouillon made with sour cabbage, in which was served the entire meal—ham, potatoes, beet-root, cauliflower, peas, beans, pears, sour plums, and goodness knows what, juice and all—a dish which nobody except those born to it could possibly eat." But usually the soup, formidable as it might be (and always consumed from a large soup plate, never in small portions from a cup), was only the prelude to what was to come. In a celebrated episode in the same novel, Mann tells of a housewarming dinner at the mansion of Consul Buddenbrook in 1835 at which some of the family and guests were all but overcome. It began with cabbage soup and proceeded through fish and boiled ham served with an onion sauce, huge dishes of vegetables, and "Frau Consul's celebrated 'Russian jam,' a pungent fruit conserve flavored with spirits," to a rich dessert known as *Plettenpudding*, composed of "layers of macaroons, raspberries, ladyfingers, and custard." For the children there was also a blazing plum pudding. In addition, there were cheeses and fruits and, after the Rhenish and Bordeaux, several bottles of sweet golden-yellow Malmsey. There were toasts; the gentlemen considered unbut-

toning their waistcoats; all were a bit unsteady, and one had distinctly eaten too much. But it was the little son and heir of the Buddenbrooks who became ill and had to leave the party.

"It's nothing much, Frau Consul," assured one of the guests, the physician Doctor Grabow. "A touch of indigestion. . . . Better put him to bed and give him a Dover powder. . . . And a rigorous diet, you know, Frau Consul. A little

Scandinavian butter mold

pigeon, a little French bread. . . ." "I don't want any pigeon," the boy bellowed. "I don't want to eat anything, ever any more. . . ."

Then Doctor Grabow smiled to himself and mused that "He would soon eat again, this young man. He would do as the rest of the world did—his father, and all their relatives and friends: he would lead a sedentary life and eat four good, rich satisfying meals a day. Well, God bless us all!" The good Doctor "was not the man to upset the habits of these prosperous, comfortable tradesmen and their families. He would come when he was sent for, prescribe a few days' diet of a little pigeon, a slice of French bread, yes, yes, and assure the family that it was nothing serious this time. Young as he was, he had held the head of many an honest burgher who had eaten his last joint of smoked meat, his last stuffed turkey, and, whether overtaken unaware in his counting-house or after a brief illness in his solid old four-poster, had commended his soul to God. Then it was called paralysis, 'a stroke,' a sudden death. And he, Friedrich Grabow, could have predicted it, on all of these occasions when it was 'nothing serious this time'. . . . Well, God bless us all! He, Friedrich Grabow, was not the man to despise a roast turkey himself. That ham with onion sauce had been delicious, hang it!"

Though Thomas Mann was writing about nineteenth-century Germany, he could easily have been describing bourgeois life of the century before. The small provincial courts of the time of Frederick the Great were themselves quite *bürgerlich* in character, with only a thin French veneer of sophistication. A little principality like Gotha had an array of high-titled retainers, including an *Oberhofmarschall* (Lord High Marshal), an *Oberlandjägermeister* (Lord Master of the Hunt), and an *Oberschenk* (High Steward of Wine), but the prince had little to do but hunt, dine, play cards, and attend the local opera, while his ladies busied themselves with embroidery, sketchbooks, and water colors. Duke Ernst August of Weimar rose at midday after breakfast in bed, talked with his gardeners, and inspected and drilled his guard of thirty-three men;

Festive procession in eighteenth-century Germany

then, sometime in midafternoon, he settled down to a three to five hour main meal, after which he might play cards with his ladies in waiting. Apart from such pleasures, the role of the German woman of whatever class save the high nobility was that of housekeeper. A visitor from early Victorian England, William Howitt, wrote in 1842 in *The Rural and Domestic Life of Germany* that he was surprised to find that "Ladies of rank and fortune are still plentiful, who spend their mornings in the kitchen up to the elbows in flour."

Along steep slopes above the Rhine and Moselle rivers, and in favored hillsides of the Palatinate, German landowners made advances in one aspect of dining—the cultivation of their fragrant white wines. Great care was taken over the years to refine growths and to differentiate them by accurate place names of origin as well as by year of vintage. The first dated wine in Europe appears to have been bottled in the commune of Hochheim on the Rhine and labeled "1711." (Hochheimer became so prestigious that Englishmen derived from the name their generic term "hock" to denote Rhine wines in general.) It was at Johannisberg that the method of leaving the grapes of a fine growth on the vine well after normal harvest was developed. If the weather remained favorable, the grapes of the *Spätlese*, or late gathering, technique yielded an exquisitely aromatic wine, velvety in texture. With the *Beerenauslese* technique, a venturesome vintner might leave some berries on the vines a few weeks longer, then pick them one by one with small scissors, selecting moldy, overripe, half-shriveled grapes which yielded wine of an even rarer flavor. (The presence of *Edelfäule*, the "noble rot" sought by ancient Roman vintners and exploited later in the production of French Sauternes, evaporated the water from the juice of the grapes and concentrated the sweetness and flavor.) A bottle might bear such a magisterial label as "Deidesheimer Kieselberg Riesling Trockenbeerenauslese," meaning a late selection of dry Riesling grapes from the Kieselberg vineyard of the commune of Deidesheim. To consume such a treasure became for the discerning German a memorable gastronomic experience.

Though Austrians of every class had always been drinkers of wine (mostly white) rather than of beer (a taste for beer did not develop until later), their vineyards produced nothing so distinguished as the German wines. Nonetheless, Lady Mary Wortley Montagu—another of that lively company of English travelers who crisscrossed Europe, saw everybody, and wrote home about everything—appears to have shared the Viennese' fondness for their wines when she visited Vienna in 1716. She was en route with her husband on his diplomatic mission to Constantinople and paused in Vienna long enough to dine

at all the best tables. She was particularly surprised, she wrote, by "the variety and richness of their wines." At one dinner a list of wines was placed before each guest, and Lady Mary "counted several times to the number of eighteen different sorts, all exquisite in their kinds." It is doubtful that she sampled all eighteen

Wooden cheese mold

wines; and, though the Austrians then and later were fond of displaying their own wines to foreign guests, one can assume that much of what she did sample was either German or French, with possibly a sweet Tokay from Hungary with the dessert.

But if the chemistry of the mid-Danubian soil and climate could not bring forth a Johannisberger any more than a Clos Vougeot, the land had other attributes that made both eastern Austria and Hungary more varied in produce than Germany. Though this plenty did not result in a high cuisine, it served to shape the pleasurable, easygoing, vivacious life of Vienna and Budapest in their prime. What also helped make this life so colorful was the circumstance that both capitals, especially Vienna, were meetingplaces of numerous influences—western European, Slavic, Balkan, and Mediterranean—and drew on foods and culinary traditions from every side.

As early as 1528, one year before the first Turkish invasion, a Venetian envoy had reported that in Vienna "Bread is cheap, the meat, beef as well as veal, excellent, and there is wine in abundance, though dear." A little less than two centuries later, Lady Mary wrote: "The plenty and excellence of all sorts of provisions are greater here than in any place I was ever in, and it is not very expensive to keep a splendid table. It is really a pleasure to pass through the markets, and see the abundance of what [in midwinter] we should think rarities, of fowls and venison, that are daily brought in from Hungary and Bohemia. They [lack] nothing but shellfish, and are so fond of oysters, they have them sent from Venice, and eat them very greedily, stink or not stink." By 1781 good fare in Vienna had become so ubiquitous that for a modest sum one could obtain a six-course à la carte meal including a choice of seven soups and five kinds of fish. A visiting Prussian bookseller and amateur musician named Nicolai observed with Prussian severity that such ease and cheapness of food led to gluttony and laziness. "The Viennese," he sniffed, "are not fond of hard work." Moreover, he noticed many florid faces and stout figures and acidly commented that many of the these self-indulgent people would no doubt die an early death of apoplexy.

Indeed the Viennese were more fond of good living than of hard work. Amid its growing prosperity the city had a large population of drifters and beggars who found themselves perennially aided by the dole and soup kitchens of a paternalistic government and by private handouts. In fact, with begging a recognized occupation and many of its professionals working well-defined stations in this or that district, some beggars even became affluent. At a late eighteenth century wedding feast given at an inn in the Viennese suburb of Penzing, the bride's parents were well-known almstakers who had become so prosperous that they were able to give their daughter a dowry of several thousand silver florins.

For common people, whether gainfully employed or not, the favorite resort was the Prater, a popular park and playground along the Danube, with band music and operatic concerts, booths selling *Wiener Würstchen* (the sausages that are the forerunners of the American "wieners"), and purveyors of Heurigen wine—the new "green" wine pressed perhaps only a few weeks before on the hillsides just outside Vienna. For those

Water ladle from a Slovakian kitchen

who could afford the price of a carriage, a trip up the slopes to Grinzing, the source of the Heurigen, was a regular diversion. There, at a rustic tavern, the new wine could be enjoyed at garden tables beside its vineyard to an accompaniment of zither players and fiddlers and a short distance from the Danube to the east.

Just as the cosmopolitan Viennese danced the czardas, the polonaise, and the quadrille, and later the waltz, the

Sancho Panza

*T*he exigencies of nature meant little to Don Quixote as he sallied through Spain. Sustained mainly by visions of "glorious Fame" and his fair Dulcinea, the knight occasionally ate roots and herbs or some pieces of salt cod known as "*Abadexo* in Castile, *Bacallao* in Andalusia . . . or Little Trout." Such food for thought, however, did little to alleviate the hunger pangs of his pot-bellied squire, Sancho Panza, who was more than eager to placate his adversaries for the sake of a meal. Abiding by the tenet that Spaniards might eat anything

except that which is "contrary to the holy mother church, to orthodoxy, and to good manners," Sancho always made do with the products at hand. In his native La Mancha he might stuff himself on leg of rabbit, roast pigeon, ewe's milk cheese, eggs and bacon, *gazpacho manchego* (a bread porridge with cooked game—quite different from the cold vegetable soup which the Moors popularized in Andalusia), and a skinful of Valdepeñas wine. Or, amongst shepherds on the dry plateau of central Spain, he would share a humble repast of kid stew, curds and whey, and acorns. Once when in jest a duke and duchess made Sancho lord of an "island" on their estate in Aragon, the squire was concerned more with the governance of his stomach than of his constituents. In preparing Sancho for his new office, Don Quixote advised him to avoid onions and garlic "Lest thy Breath betray thy Peasantry," but Sancho believed it was "Not with whom thou wert bred, but with whom thou hast fed" that made him qualified. During his brief incumbency, Sancho never developed a taste for such foods befitting his position as the aristocratic *guisados* (civets of fowl or hare), "*Moron* Partridges," or "*Lavajos* Green Geese." Sancho's likes were simple, and he relished above all an *olla podrida*, a "Hodgepodge of . . . many Sorts of Victuals . . . both wholesom and toothsom," including garbanzo beans, bacon, chicken, chorizo sausages, garlic, and pimentos cooked in an old earthen pot (and which in Cervantes' time as well as now was a Spanish national dish). Unfortunately, when this stew was set before him, his physician cried, "*Absit* . . . no Diet in the World yields worse Nutriment than those Mishmashes do. No, leave that [to] Masters of Colleges, and lusty Feeders at Country-Weddings: But let them not incumber the Tables of Governors." With that Sancho swore, "let me eat, or let 'em take their Government; for an Office that won't afford a Man his Victuals, is not worth two Horse-Beans."

polka, and the schottische with equal enthusiasm, their taste for sweets was catholic. The famed Viennese *Apfelstrudel* is said to have come from Hungary and before that from Turkey, where it took the form of *baklava*. The caramel encrusted, many-layered pastry known in Vienna cafés as the *Szegedinertorte* came from down-river Szeged in Hungary. The *Gugelhupf*, a fruitcake popular at domestic coffee parties, recalled Vienna's victory over the Turks (it was baked in the shape of the sultan's turban). The curious curled pastry called *Schillerlocken* (after the curly locks of Friedrich Schiller, a German poet deeply opposed to absolutism) had some political overtones as well. Vienna's most celebrated pastry was the *Sachertorte* —a chocolate-frosted cake with two layers of apricot jam; it bore the name of Franz Sacher, a noted confectioner and the proprietor of the city's liveliest hotel during the latter days of the empire. (From 1938 to 1962 a series of lawsuits regarding rights to the name "original *Sachertorte*" was waged in the Austrian courts to the vast entertainment of Austrians everywhere.)

Another instance of the eclecticism of central European cuisine was to be found in Hungary, ruled by Hapsburg Austria after the Turks were routed, but racially different from it. The Magyars who settled in Hungary in the ninth century had preserved many of the rough-and-ready eating customs of their nomadic Asian forebears. The traditional *bogrács*, a great copper kettle suspended from a tripod over a blazing fire, remained the proper vessel for cooking the hot Hungarian *gulyás*. The same vessel was used for making a pungent soup of fresh-water fish, including carp and perch, from the Tisza River. Hungary had stuffed sour-cabbage dishes, sour cream, seasonings of dill, aniseed, and pimento, mutton, and some of the finest poultry in Europe, including turkey and goose. Hungarians also liked macaroni and garlic. In this they were influenced perhaps by the Italian cooks whom Beatrice of Aragon brought with her when she arrived to become Matthias Corvinius' queen in the last half of the fifteenth century.

Paprika, today thought of as a vital ingredient of Hungarian cuisine, actually reached Hungary with the Turks, who occupied the country from 1526 to 1686; it was not widely used by Hungarians until the second half of the nineteenth century. Like the thick coffee which the Turks had brought to the Danube valley, paprika traveled upriver, and a Viennese addressing himself to a *Paprikaschnitzel mit Ungarischem Kraut* found himself consuming a truly international veal cutlet, the meat raised in Austria or Bohemia, the technique of sautéing the very thin slices of meat in batter Franco-Italian in origin, the principal condiment indigenous to India, and the sour cabbage a dish dating back to mongol incursions.

Spanish gentlefolk drinking chocolate, 1700's

273

It was after the Congress of Vienna, marking what appeared to be the end of the French threat and the setting up of a permanent order in Europe, that the middle class under the Hapsburgs fully came into its own. Domesticity mixed with pleasures outside the home. The Biedermeier house, with its circle of chairs for the family coffee gatherings, its potted geraniums in window boxes, its bird cages, its table under the arbor back of the house, was an upper middle-class setting portrayed by many sentimental painters of the period. At the same time, the Vienna cafés, with their mirrors,

Winter market in nineteenth-century Moscow

hangings, and deep plush seats, were always crowded with men escaping either their family or their office. Newspapers, writing materials, and chess sets were provided as a matter of course; one could sit as long as one wished over a single cup of coffee, the waiter bringing a fresh glass of water every half hour as a kind of time-clock courtesy. In the evening much of Vienna went out to dine and dance. Josef Lanner, a dashing composer of waltzes, led the orchestra at numerous balls held in Dommayer's Casino. His rival, the elder Johann Strauss, conducted at Sperl's. At the Coliseum, chefs were

engaged in producing such dishes as a "Trout minuet," a "Fresco of boiled lobsters," and something called "Orpheus sailing on a giant salmon."

Beethoven late in his life echoed an old criticism when, during a meal after a walk in the woods, he was so oppressed by the amounts heaped on his table that he grumbled, "Why so many different dishes? Man sinks almost to the level of an animal when eating becomes his chief pleasure." Yet for most people there could not be enough of good things; such festivities as the annual round of Fasching balls brought six weeks of high living and dining, and there was every reason to assume that this happy condition would last indefinitely.

The fatal collision that was to come in 1914 would for many end such pleasures. The power struggle that arose among Vienna and Berlin and St. Petersburg made deadly enemies above, and proletarian friends below. As has often been remarked, the landed gentry, the closest thing Russia had to a middle class, was naïve politically, insecure in status, leaning westward in social aspiration but eastward in its slowness to convert from feudalism to a modern industrial state. Gogol, Pushkin, Tolstoy, Turgenev, Dostoevsky, Goncharov, and Chekhov have all written widely of these people, proud in their ways, often entrapped by their longings and their insufficiencies, yet all enjoying themselves volubly over samovars and at buffets and long dinners.

No literature, in fact, has set so many of its scenes around the table. One thinks of the student Raskolnikov indulging himself with champagne and rich dishes far beyond his means after committing murder in Dostoevsky's *Crime and Punishment;* of the lonely, provincial ladies offering the officers of the garrison lunch, a supper of roast turkey and apple tart, and almost continuous tea in Chekhov's *Three Sisters.* Tolstoy has a particularly thematic scene in *Anna Karenina* in which the sensual and polished Oblonsky and the spiritual Levin go out to dine together at a fashionable Moscow restaurant. Oblonsky wants to order elegant dishes in the French style: oysters, *soupe printanière,* turbot with a *sauce Beaumarchais,* capons *à l'estragon,* a *macédoine* of fruits;

Embroidered matzo cover

Levin (who in Tolstoy's mind is evidently a symbol of virtuous Russian simplicity) is unhappy at this and would have preferred plain porridge, cabbage soup, bread, and cheese.

Gogol, in his satirical *Dead Souls,* sets a dinner-party scene that is equally revealing of upper-class tastes. Before entering the dining room, the gentlemen take a few appetizers and a tot of vodka. Then the meal begins: " 'The cabbage soup is particularly good today,' said Sobakevitch, taking spoonfuls of the soup and helping himself to an immense portion of a well-known delicacy which is served with cabbage soup and consists of sheep's stomach stuffed with buckwheat, brains, and sheep's trotters. 'You won't find a dish like this in town,' he went on, addressing his friend Tchitchikov, 'the devil only knows what they give you there!'

" 'The governor keeps a good table, however,' said Tchitchikov.

" 'But do you know what it is all made of? You won't eat it when you do know.'

" 'I don't know how the dishes were cooked . . . but the pork chops and the stewed fish are excellent.'

" 'You fancy so. You see I know what they buy at the market. That scoundrelly cook who has been trained in France buys a cat and skins it and sends it up to the table for a hare.' "

A dinner table dispute develops: " 'If you sprinkle frogs with sugar I wouldn't put them in my mouth, and I wouldn't taste oysters, either,' says the host Sobakevitch. 'Take some mutton. This is saddle of mutton with grain, not the fricassees that they make in gentlemen's kitchens out of mutton which has been lying about in the market-place for days. The French and German doctors have invented all that; I'll have them all hanged for it. . . . They talk of enlightenment . . . faugh!' " He goes on railing, while the mutton is followed by cheesecakes, each larger than a plate, then by "a turkey as big as a calf, stuffed with all sorts of good things: eggs, rice, kidneys, and goodness knows what." After that, saucers of radish preserve are offered, and the men, who had intended to talk business, settle sleepily into their easy chairs.

The most entertaining element of Russian cuisine remains that of the *zakuski,* an impressive display of hors d'oeuvres related to the Scandinavian *smörgåsbord*. An upper middle-class house would present platters of smoked sturgeon, herring fillets, suckling pig in horseradish, salmon, cucumbers in brine, little warm pâtés of meat baked in pastry (*pirozhki*), and small pancakes (*blini*) filled with sour cream and the finest caviar from the Caspian Sea. It was with the *zakuski* that exuberant drinking commenced. One never drank without eating; and the rich fish and tidbits that were small meals in themselves provided a firm foundation for tot after tot of vodka. Long regarded as indigenous to Russia, vodka now appears to have come from southwestern Europe. Or so the Russian historian Uspensky argued, stating that its distillation began on the island of Majorca and was transmitted by the Majorcan philosopher and alchemist Raymond Lully to the Genoese, who thereupon passed the technique to eastern Europe. The best Russian vodka was distilled from grain, the poorer varieties from potatoes. In either case, one could have it plain or iced, peppered (*pertsovka*) or flavored with a Siberian herb (*zubrovka*). And if one's purse matched his thirst, he could afterward indulge in what the Russians called *champanskoe*, served not just chilled, as in France, but half-frozen.

Yet, of all the European cuisines, none was more international than that of the Jews, the world's greatest migrants since the time of the Diaspora. Carrying their dietary laws, customs, and some of their ancestral dishes with them, they assimilated the foods of the many peoples among whom they settled. The traditional *knaidlach*, or dumplings made with *matzo* meal, are said to date back to the time of Moses; and for Austrian Jews, who observed a special rite at Passover, they symbolized the round stones which Moses threw against the wall that imprisoned the Jews in Egypt. *Matzos*, the only bread eaten during the Passover, were unleavened in memory of the hasty departure of the Jews and the unleavened dough which they baked in the desert sun. Jewish *blintzes*, inspired by Russian *blini*, were traditional at the spring festival of Shavouth and were usually filled with cheese, recalling that when the Jews returned from their long watch at Mount Sinai, the milk had soured in its jugs. Cheese or spinach turnovers called *borekas* were of Spanish-Jewish origin and closely resembled in name and taste the Middle Eastern *burek*, introduced on the peninsula perhaps by the Moors. *Gefüllte fish*, a dish prepared with ground, fresh-water fish such as pike or carp, and served on the Sabbath and during Passover, may have come into being in Holland, where Jews were welcomed after their expulsion from Spain in 1492. *Holishkes*, rolls of chopped meat cooked in grape leaves, are a traditional dish at the harvest festival of Sukkoth and commemorate the vineyards on the hillsides of the ancient Palestine homeland. They are, however, eaten by peoples throughout the Middle East and the Balkans. There was even a special curry of chicken, spices, peppers, and fruit which Jews, who had lived for centuries in Cochin, India, adopted from their Hindu neighbors and brought with them when they emigrated to the modern state of Israel. But had not every culture been borrowing from its neighbors since the beginning and making adaptations, even while priding itself on originality?

GOOD TIMES
AND
GEMÜTLICHKEIT

An Italian peasant wolfing dinner: "The Bean-Eater," by Annibale Carracci, c. 1585

In Celebration

Business, for the resolute, frugal Dutchman, always preceded pleasure, but when the day's work was done, some excuse for celebration could often be found, were it a religious holiday, a child's weaning, or another victory for the republic. The inverted "wager cup" at right was so designed that it could not be set down until empty. Practiced drinkers who could blow on the windmill and drain the cup before the sails stopped turning won a bet. Games, however, were not really needed to stimulate drinking at parties. Liquor flowed like water and was, considering the sanitation of the day, less dangerous.

The only stigma connected with drunkenness fell on the host who failed to get every man, woman, and sometimes child properly inebriated. The voracious Dutch made sure that plenty of food accompanied the wine, beer, and gin; special delicacies were prepared for feast days. In Jan Steen's painting of the Saint Nicholas Feast, opposite, traditional nuts and waffles fill the foreground. A lascivious old lady in the background beckons to her nubile granddaughter to look at what awaits her in the bedroom. If she does peek, the girl will find a *vrijer*, a gigantic cake shaped like a man, in her bed.

Pieter Bruegel's "Peasant Wedding," painted c. 1567, shows the Flemish in the flush of festivities. Unsteadied guests wisely keep their seats and leave the serving to sober cooks and waiters.

These cast-iron disks came in hinged pairs which, with handles attached, were used in the sixteenth century to cook German Waffelen. The iron above shows a hunting scene, that below, the holy day of Resurrection.

Pancake Day

From the frying pan to the waffle iron, flat breads have always enjoyed a special place in European tradition. As a symbol of the Eucharist, the wafer provoked a schism in the Protestant church. As the substance of self-indulgence, the rich, fat Shrovetide pancake was eaten in a ritual of pre-Lenten merrymaking that was celebrated from England to Russia. An Englishman, who may have perceived some sort of popish plot in such delicious fare, wrote, "there is a thing call'd wheaten floure, which the cookes do mingle with water, eggs, spice and other tragicall, magicall enchantments, and then they put it by little and little into a frying-pan of boiling suet, where it makes a confused dismall hissing, untill at last . . . it is transformed into the form of a . . . Pancake, which ominous incantation the ignorant people do devoure very greedillie." For the Dutch family in Pieter Aertsen's painting, c. 1560, above, the "magicall enchantments" of "Fat Tuesday" have already lost their charm. Perhaps their thoughts have turned to the forty lean days ahead. Undeterred, the old crone continues to cook while the waffles and pancakes cool.

In the Shops

In the Netherlands self-regulation of trades permitted customers to shop with a confidence rare on the rest of the Continent. The bakery above sells bread whose contents, size, shape, and price are set by a local guild; the pocket scale, left, gives inspectors a quick reading on the specific weight—hence quality—of the grain that goes into various rye, barley, oat, buckwheat, and luxury wheaten flours. Hours are also regulated, and though this proprietress has only her tatting to occupy her while the next batch is in the ovens, she must remain open for business. When the breads are done she will summon clients with a blast on the ox horn at her elbow. The liquor store opposite, with its shelves of bottles and alembics for distilling spirits, is also regulated—what the guild does not supervise, the distiller's cashier-wife does. The dram of hospitality her husband dispenses must be accounted a short-term investment, a stimulant to new business, for as one foreigner remarked, "in dull air [liquor] may be necessary to thaw the frozen. . . brain."

On the Square

Butter, cheese, fish, meat, and produce were sold in outdoor markets, usually held in the town's main square, literally under the noses of the municipal authorities, who rented out stall space to farmers. Some markets were held once a week, but Pieter Aertsen's sixteenth-century vendor below most likely set up shop every day, for the Dutch doted on the vegetables—particularly beets, carrots, turnips, and parsnips—that their rich soil produced. In this they were advanced over other Europeans, one Englishman scoffing: "the poore Dutch men, like swine, digge up the rootes."

Dutch Treat

In the fourteenth century an enterprising Zeelander discovered a way to preserve herring by curing and pickling it in brine. The Netherlands promptly snatched the international herring monopoly from the northern Hansa towns. Their skill as sailors and as merchants, the latter based on a sturdy system of guilds, seems to have especially galled the English, one of whom complained in 1614, "We are daily skorned by these Hollands for being so negligent of our profite, and carelesse of our fishing, and they do daily floute us . . . at sea." The Spanish also attacked, hiring privateers in Dunkirk to destroy the Dutch fleet and, thereby, its prosperous economy. Though the French pirates sunk hundreds of boats during sixty years of harassment operations, it was herring as usual in Dutch households. They ate their profits fresh and raw when they were able; pickled, mashed, smoked, or boiled the rest of the year. They mixed herring with all manner of ingredients and consumed it zealously from dawn to dark.

Even the tableware celebrated Holland's good fortune; at left are Delft plates showing three phases of the herring industry: fishing, packing, and door-to-door selling. In Steen's "L'Offre Gallante," opposite, salesmanship of another nature has won the heart of a buxom young maiden.

Bread and Bratwurst

Sandwich fixings have never reached more heroic proportions than in Germany, where in the eighteenth century the two demonstrations here took place. The *kuchen*, or sweet loaf above was prepared by the bakers of Dresden in 1730 in honor of a victory in Saxony. The recipe included 3,600 eggs and 126 pails of milk, and a twenty-foot-long knife was needed to cut it. The sausage below, which the engraver would have us believe is one single extrusion, is coiled around a long pole, the easier to parade it through the streets past an admiring throng of townspeople.

In a Spanish Kitchen

At a time when the Inquisition raged, even cookbooks warned that a señora with an unswept floor, a misplaced saucepan, or a neglected cooking oven would be duly punished by hell-fire. Thus, the Spanish housewife kept the kind of meticulously clean kitchen that inspired Velázquez' *bodegon*, or kitchen scene, above, with its brick oven, austere arrangement of copper and earthen soup pots, mortar and pestle, and shallow *paellera*, an iron skillet used for simmering Spain's classic rice dish. A different kind of fire flows through the veins of Goya's nineteenth-century peasant, below, who has consumed so much wine that he is well on his disheveled way to a not quite eternal siesta.

290

*The lean old woman in Velázquez' painting of
1618 prepares her* almuerzo, *or mid-morning
meal, on a brazier. The eggs frying in olive
oil, along with some onion, minced garlic, and
pimento, may constitute her only meal of the
day. Perhaps she can tempt the boy to share his
wine and melon with her. Consoling but not
filling is the native proverb "With a handful
of olives and a crust of bread, one can live."*

291

Keeping the Feast

The German Jewish family above remains impervious to the elements as it celebrates the Festival of Tabernacles, or Laubhuttenfest. Instead of building the traditional *sukkāh*, or outdoor booth of latticework festooned with fruits, vegetables, vines, and branches, its members prefer the comforts of home; they have created a miniature *sukkāh* above the dinner table and have decorated the ceiling. The father, who has ushered in the holiday by lighting candles and saying a prayer, is now ready to dig into such delicacies as *gebrutenah euter* (roast beef udder), *kreplach* (stuffed dumplings), *holishkes* (stuffed vine leaves), *challah* (white bread twists), and *strudel* filled with fruits of the harvest. The eighteenth-century engraving at right portrays the bustle of a Jewish community baking *matzos* for Passover. Under a rabbi's careful scrutiny, a woman mixes the flour-and-water dough, while men roll out the round, flat wafers. Few foods are surrounded by more ritual than the matzo, or "bread of affliction," symbolizing the unleavened dough carried by the Jews in their hasty exodus from Egypt. On the top floor, a bespectacled man with a candle and a goose-feather brush searches for the *chometz*, or remaining crumbs of leavened bread, which he will sweep up and burn before Passover begins.

The nine-inch Gothic tower, left, made in Frankfort c. 1550 to contain spices, recalls the Middle Ages when spices were so precious that they were locked in the strongholds of city halls. The faience plate from Delft, above, inscribed with "Rosh Hashanah" (New Year), is used on the holiday to serve apples dipped in honey.

KIRCHNER, Jüdisches Ceremoniel, 1726

Pasta con Amore

The origins of pasta remain obscured in the vapors of ancient cookery. Except for parts of northern Italy, where *polenta* (corn meal mush) and *risotto* (a rice dish) traditionally prevail, pasta has been for centuries the daily bread of rich and poor alike. Marco Polo is often credited with introducing Chinese "spaghetti" to his countrymen, but an ancient tool identified as a macaroni-maker can be seen in the frescoes of an Etruscan tomb; and there is evidence that *ravioli* and *fettucini* made from semolina paste were prepared in the Middle Ages. By the seventeenth century, when the anonymous portrait of the merchant, opposite, was painted, business was so good that a crude sort of assembly line was often needed to satisfy the demand. At the back of shops like his, teams of muscular young men, stripped down to shorts and barefooted, waded into the dough to knead it. Then, after the dough was shoveled into a cylinder, more boys operated a huge wooden lever to press the dough through the *trafila*, a plate perforated to form the paste into one of the dozens of distinctive shapes that the local trade favored. There were marked preferences from one town to the next, and each variety, from the sublime *capelletti d'angelo* (angel's hair) to the ridiculous *ziti* (bridegrooms), was said to have its own flavor, though all were prepared from the same basic recipe. The final job was laying the pasta out to dry, a task in which the merchant, bearing a scepter of wet noodles, has taken a hand.

Whenever a Neapolitan was seized with a passion for pasta, there was a cooperative vendor nearby. At top, a pizza salesman; above, a macaroni booth at rush hour; below, clowns eating handily.

Tea and Hospitality

BELOW: HARRY W. BRENNER, NEW YORK

Enameled tea strainer

Khlebosolstvo—literally translated "bread and salt" but in practice the Russian word for "hospitality"— centered on the great samovar which every household owned. This uniquely Russian device for keeping tea water always at the boil ensured visitors a welcome all day long. It consisted of a charcoal-burning base, a central chimney surrounded by an urn of water, and a top rack for holding a pot in which the infusion steeped. The hoary gentlemen at the stall above evince a proper respect for their host's samovar by gathering around it for a portrait. The men are merchants, come to the east-west entrepôt of Novgorod for the summer trade fair; one of the major commodities they will buy is China tea, perhaps from this very stall. If the tea passes the test, it will be shipped in bales or bricks to their local markets. Meanwhile, the merchants sip, grit their teeth (to hold the piece of sugar that sweetens the tea on its way down), and listen to the latest news of business.

When Czar Alexander III gave a picnic, a staff of seven men with a battery of equipment reported for duty. One of the juggernauts above combines the function of samovar with cookstove. The other carries everything from caviar to camp stools, for when the party below "roughs it," everything must be just right.

Sanctum Sanctorum

HAMBURGER KUNSTHALLE

From London to Budapest, the café was the bourgeois gentleman's bastion of privilege, his political club, his amusement hall, his snack bar. A century after the Continent's first café had opened in Paris, the city of Vienna listed over a hundred establishments where coffee and conversation shared space with zithers, poetry improvisers, and billiard tables (a law required that the game be played on the ground level lest throngs of spectators come crashing down on coffee drinkers). In warmer climes, cafés spread out over the sidewalks, and when hotbloods were not planning a revolution, the passing scene was entertainment.

Except for the winsome cashier, women were not welcomed at Vienna's Silbernen Kaffeehaus, above, an establishment which boasted silver coat hangers and such distinguished patrons as waltz kings Lanner and Strauss. The Café Greco was, in 1850 when Passini painted the scene at left, a hangout and mail drop for foreigners in Rome—Mendelssohn, Schopenhauer, Buffalo Bill. It still stands near the Piazza di Spagna.

The first pineapple harvested in England, presented to Charles II by his gardener, c. 1670

PLEASURES
OF
ENGLISH
COMPANY

No people have held more tenaciously to their traditions than the British—or so the commonplace has it. Actually, few people have shown themselves so responsive to new whims of fashion, or so inventive in their customs of the table. After the stately exuberance of the Elizabethans and the hauteur of the first Stuarts, English manners passed within three centuries from the dour restraints of the Puritan Commonwealth, through the lustiness of the Restoration, the decorous period of Queen Anne, the robust self-indulgence of the Georgian era, and the dandyism of the Regency, to the ponderous and sometimes suffocating ways modeled by that commanding arbiter of English style, Queen Victoria.

These shifts found their embodiment in a succession of public and private institutions. In the seventeenth century the coffeehouse flourished as a major political and cultural center, one quite different in tone from the cafés and *Kaffeehäuser* of the Continent. From this evolved that particularly

English establishment, the exclusive gentleman's club. Great, comfortable country mansions and fashionable summer resorts also came to distinguish the English upper-class way of life. Finally, in the later years of Victoria's reign, the daring fashion of "dining out" in public was to lead to still another invention, that of the "grand hotel" with its fine restaurant, marked by the opening of the Savoy in the 1880's.

Startling contrasts also marked each period. Even as Restoration England cast off Puritan restraints, men of all classes who mingled at coffeehouses were enjoined by the management to avoid cards and dice; fines were imposed for swearing and quarreling; and anyone wanting alcoholic drinks usually took his trade elsewhere. Though exquisite silver, porcelain, and formalities of the tea table were fashionable in Queen Anne's day, a Swiss visitor of that time was aghast that even in the best society "belching at table, and in all Companies whatsoever, is a thing which the English no more scruple than they do Coughing and Sneezing. This is full strange to us that come from a Country where Custom has ordain'd that Belching should be a Privilege reserv'd totally to Hogs."

French cuisine was favored among the elegant, who imported French chefs, but the rest of England persisted in cooking in a generally unimaginative manner much as their Elizabethan forebears had, as if patriotism itself resided in boiled beef and cabbage. Thus, one Robert Campbell inveighed against highly seasoned French dishes in his tract *The London Tradesman* of 1747: "In the Days

of good Queen *Elizabeth*, when mighty Roast Beef was the *Englishman's* Food, our Cookery was plain and simple as our Manners; it was not then a Science or Mistery. . . . But we have of late Years refined ourselves out of that simple Taste, and conformed our Palates to

Seventeenth-century spice box

Meats and Drinks dressed after the *French* Fashion: The natural Taste of Fish or Flesh is become nauseous to our fashionable Stomach; we abhor that anything should appear at our Tables in its native Properties; all the Earth . . . must be ransacked for Spices, Pickles, and Sauces, not to relish but to disguise our Food. Fish, when it has passed the Hands of a *French* Cook, is no more Fish . . . . It, and every Thing else, is dressed in Masquerade, seasoned with slow Poisons, and every Dish pregnant with nothing, but the Seeds of Diseases both chronick and acute."

Upper-class Englishmen and their ladies took most of their pleasures apart. Great hostesses were rare and nothing comparable to the French *salon* existed. Rather, great hosts were the rule, and lavish stag dinners the preferred entertainment; even when the sexes dined together, ladies generally retired soon after for cards and gossip, while the cloth was removed and men gathered closer over the mahogany for round after round of port. Yet, English women emerged as taste makers where French women had rarely ventured—as cookbook writers, beginning with the publication in 1670 of Hannah Woolley's *The Queen-like Closet: or, Rich Cabinet*, packed with household advice.

Were there no immutable English traditions? One thinks of the hearty breakfast. On New Year's Day, 1661, Samuel Pepys gave a breakfast party at which he regaled his friends with "oysters, neats' [oxen's] tongues, anchovies, wine, and Northdown ale." It was not as massive a morning meal as that taken at many a Tudor or early Stuart table (it appears to have included no mutton or beef), but it was in the handsome old style. Yet by the end of the seventeenth century, and throughout most of the eighteenth, a breakfast feast such as Pepys' was rare. The most that the gentry took then was a cup of coffee, chocolate, or tea, accompanied by bread or rusks or by that new invention, toast. ("The slices of bread and butter, which they give you with your tea, are as thin as poppy-leaves," reported the Swiss traveler Charles P. Moritz, who otherwise had little use for English cuisine; "But there is another kind of bread and butter usually eaten with tea, which is toasted by the fire, and is incomparably good. This is called toast.") Moreover, breakfast was often taken at about ten o'clock, after several hours of household activity—ladies instructing their servants, children receiving their lessons, fathers riding out or preparing their correspondence, and calls paid.

Less than two centuries later, breakfast customs had come full circle. We read, for instance, of a meal offered at one of the better provincial inns of England, the White Lion in distant Merionethshire, to fortify guests one rainy Sunday morning in 1854. The host offered a "pot of hare; ditto of trout; pot of prepared shrimps . . . tin of sardines; beautiful beefsteak; eggs, muffin; large loaf, and butter, not forgetting capital tea."

Equally substantial but less sociable were the breakfasts served in upper-class Victorian households. Sideboards were laden with silver-domed platters of eggs and bacon, grilled kidneys, sausages, kippers, plaice, from which the family took their choice. Punctuality at breakfast was counted among the Christian virtues. By eight o'clock everyone was expected to be in his place, and the head of the household was likely to be found already seated, surrounded by salvers of crumpets and pots of marmalades, reading from the immense pages of the morning *Times*.

Perhaps the sturdiest English tradition resulted from the "clubbable" character that Samuel Johnson noted in his friends, men who loathed being alone and who liked nothing better than to gather with friends and acquaintances for good talk and cheer. A "club," in the early part of the period, did not signify a formal institution housed in its own building; it was more accurately a circle of men of like interests who met frequently at their favorite tavern, chophouse, or, in later years, coffeehouse. Ben Jonson prefigured the custom by organizing the Apollo, a literary circle, at the Devil Tavern in Fleet Street. Rooms upstairs were reserved for the "private amusements" of the playwright and his fellow "clubbers." On the eve of the Restoration the Coffee Club of the Rota began to meet at Miles' Coffeehouse in New Palace Yard, Westminster; termed a "free and open society of ingenious gentlemen," it was, in effect, a debating circle. Pepys was one of its regular visitors, and the talk ranged far and wide over political as well as literary matters, the Rota often taking a vote on issues before Parliament.

The early years of the eighteenth century saw the nation bitterly divided between Whigs and Tories, particularly over the War of the Spanish Succession and the successor to Queen Anne herself: Should the next monarch be the Hanoverian George or Anne's exiled half brother, James, "the Pretender"? Men gravitated increasingly to political "clubs" of their own persuasion. Jonathan Swift was one of those who joined a Tory circle known as the October Club, which met at a tavern near the House of Commons. It was, he wrote, "a set of about a hundred Parliament men of the country who drink October beer at home, and meet every evening . . . to consult affairs and drive things on to extremes against the Whigs." In 1714 he formed his own Scriblerus Club of Tory partisans and men of letters, including the poet Alexander Pope, the statesman Lord Bolingbroke, and the playwright John Gay. The Whigs had their Kit-Kat Club, founded about 1700. It took its name from Katt, the proprietor whose reputation as a pieman had first attracted members there. Its luminaries included at various times such men as Addison, Steele, Congreve, Robert Walpole, and the architect Vanbrugh.

The Whig cause, because of prosperous middle-class support, ultimately prevailed, leaving Jacobites, when called upon to drink to His Majesty George I, to pass their wineglasses across their finger bowls in a covert toast to their exiled king "over the water." Finger bowls were consequently abolished, not to be restored until the twentieth century. Among themselves the Jacobites may have raised the following cheer:

God bless the king, our Faith's defender;
God bless—sure there's no harm in
  blessing—the Pretender;
But who Pretender is, and who is king,
God bless us all, that's quite another thing.

Yet peace and prosperity brought a degree of reconciliation, and no man in England was more clubbable than Johnson himself, who formed first the Ivy Lane Club, which met every Tuesday at the King's Head Tavern, a beefsteak house; then the Essex Head Club, meeting three evenings a week at the Essex Head Tavern off the Strand. He was also a regular at the Turk's Head Club, whose roles included Sir Joshua Reynolds, Oliver Goldsmith, Edmund Burke, and the actor David Garrick (though Johnson thought to blackball him for possible "buffoonery"). Here the select —first restricted to nine in number, though the quota was eventually raised to thirty-five—could match wits as well as drinks with the encyclopedic sage. Before long the Johnson circle had become, in effect, a congress of leading men of letters.

The coffeehouse was itself a club of sorts, but a democratic one, open to all who came. The first coffeehouse was

The Kitchen Conspiracy

"The honour of every family," Jonathan Swift observes, "is deposited in the hands of the cook, the butler, and the groom." In his ironical *Directions to Servants*, written c. 1731, he offers some helpful advice on how to keep this sacred trust to the advantage of everyone but the "common enemy, which is your master and lady." No one, it seems, is better situated to wage inter-necine war than the female cook. Her first order of business is the affections of the butler: "Let there be always a strict friendship between you and the butler . . . the butler often wants a comfortable tit-bit, and you much oftener a cool cup of good liquor. However, be cautious of him, for he is sometimes an inconstant lover, because he hath great advantage to allure the maids with a glass of sack; or white wine and sugar." The cook's relations with the lower ranks are less agreeable. "To keep troublesome servants out of the kitchen, always leave the winder sticking on the jack to fall on their heads." Swift ad-vises the footman to counterattack: "Whenever she turns her back, throw . . . a handful of salt in the pot, or smoking coals into the dripping-pan, or daub the roast meat with the back of the chimney . . . ." In the cook's dealings with tradesmen, too, strategy is recommended. "If you be employed in marketing, buy your meat as cheap as you can: but . . . set down the highest rate; which besides is but justice; for no body can afford to sell at the same rate that he buys. . . . Do not accept a treat of beef-stake and pot of ale from the butcher,

which I think in conscience is no better than wronging your master; but do you always take that perquisite in money. . . . If you find it necessary to go to market in a wet day, take out your mistress's riding-hood and cloak to save your cloaths." Management of the stewpots Swift leaves, for the most part, to the cook's imagination, though he does caution, "Never send up a leg of a fowl at supper, while there is a cat or dog in the house, that can be accused of running away with it: but, if there happen to be neither, you must lay it upon the rats, or a strange greyhound. . . . If a lump of soot falls into the soup, and you cannot conveniently get it out, scum it well, and it will give the soup a high French taste. . . . When you find that you cannot get dinner ready at the time appointed, put the clock back . . . and, if your dinner miscarries in almost every dish, how could you help it."

probably the Angel, which opened about 1650 in Oxford, at a time when no fewer than 350 alehouses were in operation there. By 1700, due to the rising vogue of coffee and the new political awareness of the middle classes, the popularity of these forums climbed to a point where more than two thousand were flourishing in London. Fifteen years later the number was close to three thousand. For the admission price of a penny, anyone could seat himself at a

Queen Charlotte frying sprats

table, pick up conversation, and gather news of the day. This was a boon in a time when newspapers were scarce and when political and commercial news was normally borne by word of mouth.

King Charles II was perturbed at the growth of coffeehouses, with their free talk and their potentialities as centers of dissent, and in 1675 he ordered them suppressed—a foolish move, never carried out and soon forgotten. Like the clubs, the coffeehouses gradually became specialized as men of varying businesses and professions congregated in their favorites. Lawyers were likely to be seen at the Rainbow in Fleet Street.

Shippers and buyers gathered at Edward Lloyd's in Lombard Street—a coffeehouse where so much maritime information was exchanged that it was to become not only the center of ship auctions but the headquarters of the famous body of underwriters known to the world as Lloyd's. Stock jobbers and financiers met at Jonathan's in Change Alley, where such schemes as the speculative "South Sea Bubble" were promoted. At Hogarth's Coffeehouse lessons in Latin were given daily at four o'clock to those who aspired to higher learning. As Macaulay remarked in his chronicle of the period, "the coffeehouse was the Londoner's home, and . . . those who wished to find a gentleman commonly asked, not whether he lived in Fleet Street or Chancery Lane, but whether he frequented the *Grecian* or the *Rainbow*." But above all, said Macaulay, "There was Will's [in Covent Garden] . . . sacred to polite letters, where earls in stars and garters, clergymen in cassocks, pert Templars, sheepish lads from Universities, translators and index-makers in ragged coats" could be found gathering about the chair of John Dryden, the poet laureate, who sat enthroned beside the fire in winter and on the balcony in summer, receiving literary aspirants and passing judgment on their work.

Alexander Pope was not yet twelve when he was presented to the presiding genius ensconced at Will's. He had already composed some verses ("I lisp'd in numbers, for the numbers came," as he later remarked proudly of his childhood efforts) and was long to write under the influence of the mighty, witty man in that high-backed chair. He had far less use for Joseph Addison, who decades later was the presiding spirit at the Whig coffeehouse known as Button's just across the street from Will's, and whom he castigated in savage verse:

Alike reserv'd to blame or to command
A tim'rous foe, and a suspicious
*   friend. . . .*
Like Cato, give his little Senate laws,
And sit attentive to his own applause."

Jonathan Swift, in turn, had little use for Will's in its post-Dryden days, scoffing at the "wits" who assembled there: "The worst conversation I ever remember to have heard in my life."

These were the cutting edges of London life. Boswell, ever bent on adventure and welcoming almost any company, male or female, was not inclined to be so haughty. He "pub crawled" from one tavern and coffeehouse to the next. His *London Journal* of 1762–63 records a day-long tour in January with friends, beginning with "an excellent breakfast at the Somerset Coffeehouse," continuing with a visit to London Bridge to view the ice floes in the river, and a stop at a little "public house" in Whitechapel to drink "some warm white wine with aromatic spices, pepper, and cinnamon." After this the gay party adjourned to a private tavern room for "a jolly profusion of smoking, juicy beefsteaks." Next they proceeded to the Bedford Coffeehouse for coffee and tea. Thereupon they attended the theater and, undoubtedly sozzled, raised an uproar against David Malloch, the playwright. Finally, Boswell relates, "After the play we went to Lady Betty's" (who presided over a literary salon of dubious reputa-

tion) and, "as . . . we were very hungry after fatigues, we were set down in the parlour by ourselves to an excellent warm supper. We were in high glee. . . ."

By this time the serious and sober coffeehouse had passed its prime. Many had become sheer gaming resorts for well-dressed rakehells. Gentlemen of high rank and fashion, having savored the pleasures of the intimate circle, now desired permanent establishments of their own behind closed doors and away

George III toasting a muffin

from the rabble. So out of White's Chocolate House in St. James's Street grew the Tories' retreat, White's (founded in 1693), and out of William Almack's Assembly Rooms grew Boodle's (1762) in Pall Mall—the first clubs to have their own buildings, with liveried staff, fine furnishings, and well-stocked wine cellars. Together with Brooks' (1778) these clubs became enduring centers of English political and male social life at the top, and were the models for many others to come. (Such was the Reform Club, spacious headquarters of the new Liberal party from the 1830's onward and in whose kitchen the great chef

307

Alexis Soyer ministered, and the Athenaeum, opened in 1824, where leading patrons of the arts enjoyed superlative furnishings, classical busts, roomfuls of books, and a formidable table.)

Another reason for the decline of the coffeehouse was that the government, to foster trade with India and China, promoted tea drinking. Beginning with Charles II's queen, Catherine of Braganza, the court had taken to tea. Thus Alexander Pope, referring to teatime at Hampton Court during Queen Anne's reign, wrote a rhymed couplet using the then-current pronunciation of tea:

> *Here, thou, great ANNA! whom three realms obey,*
> *Dost sometimes counsel take—and sometimes tea.*

Tea was also a favorite among English women of lesser rank, whose tastes were probably influenced by the fact that they were excluded from the coffeehouses. The "genteel" brew was served in pleasure gardens such as Vauxhall and Ranelegh. Tea drinking, particularly as tea tariffs were lowered, spread at such a rate that in the early decades of the eighteenth century annual imports rose from twenty thousand pounds to sixty thousand pounds, and by the end of the century, they had reached some twenty million pounds. Brewers, distillers, and importers of wine feared that tea would heavily cut in on their trade. Yet, the consumption of wines and spirits also rose enormously in the same period, from a half-million gallons of taxable gin in 1700 to five million in 1735, not to mention the illicit, and thus unaccounted, liquors drunk.

Mention of good claret and rich port also comes up constantly in the context of Georgian life. What wine a gentleman drank often reflected his politics or the dictates of English foreign policy. The immense popularity of port was an outgrowth of the power struggle between England and France for influence in Spain and of the Methuen Treaty of 1703: the Whigs, anxious to bring Portugal over to the English side and to boycott French trade, dropped the duties on Portuguese wines to only £7 a tun, raising those on French wines to a forbidding £55 a tun. Port, readily available, thus became the Whigs' patriotic drink; one proved his loyalty by the quantities he drank, while to resort to clarets or Burgundies was to drink the wine of the enemy. The Tories, on the

Brass nutcracker, 1700's

other hand, made a point of demonstrating their opposition to the war by acquiring the best French wines available, no matter what the price.

Another drink long identified with Whiggery and its political jollifications was punch. The drink derived its name from a Hindustani word meaning "five," a reference to its five basic ingredients

—rum, citrus-fruit juices, sugar, water, and spices—and was brought to England in the seventeenth century by merchants returning from India. Since it combined the principal imports from successful English enterprises in the West Indies, it enjoyed a double popularity. Punch was served hot or cold from great bowls, and in its potency and sweetness it resembled the spiced wines of the Middle Ages. At poorer clubs and taverns, the punch was often made with rum substitutes, either Eastern arrack—a distillation of coconut, rice, or sugar cane—or other nondescript brandies. By the 1780's it was one of the standard libations even at Tory Cambridge.

The rich never ate or drank so much as in Georgian England, and gout was the common price the overindulgent paid. If a man was long to survive a regimen of several bottles a day, he needed to pursue a highly active life to offset some of its effects, and this most gentlemen did. Amid all their clubbing and late evenings at wine, they were earnest horsemen, travelers, collectors, letter writers, amateur antiquarians, and above all mansion builders and developers of country estates. On a typical day in town, a Georgian gentleman might do business with his solicitor at breakfast; then ride out in St. James's park, pay social calls, take a light lunch at midday (the "dinner" hour in England, once observed before or close to noon, had been advanced to two o'clock at the beginning of the eighteenth century, and to three, four, and even five or six o'clock by the end of the century). After the meal he might visit London's smart art dealers to pass judgment on the latest fashion in painting and sculpture, or retire to his study to try a translation of Horace or Ovid (a fashionable exercise of the time) before showing his prowess at the dinner table. Then, on to his club for an hour or two; and afterward to Parliament where, if steady enough, he might deliver a speech; after adjournment he would visit his mistress.

Silver gilt punch bowl, c. 1715

In the country the gentleman's life took another turn. Generally, his wealth came from his lands, which had to be tended carefully if they were to thrive. Unlike the French courtier who under the spell of Versailles often saw little from year to year of his own holdings, the English landlord, from duke to squire, spent months on end at his estate, conferring with overseers, visiting tenants, serving as local justice of the peace, and supervising crop management. Many a landed lord, absenting himself from clubs and boudoirs, particularly during the spring and summer, became an expert on selective cattle breeding, crop rotation, and experiments with new vegetables and fruits. The effort he expended was salubrious for both his health and his table.

Many wealthy and titled heirs—Bathursts, Pembrokes, Burlingtons, Oxfords, Leicesters, Bedfords—took to erecting ostentatious country showplaces designed after the style of Palladio, Inigo Jones, Sir Christopher Wren, and Sir John Vanbrugh. From these handsome seats they administered self-sufficient sources of varied food supply, tending their own orchards, raising poultry, cattle, hogs, and often producing their own cheese, ale, and cider. Tobias Smollett, author of the Georgian novel *The Expedition of Humphry Clinker*, wrote authentically, if in high-flown style, when he had one of his characters, Matthew Bramble, describe life at his own Brambleton Hall in the Midlands: "I drink the virgin lymph, pure and crystalline as it gushes from the rock, or the sparkling beverage home-brewed from malt of my own making . . . my bread is sweet and nourishing, made from my own wheat, ground in my own mill . . . my table is, in a great measure, furnished from my own ground; my five-year-old mutton, fed on the fragrant herbage of the mountains . . . my delicious veal, fattened with nothing but the mother's milk . . . my poultry from the barn door, that never knew confinement but when they were at roost; my rabbits panting from the warren; my game fresh from the moors; my trout and salmon struggling from the stream. . . . My salads, roots, and pot-herbs, my own garden yields in plenty and perfection. . . ."

Some estate owners, in their efforts to outdo one another, leaned to the exotic. The extravagant Duke of Chandos—who maintained at Canons an aviary of rare birds, along with 93 household servants, 19 gardeners, and an orchestra of 27 players—called upon overseas suppliers to furnish him with unusual produce: "From Captain Massey in Carolina came rice, kidney beans (said to grow prodigiously, like hops or vines), ananas (or pineapples), and pickles, not to mention certain fauna—a Mexican squash [*sic*], 'which we take to be a little beaver,' rough coated, very tame and entertaining, and flamingos. Mr. Ashley of the Barbados [sent] pineapples, cinnamon, coffee trees and berries, and 'Avigator [*sic*] Pears'. . . . Messrs. Harriman of Leghorn supplied broccoli seed and fennel . . . orange-flower water, capers, *muscatello di Castello* vinegar, preserved citron, anchovies. . . . While from Oporto the Duke procured Lamiego hams, more appetizing, let us hope, than those from Pennsylvania, and, from Lisbon, sugar, raisins of the sun . . . currants, lemons, oranges, musk and water-melon seeds." The Duke of Bedford, at Woburn, rejected the offer of a tiger from a supplier abroad, but accepted a huge turtle. "His Grace had about twelve ladies and gentlemen at the eating of it," his steward reported. "We dressed it after the West India manner and the Duke said he never eat [*sic*] a better in his life."

However the fare might vary from one great country house to the next (de-

Before: top-hatted Britisher landing in France

pending largely on whether the owner had imported a French chef), it was customary that the company be large. The day might find the house guests broken into small groups, pursuing various diversions and sports in the surrounding "park" and the preserves beyond; but the dinner hour brought the company together in the drawing room for a formal entrance into the dining room, each lady on the arm of a gentleman. Liveried house servants lined the way, sometimes with the personal attendants of the visitors forming a second rank. Lord Hervey recalled an extended visit to Robert Walpole's stately Houghton Hall in Norfolk—a rural palace surmounted by domes and statuary: "we used to sit down to dinner a little snug party of about thirty odd, up to the chin in beef, venison, geese, turkeys, etc.; and generally over the chin in claret, strong beer and punch." In a later generation we hear of a house party of forty at the Duke of Devonshire's Chatsworth, and of eighty at Thomas Coke's Holkham Hall. At Woburn, in 1800, at a four-day-long Sheepshearing Party, nearly two hundred people, ranging from noblemen to yeomen from the countryside—a company reminiscent in size of Tudor days—sat down together for dinner at three.

Despite the profusion of servitors in attendance on such occasions, dining procedure in many mansions appears to have been self-service. The table was set with platters before the guests entered, and each gentleman helped himself and his table partner to the dishes nearest him; if he liked some other dish several places away or across the table, he asked for a helping to be passed to him or sent a servant to fetch it. In the eyes of the German prince Pückler-Muskau, visiting estates during the Regency, this was "a very troublesome custom," and he was pleased to discover that "some of the most elegant travelled gentlemen have adopted the German [and French] fashion of sending servants round with the dishes."

As for wine, the prince observed that "It is not usual to take [it] without drinking to another person. When you raise your glass, you look fixedly at the one with whom you are drinking, bow your head, and then drink with the greatest gravity." Such toasting was another custom hallowed by generations of the gentry, a French visitor having written as early as 1698 that "To drink at table without drinking to the health of some one in especial, would be considered drinking on the sly, and as an act of incivility." The larger the company, the more numerous the pledges. After this, and the port and the cards and the other indoor games that followed, the house guests retired to gather strength for the next day's exertions.

Though the urban upper middle classes possessed no Woburns or Holkham

After: rolling home with a well-developed paunch

311

Alexis Soyer

The finest chef in mid-nineteenth-century England was a Frenchman. Dining at the Reform Club, where Alexis Soyer was head chef, was the goal of every gourmet in London. The talented, flamboyant, egocentric character could have capitalized on his reputation socially, but he chose to use it to launch some of the projects that crowded his brain. The astonishingly vulgar ambience and delectable food of The Gastronomic Symposium of All Nations, a restaurant that he designed, decorated, and operated, attracted a thousand customers a day, but he happily sold recipes to the firm of Cross & Blackwell so that the poorer, stay-at-home public could sample his culinary artistry, too. In spare moments he invented things—stoves, jelly molds, mime scenery—and even there succeeded with surprising frequency. But Soyer was above all

a humanitarian. Organizing soup kitchens for starving Britons and providing nourishing food on the Crimean battlefield were his proudest achievements. His enormously popular cookbook for the rich was followed by one for poor cottagers. His style can best be described as purple, his English fractured; but Soyer's advice was always thorough and appropriate for the audience he meant to reach. The following is from his *Shilling Cookery*, which is set up as an exchange between two ladies gathering recipes. "*Mr. B.* [husband of one of the ladies] 'In my wife . . . you see almost an accomplished woman (hearing such praise, Mrs. B. retired, saying, 'How foolish you talk, Richard'); she . . . as an amateur, is rather proficient in music, but her parents, very wisely considering household knowledge to be of the greater importance, made her first acquainted with the keys of the storeroom before those of the piano.'" Mrs. B.'s recipe for toast: "Procure a nice square loaf . . . that has been baked one or two days previously (for new bread cannot be cut, and would eat very heavy) . . . contrive to have rather a clear fire; place a slice of the bread upon a toasting fork . . . then begin to move it gradually to and fro until the whole surface has assumed a yellowish-brown color . . . have some fresh or salt butter (which must not be too hard, as pressing it upon the toast would make it heavy); should you require six such slices for a numerous family . . . cut each slice into pieces as soon as buttered . . . as often in cutting through four or five slices with a bad knife, you will squeeze all the butter out of the upper one and discover the under one, at the peril of its life, swimming in an ocean of butter at the bottom."

Halls, they were not far behind their betters in the pursuit of good living. And in the country, even a man of lesser means might be found serving an original and varied dinner. A particularly gregarious host, a rural parson named James Woodforde, recorded an entertainment he had given (on a clerical salary of some £400 a year) to a small party in 1770: "I gave them for dinner a dish of fine Tench . . . Ham and 3 Fowls boiled, a Plum Pudding; a couple of Ducks rosted, a rosted neck of Pork, a Plum Tart and an Apple Tart, Pears, Apples and Nutts after dinner; White Wine and red, Beer and Cyder." The meal began at four o'clock. At six he served coffee and tea. Later, at ten, he offered a supper of "Hashed Fowl and Duck and Eggs and Potatoes, etc." Four years later he told of a more "elegant" dinner he had presented on his stipend: "The first course was, part of a large Cod, a Chine of Mutton, some Soup, a Chicken Pye, Puddings and Roots, etc. Second course, Pidgeons and Asparagus. A Fillet of Veal with Mushrooms and high Sauce with it, rosted Sweetbreads, hot Lobster, Apricot Tart and in the Middle a Pyramid of Syllabubs and Jellies." There were fruits as well as Madeira and port to wind up the evening, and "We were all very cheerful and merry."

Regarding desserts, Mrs. Raffald in *The Experienced English Housekeeper*, a compendium of some eight hundred recipes published in 1769, advised her many readers to "lay up" in summer all manner of preserves and dried fruits for the January table; such unexpected fare in winter would be "entertaining to the company," making "a pretty appearance after the cloth is drawn"—that is, after the table was cleared for dessert. She counseled that all sweetmeats and fruits be readied in China dishes or baskets; that it would be easy to make "five different ices" for the centerpiece, "with four plates of dried fruit round them, apricots, green-gages, grapes, and pears —the four outward corners, pistacho [*sic*] nuts, prunellas, oranges, and olives —the four squares, nonpareils, pears, walnuts, and filberts—the two in the centre, betwist [*sic*] the top and the bottom, chestnut and Portugal plums—for six long dishes, pine-apples, French plums, and the four brandy-fruits, which are peaches, nectarines, apricots, and cherries." For reasons that were never made clear, each course in a given meal was to have the same number of dishes —twenty-five in the meal whose dessert is described above.

Such good eating required food industries on a scale never before known. Large specialty markets dotted London in the eighteenth century—fish at Billingsgate, poultry at Leadenhall, fruits and vegetables at Covent Garden and Spitalfields, meat at Smithfield. Over 75,000 head of cattle were driven to London yearly in the first half of the century; some 100,000 toward the end. Salmon came from Scotland, oysters from Colchester, butter from Yorkshire and East Anglia (the trip by sea left some of it tasting like "train-oil thickened with salt," said Smolett), and the cheesemongers of London maintained a fleet of more than a dozen ships to bring huge wheels of Cheshire cheese around Land's End from the port of Liverpool.

Still, amid this prosperity, the laboring class fell prey to the gin craze of which William Hogarth has left vivid testimony. The *laissez-faire* attitude of the government was, without doubt, partially at fault. It had long regulated the sale of ale and beer, requiring that they be dispensed only at licensed houses. But it had imposed no like restrictions on spirits, and only the lightest of taxes. It appears to have been unprepared for

Milk for sale in St. James's Park, 1790

the sudden proliferation of back-alley gin mills—where signs such as "Drunk for a penny, dead drunk for twopence, straw provided free" lured many of the cities' poor to their ruin. The "gin," moreover, was often not a true product of grain and juniper at all, but a potion of lethal substitutes. One recipe called for oil of vitriol [sulphuric acid], oil of almonds, oil of turpentine, spirits of wine, lump sugar, lime water, rose water, alum, and salt of tartar. The novelist Henry Fielding, in outrage, wrote in 1751 of "that poison called *gin* . . . the principal sustenance (if it may be so called) of more than a hundred thousand people in this metropolis." Though belated steps were taken to bring spirits

under control, by taxation and curtailment of illicit stills, enormous social damage had been done.

Other social ills overtook the poorer classes from about mid-century on. The "enclosure" movement, under the pretext of putting more land under cultivation, benefited rich landowners while uprooting many a cottager from his farm land and pasturage. The deprived and the landless were forced into the cities, there to become the work force of the new Industrial Revolution. Food prices soared, particularly during the Napoleonic Wars, and the Corn Laws of 1815 made matters worse by restricting grain imports and keeping home prices high. Adulteration of foods by unscrupulous producers, along with a high rate of spoilage due to the increasing distances and inadequate roads over which food was brought into teeming cities—all this added to turmoil and unrest. The quality of English bread so deteriorated that an uproar was raised against both its price and content. Critics charged that chalk or alum was added to make it white, and one pamphleteer, in *Poison Detected, or Frightful Truths*, charged that bakers were snatching bodies from the morgue and grinding up the bones for flour. Some vegetables were made to look greener with poisonous copper oxide additives. Milk was almost unknown to the urban poor, except in a watered or half-spoiled state (though in the fashionable West End of London, cows were still driven through the streets and milked at curbside for wealthy clients).

In novels such as *Oliver Twist* and *Nicholas Nickleby*, Charles Dickens described the ravages of near starvation among the poorest of all, the children of the poor: "Pale and haggard faces, lank and bony figures, children with the countenances of old men . . . boys of stunted growth, and others whose long meagre legs would hardly bear their stooping bodies." In the 1840's—the "Hungry Forties," as they are often called—wages were to sink to their lowest level in a century, and the diet of the poor, then composed chiefly of potatoes and gin, reached its nadir. The disease which destroyed the Irish and English potato crops, and the resultant famine of 1845–46, sent a specter through the land, and vacant-eyed, corpse-like figures could be seen in numbers in gutters from Thamesside to Merseyside. There were innumerable reformers on hand, to be sure, to proclaim that the best medicine for poverty was temperance.

Perhaps few men cared less about the condition of the poor than the raffish George IV, whose first notable act as regent for his insane father was to invite two thousand guests to Carlton House for a stupendous banquet and benefit for artists in 1811. As if to emulate Louis XIV at Versailles, he had an artificial rivulet constructed for the festivities. It sprang from a silver fountain housed in a "temple" in front of his own chair, ran

Street cars carrying hot and cold drinks, 1842

through a channel in the main table, and was spanned by numerous little bridges; "gold and silver fish were by a mechanical invention made to swim and sport through the bubbling current." At Brighton the regent erected the gossamer pavilion that was his Oriental pleasure dome, and he imported the great Carême to be his chef at a salary of £1,000 a year. To be stylish under the Regency, one needed to be carefree, a trifle exotic, and Francophile; yet, as the Frenchman Louis Simond wryly observed after a tour of great houses in 1810–11, it was remarkable that English gentlemen who prided themselves on their "scrupulous delicacy" of taste adhered to an odd custom—that of using a chamber pot placed in a corner of the dining room to relieve themselves as the hours over wine wore on.

Nor were the privileged classes of the early Victorian age greatly concerned with the state of England's society as a whole. They were much more involved in the change of manners affecting upper and middle classes. Everything was in flux, from mealtime hours to food and method of table service. The gradual advance of dinner to the evening hours (Queen Victoria, at the time of her coronation in 1837, took dinner as late as eight o'clock) resulted in a general upheaval of the established eating order and the introduction of two new forms, the substantial luncheon and the ritual of afternoon tea. The confusion over what to call each meal seems to have been so troublesome that Thomas De Quincey offered his readers an all-purpose definition: "dinner" was "that meal, no matter when taken, which is the principal meal, i.e. the meal on which the day's support is thrown . . . in which [meat] predominates."

In 1853 *The Family Friend* counseled wives that luncheon be taken about five hours after breakfast, "to allay the cravings of nature, but not entirely to destroy the appetite." With this the magisterial arbiter Isabella Beeton agreed, instructing ladies in her *Book of Household Management*, published in 1861, that the "solidity" of luncheon "must of course in some degree be proportionate to the time it is intended to enable you to wait for your dinner and the amount of exercise you take in the meantime." And as the fashionable dinner hour grew later and later, the more important became the palliative of afternoon tea, which evolved from its origins as a polite refreshment into a virtual submeal involving tea cakes, sandwiches, and scones, and thus into an institution.

Traditional English fare and Continental cuisine, and their various manners of presentation, were also a subject of dispute. No man was a warmer advocate of the joys of the hearty English meal uncontaminated by foreign influences than Dickens, with his glowing descriptions of great beefsteaks and smoking potatoes, of flaming Christmastide plum puddings, of a board "groaning beneath the weight of fowls, fish, boiled beef . . . [and] heavy vegetables," accompanied by tankards of "the most stupendous Wiltshire beer." Generally, the meal was set before diners all at once.

But for the upper class it became the fashion in Regency times to present a dinner *à la française*—a bastard scheme in which standard English dishes high-lighted by some Frenchified dishes were served in the French manner, that is, in ordered sequence. A menu at a party for eighteen given by the Duke of Richmond in London in the 1830's offered twenty-eight dishes, ranging from lightly garnished calf's head and ramekins of cheese to such elaborate dishes as mutton cutlets with soubise sauce, cassolettes of salpicon of beef palates, lark patties with truffles, and so on, apportioned or carved at table. Much later, the modern idea of serving *à la russe* came in—joints were fully carved by stewards, arranged on platters, then formally presented in well-defined courses to each diner.

Meanwhile, perhaps chiefly as a result of Prime Minister Gladstone's relaxation of import duties on table wines in 1861, the drinking of French wines came into favor once again. Port was no longer the preferred drink of the aristocracy. No doubt their health improved. They continued to eat heartily. Prime Minister Lord Palmerston was reported by a companion at a dinner in 1865 to have consumed "two plates of turtle soup; he was then served very amply to a plate of cod and oyster sauce; he then took a pâté; afterwards he was helped to two very greasy looking entrees; he then dispatched a plate of roast mutton; there then appeared before him the largest, and to my mind the hardest, slice of ham that ever figured on the table of a nobleman, yet it disappeared, just in time to answer the inquiry of his butler, 'Snipe, my Lord, or pheasant?' He instantly replied 'Pheasant,' thus completing his ninth dish of meat at that meal." The prime minister was then eighty-one and in thriving health.

COFFEE,
TEA,
OR GIN

Three ways to hold a Chinese tea cup, demonstrated by an eighteenth-century family

Robert Wass, the Red Lion's most popular waiter, is seen in the sketch above carrying a bowl of punch, perhaps to some coffee-sated patrons. Most coffeehouses made extravagant health claims like those in the broadside below and sold tokens (below right) redeemable in coffee. The seventeenth-century painting at the right conveys the conviviality that turned customers into habitués.

The CHEAPEST & SAFEST Way of bringing forth y'ᵉ Venom of y'ᵉ Secret Disease, and Perfectly Curing it in Man or Woman, By only y'ᵉ Paris Pill, & a Balsamick Electuary, without Prejudice to the Body, or Hindrance of any Business, & that so Privately that a Friend in Bed shall not know it. The Price of a Box of the Pills is 2ˢ.⁶ᵈ and a Pot of the Electuary 1ˢ.⁶ᵈ of n'ˢ Pills and Electuary two Boxes & one Pot will be sufficient for any one not very far gone in the Distemper and Double the Number will heal the Patient if in great Extremity. Sold by I. Sherwood Book Seller at Popings aley Gate fleet street With a paper of Directions.

Seminaries of Sedition

Puritans condemned England's love of coffee as excessive and coffeehouses as dens of dalliance; Charles II saw them as centers of political dissent; tavernkeepers and vintners resented the inroads coffee made on their business; and one alarmist termed it "the black enemy of sleep and copulation." Despite these churlish demurrers, coffeehouses prospered from Dublin to Edinburgh. Drawn by the delicious aroma and an atmosphere of sobriety difficult to find elsewhere during that hard-drinking age, assorted groups of wags and intellectuals, bards and blackguards, gathered in their favorite haunts, day after day, to match wits with their peers.

The Beaten Path

Before the days of the Salvation Army, there was little organized attempt to instill temperance in the masses. At the height of the gin era in the 1740's, every fourth slum dwelling sold cheap gin; and people on the verge of starvation went to any length to secure their "Royal Poverty," defined by a contemporary lexicographer as a "nickname for the liquor called geneva. . . . When beggars are drunk they are as great as kings."

William Hogarth, whose "Gin Lane" appears above, was one of the few to realize the dangers of the gin craze and to pressure Parliament into passing the "Tippling Act" of 1751 which taxed and checked the illicit sale of liquor. Here, drink has drained the energy of the underfed populace, and the pawnbroker alone does a thriving trade. While one woman pours a shot of the potent pacifier down her baby's throat, another neglected child plunges to his death. To entice the people back to the fold, Hogarth advocated beer as a more healthful drink. In "Beer Street," opposite, prosperous cockney laborers pause for a tankard of "that invigorating liquor" and some good-natured banter. As two fishwomen read a ballad about herring, a blacksmith displays his strength. Even the sign painter is likely to be rewarded with the Barley Mow's brew.

321

The Beefeaters

"I eat like a very Turk, or rather indeed like a very John Bull, whose supreme joy is good beef," Boswell confided to his diary. Beef was not only a joy; it was the essence of inviolable English tradition, prompting Henry Fielding to quote a patriotic song in its praise. One verse ran: "Then, Britons, from all nice dainties refrain, Which effeminate Italy, France, and Spain; And mighty roast beef shall command on the main." At right, Hogarth's "Calais Gate" takes another swipe at food across the Channel. A cook returns from the docks with a juicy side of beef, imported by a Calais hotel catering to English travelers, but not before the soup-eating soldiers have cast a lean and hungry look his way and the friar has given the meat a covetous poke. The cartoon above draws a comparison between food prices and wages, indicating that to a laborer in 1795 symbols of plenty had a hollow ring.

Cucumbers by the cartload

Oysters on the half shell

Sweet milk, sweeter words

Hot cross buns in season

Casseroles from the baker

Cherries for cheer

Alive, Alive, Oh!

By 1850 thirteen thousand hawkers were doing a brisk trade in London's streets. Some sold pies, sausages, breads, and other foods that were literally "homemade" in neighborhood cookshops and houses. Other vendors resold at small profit produce bought at outlying farms or at one of a dozen entrepôts like Billingsgate Fish Market above. Though anyone was free to buy from these cheaper markets, stalls were so filthy and smells so bad that customers risked "carrying home the shop-bill upon their clothes," as one veteran complained. Haggling on one's own doorstep, to judge from Thomas Rowlandson's scenes opposite, was a far more pleasant exchange.

"Prince of Whales"

This 1792 sketch by the caricaturist James Gillray, entitled, "A Voluptuary Under the Horrors of Digestion," is actually a picture of the future George IV at table. It is not difficult to understand why contemporary satirists referred to him as a fat Adonis and the Prince of Whales.

The prince regent who became George IV was a prodigious drinker, eater, and whoremonger; he was also able to find time to spend the state's money building and rebuilding various residences. His greatest extravaganza was Brighton Pavilion, an Oriental pleasure palace that was the scene of activities as unorthodox as the decor. The prince conducted drinking bouts from which no man could easily excuse himself; female guests fulfilled their roles, in part, by supporting the swaying sovereign on the dance floor, pretending the while that it was they who had overindulged. As befitted a man of his interests, George gave Brighton's kitchen (below opposite) special attention. Not only did it carry on the decorative themes of the grand dining room (above); it was adequately equipped to serve hundreds. Its facilities comprised a veritable showcase of the latest cooking gear: "contrivances for roasting, boiling, baking, stewing, frying, steaming, and heating; hot plates, hot closets, hot air, and hot hearths." In 1816 the regent persuaded Carême to preside over the belowstairs wonderland, but the famous French chef left within eight months. He confided to an English lady that "the tastes of his royal majesty were too bourgeois." George, however, knew what he liked—and usually got it. In later years, when he was so corpulent he had to be lowered onto his horse by a machine, and a specially tailored coat failed to hide the well-corseted royal paunch, George IV, publicly exposed, abandoned Brighton.

The Norfolk coach speeding toward London with a cargo of fresh-killed geese and turkeys

A merry throng of shoppers converging on the baker's for traditional Twelfth Night cakes

Four generations of a family finishing their second gigantic Christmas meal of the day

Twelve Days of Christmas

Victorian sentimentality swelled to a climax during the Christmas season; apparently, the only way Englishmen could stop choking on the lumps in their throats was to keep eating and drinking. The season traditionally began with a plump bird and a plum pudding, the latter steamed to a soggy deliciousness in a huge cauldron like that pictured above. Artist Robert Seymour's cook presumably worked for a household where the merriment lasted a full twelve wassailing days, but even the likes of Bob Cratchit could look forward to at least one memorable meal. As Dickens described the occasion, "There never was such a goose. . . . Its tenderness and flavor, size and cheapness, were the themes of universal admiration. Eked out by apple-sauce and mashed potatoes, it was a sufficient dinner for the whole family." At the climactic moment, Mrs. Cratchit brought forth the pudding, "like a speckled cannon-ball, so hard and firm, blazing [with] ignited brandy. . . . O, a wonderful pudding!" As the century wore on, many families added tree decorating (a custom imported with the German Prince Albert) to the agenda. The decorations of gingerbread and bonbons were almost a meal in themselves.

The Breakfast Habit

Melton Mowbray in Leicestershire is renowned for its Stilton cheese, pork pies, and most especially its fox hunting, all in a day's pleasure for the gentlemen above. The engraving, after a painting by Sir Francis Grant, records a hunt breakfast held in 1839 at one of the district's many estates, and the morning meal which they have just finished is a traditionally sumptuous if leisurely preparation for a brisk ride to hounds. While a late-comer is served, the others are free to read the paper, scribble a few lines, or just wait impatiently.

Servants and Serviettes

To many Victorians nothing was more important than gentility, even if achieving it meant being vulgar. One way to be considered genteel was to entertain on a scale more lavish than one could afford. Only the very rich could muster the large corps of waiters necessary for a dinner party from their own household staffs. The others did what William Thackeray confessed to in an essay on dinner-giving snobs: "[I] hire sham butlers and attendants; have a fellow going round the table with still and dry Champagne, as if I knew his name, and it was my custom to drink those wines every day of my life." The properly ostentatious Victorian (whose elegant dinner is about to be enjoyed, above) also served more dishes than any normal guest could sample. It was considered fair to spirit away an untouched platter after only a slight pause, thereby preserving it for the admiration of the next night's crowd. But a good player like Thackeray's dining-out snob could easily out-maneuver his host: "Whenever, for my part, I see the head man particularly anxious to escamoter [take away] a *fricandeau* or a *blancmange* I always call out, and insist on massacring it with a spoon." A third important element of a dinner party was table decoration. A much-sought-after accomplishment in a housemaid was the ability to fold napkins into fanciful shapes, but as such a talent was not to be found just anywhere, there were many manuals of instruction in the art. A page of directions for the "Rose and Star," surrounded by several completed creations such as a double horn of plenty, slippers, and an archbishop's miter, is shown opposite.

1.—Lay the Serviette flat on the table, and fold at the dotted lines so that the corners (A A A A) meet at centre spot.

2.—Without turning the Serviette, fold the corners down again in the same manner.

3.—And repeat again.

4.—Now turn the Serviette over on to the plain side.

5.—Fold at the lines so that the corners (B B B B) meet at the centre.

6.—Hold a tumbler firmly on the Serviette at the dotted circle.

7.—Pull each of the points away from underneath.

8.—Complete.

BEETON, *Book of Household Management*, 1909 ED.

As the Queen Went, So Went the Nation

HER MAJESTY'S
DINNER
THURSDAY 27ᵀᴴ APRIL·1882·

A LA TORTUE.   AU PRINTANIER
Potages.
A LA CRÈME D'ORGES
Poissons
LE SAUMON, SAUCE HOMARD ET PERSIL
LES FILETS DE SOLES FRITS
Entrées
LES RISSOLLES À LA D'ARTOIS
LES CÔTELETTES D'AGNEAU AUX HARICOTS VERTS
LES SUPRÊMES DE VOLAILLE AUX POIS
LES FILETS DE BOEUF À LA FINANCIÈRE
Relevés
ROAST BEEF   ROAST MUTTON
HAUNCHES OF VENISON
Rôts
LES POULETS GRAS   LES CAILLES BARDÉES
Entremets
LES ASPERGES À LA SAUCE
LES ESCALOPES DE FOIES GRAS À L'ASPIC
LA GELÉE AU VIN DE CHAMPAGNE
LES CHOUX GLACÉS À LA DUCHESSE
Relevé
LES BAVARINS AU CURAÇAO SAUCE ABRICOT

REPRODUCED BY GRACIOUS PERMISSION OF HER MAJESTY QUEEN ELIZABETH II

Though a few English gourmets of the Victorian era were advocating one dish per course, state banquets continued to offer a wide selection of dishes, each as dull as the next. Among the unexotic choices on the wedding menu above are fried sole, lamb chops, and chicken livers.

The thoroughly bourgeois morals and tastes of grandmotherly Queen Victoria quite naturally were adopted by the hordes of new-rich Englishmen who had no taste at all. Her majesty sponsored the 1851 show at the Crystal Palace, where table implements like the cream ladle and fish fork, below, and furnishings of the same ilk were displayed. A catalog of the Exhibition burbled that such items ideally suited "the taste . . . and domestic refinement of those classes [for whose] use the articles were manufactured." It is not surprising, therefore, that the tables of parvenus all over England were soon writhing with silver and glass. Victorian interest in the appearance of things lapped over into the kitchen, too, producing such follies as the cake opposite, which graced the bridal table of Victoria's grandson George. Wine, however, did not flow freely at the queen's table, and after-dinner port sessions were cut short, for she objected to the bibulous and bawdy. As if to make up for it, she insisted that no one leave the table hungry. Her subjects, noting the royal behavior and waistline, dutifully overate for Crown and country.

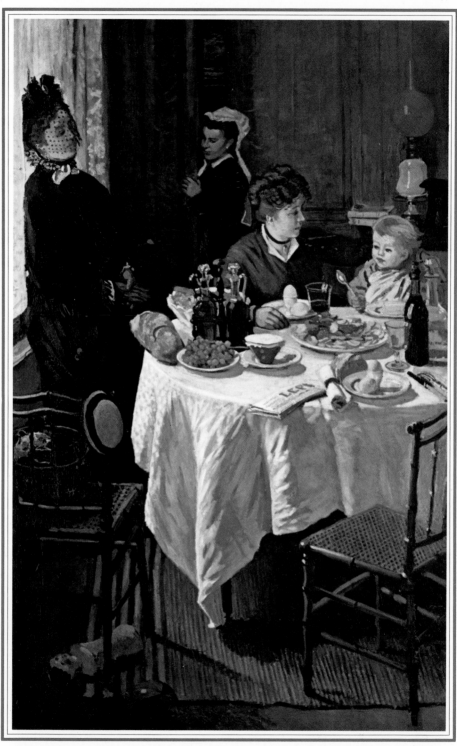

The midday meal, affectionately portrayed by the head of the household, Claude Monet, in 1868

TOWARD
AN
INTERNATIONAL
STYLE

Two men of plebeian origin, born within four years of each other in obscure Alpine villages, rose in the last decades of the nineteenth century to become all but sovereign arbiters of the privileged tables of Europe. The society into which they climbed stood at its zenith of regal splendor. Yet no one sought to bar their ascent. Georges Auguste Escoffier, born in 1846, the son of a blacksmith in Villeneuve-Loubet in Provence, and César Ritz, born in 1850, the thirteenth child of a Swiss peasant couple in Niederwald near the Simplon pass, ruled together like the royalty and millionaires to whom they ministered.

Their arrival on the scene in the 1880's was well timed. The fashionable world was beginning to lose its old ingrown exclusivity and was bursting with new money, with new personalities who found Queen Victoria staid and Emperor Franz Josef stuffy, and with a craving for new pleasures and sensations. To all this the ambitious duet of Escoffier and Ritz was remarkably attuned. Quitting smithy and farm, they had both commenced their careers at a very young age (the thirteen-year-old Escoffier as a scullion in his uncle's restaurant in nearby Nice, the fifteen-year-old Ritz as an apprentice wine steward in a hostelry in neighboring Brig). Both soon gravitated to Paris, Escoffier to become the *saucier* at the smart Restaurant du Petit Moulin, and Ritz to rise from

Auguste Escoffier

assistant waiter to *maître d'hôtel* at a series of restaurants. When at length Ritz invited Escoffier to become chef of the Grand Hotel at Monte Carlo, of which he was then manager, both were men of proven brilliance.

Escoffier, a culinary innovator of the first order, was out to do nothing less than revolutionize the whole scheme of French cookery. Ritz, for his part, was the first great entrepreneur of the fashionable hotel and resort. Over the years he extended his operations from Monte Carlo, Baden-Baden, and San Remo to London's Savoy, Carlton, and Ritz hotels. He operated additional establishments in Frankfort, Biarritz, Rome, Palermo, Madrid, Johannesburg, and

Cairo. Unlike Vatel or Carême, neither Ritz nor Escoffier ever took service in the household of a great lord. They served a select public who came to them. Taste makers of genius, both were inveterate showmen and impresarios, with all the verve of *arrivistes* and a high degree of acquired snobbery.

The era upon which Frenchmen, glowing with memories, were eventually to bestow the name *la belle époque*, was one of constant movement both in the social and geographic senses. Luxurious railroad transportation played an increasing role, enabling leisure classes to pursue more readily the cycle of the seasons, traveling across Europe from resort to resort with their servants and mountains of luggage. The list of fashionable watering places extended from Ostend and Aix-les-Bains to Hamburg and Karlsbad. Russian grand dukes arrived from distant estates in *wagons-lits* to meet with maharajas and South American cattle magnates at the tables of Monte Carlo. The Prince of Wales, the future King Edward VII and for decades Europe's biggest glass of fashion, regularly visited Biarritz, Marienbad, and Baden-Baden, and in doing so made them especially prestigious in international society. (His professed objective, like that of other frequenters of spas, was to take what was called the "cure"" to remedy the effects of too much good eating—which, however, did not interfere with his having a five-course luncheon, afternoon tea, and a seven-course dinner, with intermediate "snacks."

In Paris, as the turn of the century approached, the *Grande Saison*, or social high season, commenced ten days after

Easter and ended with the running of the Grand Prix in mid-June, after which the gentry dispersed to the seaside or the mountains. In the fall there were hunting parties at châteaux, followed in December by a *Petite Saison* of formal dinners, opera, theater, and balls in town, ending in late winter, when it was time to sojourn to the French Riviera. In England the high season began early in May, with Ascot Sunday in June, after which came the Henley boat races on the Thames. The season ended in August with the Cowes Regatta of the Royal Yacht Squadron—so brilliant under Edward's reign that the waters of the Solent might be crowded with such tall-masted yachts as the king's *Victoria and Albert* (accompanied by a battleship), Czar Nicholas' *Standart*, Kaiser Wilhelm's *Hohenzollern*, Alfonso of Spain's *Hispania*, and J. P. Morgan's *Corsair*. After banquets afloat and fireworks, lines of festooned gigs brought guests back to shore. The next thing to do was to shoot grouse in Scotland or possibly visit the Swiss lakes and mountains.

In Austria, as soon as the aging Emperor Franz Josef had closed the season's formalities at Schönbrunn palace in Vienna and retreated to his hunting lodge at Bad Ischl, the aristocracy withdrew to livelier playgrounds. (A dinner at Schönbrunn was a quite excruciating affair: several hundred places might be set, with a footman assigned to each guest, but the first person served was of course the emperor, who ate sparingly and with extraordinary rapidity. Etiquette required that the moment he had finished a course, all others suspended any further eating, with the result that many never got so much as a morsel. It was common practice in Vienna, when invited to the imperial table, to fortify one's self with a substantial dinner at Sacher's in advance.)

In England the mobility of the era showed itself in the quite sudden love affair with the grand hotel and restaurant. Until the 1880's there had been no restaurants of respectable standing in London, and none of good table other than the

César Ritz

noisy Café Royal in Regent Street; and this, owned by a Frenchman, was long patronized almost entirely by *émigrés* and visitors from the Continent. A few places such as Romano's in the Strand catered to journalists, women of "the lighter stage," and bohemian types. Kettners' nearby had numerous private dining rooms whose uses—like those in the old taverns—were notorious. But restaurants and hotels were not for the English gentry when on home ground, so it was thought. Gentlemen would not emerge from their clubs, nor ladies from their town houses, to be seen dining in public.

Yet in the 1880's Richard D'Oyly Carte, the London theatrical promoter who had enriched himself by producing Gilbert

A Gourmet's Guide

*T*he first automobile drivers were genuine adventurers, wandering where their cars would take them, daring breakdown and washout, innless nights and restaurantless days. Gradually, automobiling became a tamer sport, and in 1900 André Michelin, a French tire manufacturer, seized the opportunity to pump up good will for his product by publishing a directory of lodgings, gas stations, and repair shops throughout France. Today's annual *Guide Michelin*, some thousand pages bristling with a formidable array of symbols, blocks of text, and maps, has exactly the same goal as the first one—to provide any practical information that might contribute to the success of a trip. To restaurateurs and many of the guide's readers, the book has come to represent something else. It is the supreme judge of the quality of food served in French restaurants, and many people who purchase it are interested only in its culinary pronouncements. At present Michelin has eleven inspectors who are bona fide gourmets and connoisseurs of fine wines. The man from Michelin arrives unannounced and eats thoughtfully, comparing what he finds with last year's rating (although to avoid identification no one man appears in the same place more than once every eight years). He makes mental notes about the setting and decor, the men's room and the table linen, and is especially critical about the service. He then presents himself to the horror-stricken owner (who is often the chef too) and asks to be shown around the kitchen. The guide has

some hundred thousand correspondents a year, classified by Michelin's editors as *sympathique*, *hépathique* (jaundiced), or *fléchi* (thoughtful); if there are many complaints about the restaurant on trial, the inspector discusses them and perhaps makes suggestions for improvements, but never until the guide comes out will the anxious *propriétaire* learn what his new rating is. One qualification for an inspector is an iron stomach, for whatever his personal inclinations, professionally he must seek out and try dining rooms with meals for under $2 as often as he inspects the very expensive ones. Small owners therefore get the benefit of expert advice, too, and consequently so do drivers of *deux cheveaux*. Restaurants are rated as to the level of luxury; more important to gourmets are the stars (like those worn above by the bulbous tiremen used to illustrate the book) rating culinary excellence. No place can win more than three stars, and only twelve kitchens in France can now claim that distinction.

and Sullivan operettas at the Savoy Theatre, conceived the daring idea of building a luxury hotel next door as a haven for his patrons. While in the process of planning his new project and taking a "cure" in Baden-Baden, he was struck by the magnetism of César Ritz, presiding there at his own restaurant and hotel together with Escoffier. If these men could command the praise of the English aristocracy abroad, D'Oyly Carte would engage them in London. His Savoy became the first hotel in Europe to offer modern comforts; it boasted seventy bathrooms (the Savoy's closest rival had four bathrooms for five hundred guests) and a restaurant on a really *grand luxe* style. A new day of London fashion had begun.

Ritz, a perfectionist even in his personal attire, would answer the private bell that warned of the arrival of royalty by placing a fresh white carnation in the buttonhole of his frock coat or evening tails on the way to the lobby. He was the master of protocol, of seating, of housekeeping, of every detail. Did Grand Duke Sergei prefer his turbot prepared in a certain way? It would be done. Did Lady so-and-so fancy a particular size of bed? It would be provided. Lighting was staged in tints to set off ladies' complexions and jewels to best advantage. Dinner music, another Ritz innovation, had to be of the best— on occasion, Johann Strauss the younger was engaged to lead his own Viennese orchestra—and evening dress, if one expected to be seated in the great dining salon rather than in the accompanying grillroom, was *de rigueur*.

The bold scheme worked. Soon such fashionable hostesses as the Duchess of Manchester, Lady Randolph Churchill (mother of Sir Winston), Lady Dudley, and the American heiress and Duchess of Marlborough, Consuelo Vanderbilt, were giving style-setting dinner parties at Ritz' Savoy. Backstage, Escoffier displayed wit and genius sometimes compounded with mischief. On one occasion he served the middle-aged, sybaritic Prince of Wales a creation mysteriously and invitingly called *Cuisses de Nymphes à l'Aurore*, "Nymphs' Thighs at Dawn." The future Edward VII savored it and then learned that what he was eating for the first time was frogs' legs. On another occasion, Escoffier was coaxed from his kitchens at the Savoy to the galleys of the recently launched Hamburg-America luxury liner the *Imperator*, where he produced for Kaiser Wilhelm II a phenomenal creation of salmon steamed in champagne. "How can I repay you?" asked the emperor, summoning the chef into his presence. "By giving us back Alsace-Lorraine" was Escoffier's reply.

Escoffier's basic scheme, with which he liked to regale those not simply bent on stuffing themselves, was to construct a dinner somewhat like a symphony of contrasting movements yet with a related theme. Soups, he said, should perform like "an overture in a light opera [divulging] what is to be the dominant phrase of the melody throughout." Each diner, like the listener at a concert, was to experience the same progression. Escoffier was the first to take seriously the precept pronounced by Brillat-Savarin, namely that "The order of food in a dinner is from the more substantial to the lighter." He popularized the new style of service, *à la russe*, rebelling against the tradition in which all the entrees were put on the table at once. In place of vast centerpieces of game, of forty or more simultaneous entrees and entremets, he introduced rhythm, if not restraint.

A dinner prepared by Edward's own chef at Buckingham Palace in 1902 showed the Escoffier influence, though it lacked the refinements of the master. A rather heavy sequence of hot and cold consommés was followed by fillets of trout or whitebait, quail and chicken, then mutton and ham garnished with vegetables, followed by ortolans and salad, succeeded by asparagus vinaigrette, and a dessert course including *"gâteau Punch,"* a sweet soufflé, pastries, and, inexplicably, canapés of anchovies. A progression of Escoffier's own making tended to be more subtle. Thus, the menu he offered at Ritz' Carlton Hotel to celebrate the coronation of George V in 1911 deserves to be given in full:

Caviar
Cantaloupe

Clear Turtle Soup
Cold Velouté of Chicken Soup

Roast Chicken George V

Saddle of Welsh Lamb
Peas à l'Anglaise

Duckling Breasts in Port Wine Aspic

Quail with Grapes

Salade Orientale
Hearts of Artichokes Grand Duc

Peaches Queen Mary
Petits Fours
Fruits

Such a dinner, with its graceful overtures and its *pièce de résistance*, the quail, rep-

resented the climax of the most polished Escoffier cuisine. Glancing over the menu today, a diner might wonder whether after the soups, the chicken, and the lamb, he might really wish to go on to a round of jellied duck and quail with grapes. But there was always respite in a change of wines—Escoffier and Ritz did their best to promote dry clarets, Burgundies, and champagnes, while discouraging that old mid-prandial palliative, sherbet.

The upper-class English, encouraged by men like Ritz and Escoffier, were rapidly becoming leading consumers of fine French wines. Another dinner served at Buckingham Palace early in Edward's reign was accompanied by an old Madeira of 1816 with the soup, a Johannisberger of 1886 as the "hock" to go with the fish, magnums of 1884 Möet et Chandon champagne with the fowl, a Chambertin of the great year 1875 with the venison, a Château Latour of the same year with asparagus with mousseline sauce, and, for good measure, a Château Margaux of 1871 in addition to the usual after-dinner port, sherry, and heirloom brandy.

None was a finer judge of wines than George Saintsbury, the renowned scholar of English literature at Edinburgh, who amid his major literary treatises wrote *Notes on a Cellar-Book*, describing his delight in "laying-down" on a scholar's pay racks of the great clarets of 1858, "not very plentiful, and getting a trifle old," of 1864, "in perfection, but very dear," and of 1874 and 1875, "drinkable at forty years old [but] always what wine-slang calls 'dumb.' " (The ruinous Phylloxera disease blighted French growths for several decades following.) Saintsbury was against the emerging vogue of the pre-dinner cocktail, and of whisky and soda, although he liked a tot straight on occasion. He was to grow ripe in years, dying at eighty-eight, leaving the jot-

Short-order staff, Paris, c. 1870

tings of his *Notes* as a classic of English response to French attraction.

While Continental cookery, hotelkeeping, and fine wines invaded England, English styles and manners captivated the *gratin*, or upper crust, of France. Paris *boulevardiers'* clothes were patterned on those of Savile Row, garden parties and five o'clock tea were introduced in the Faubourg St-Germain, and the English country house party was copied in ancient châteaux. Parisian sporting fellows aspired to membership among *les clubmen*—banded together at such English-style clubs as the Jockey or Royale.

Yet Parisian life retained its own particular flavor, though this too was fast changing. The *belle époque* saw the *grande cocotte* graduate from a playgirl or a *chanteuse* performing at the Folies-Bergère or the Bal Tabarin to a dashing beauty kept by princes, magnates, or foreign potentates. Flashing with diamonds and trailing ermine or chinchilla, she often swept into Maxim's on the Rue Royale for late supper. The most gorgeous and desirable of these creatures—*les grandes horizontales*—took on spurious, aristocratic names as they rose to fame, such as Liane de Pougy, Emilienne d'Alençon, Cléo de Mérode, and Clémence de Pibrac, though this fooled nobody. Wealthy Russian nobles were particular habitués at the supper tables of Maxim's. There they could find a favorite to make the all-night "Tour of the Grand Dukes," or round of cabarets. Spectacular parties were frequent; at one the Grand Duke Sergei of Russia presented the *horizontale* Augustine de Lierre with a twenty-million-franc pearl necklace served on a bed of oysters. One bold entertainer of men who declined to adapt her name to fit Europe's social register was the devastating Catalonian gypsy known as *"la belle Otéro,"* adept at jumping on the tables of Maxim's to perform a wild fandango. Otéro, who made millions only to lose them all at the gambling tables, reached such notoriety that when she was found seated at the Comédie Francaise on an evening also honored by the Russian czar's presence, she was smartly ejected, shouting to the royal box as she left the theater, "I'll never eat caviar again!"

Maxim's was the liveliest dining place in France and perhaps the world, and one never took his wife there. Hugo, the *maître d'hôtel*, kept a discreet notebook for leading guests. It contained the names of the chief *horizontales* known to the establishment, and some notations

343

in code as to their current availability. One was "R.A.F.," meaning *rien à faire*, in other words, "occupied." Another rating was "Y.M.C.A.," which, far from implying any connection with a young men's Christian association, signified *Y a moyen de coucher avec*—or "highly cooperative."

Paris society was divided into numerous circles, the old, the newly rich, the decadent, the international, the anti-Dreyfus, and pro-Dreyfus. (In many houses that sought to keep dinner-table peace at the height of the furor, a sign was posted like a centerpiece, *"Ici on ne parle pas de l'Affaire."*) No hostess was more imperious than Madame Aubernon, who at her twice-weekly intellectual evenings jingled a large silver bell to gain the company's full attention. No host was more eccentric than the perfumed Comte Robert de Montesquiou (a model for the Baron Charlus of Marcel Proust's novel). On one occasion he gave a soiree in a darkened room suffused with exotic essences. All eyes were focused on a live turtle, its shell encrusted with diamonds, sapphires, and amethysts, that crawled among the diners. For another evening he sent out engraved cards inviting his elite friends to the christening of his cat.

But even Montesquiou was no match for the flamboyant Comte Boni de Castellane. By marrying Anna Gould, the very plain daughter of the American millionaire Jay Gould, Comte Boni gained a dowry of fifteen million dollars. He ran through her money fast, building his fantastic Palais Rose in Paris on royal, seventeenth century proportions, and at his château keeping six hundred servants in

livery to match the changing decor. For Anna's twenty-first birthday he staged a fete that among other embellishments called for 80,000 Venetian lanterns, an orchestra of 200 musicians, the complete *corps de ballet* of the Opéra, 15 kilometers

Detail from a menu sketched by Renoir

of red velvet carpeting, and 600 torches carried by lackeys in scarlet livery.

It was a great epoch for all those with bank accounts. The *demi-monde* had long been following the *haut monde* from resort to resort, often with the result of raised lorgnettes on the part of dowager duchesses. But by now all circles, from the aristocrats to the *horizontales*, were beginning to mix. In the daily morning drive in the Bois de Boulogne, the Barons Rothschild, the Aga Khan, Prince Galitzine, and Leopold II of Belgium might be found taking the air almost in tandem with the writers Edmond Rostand and Colette, and with Liane de Pougy, Cléo de Mérode, and *"la belle Otéro."* At Ritz' loftiest international establishment, the hotel that bears his name at 15 Place Vendôme, the guests regularly included, along with an array of lords and ladies, the highest-priced courtesans of the town.

Ritz and Escoffier had taken leave of the Savoy, after a falling-out with its directors, when in 1905 the Wall Street financier George Kessler staged there his startling "gondola dinner." At a cost of £4,000, the equivalent of $20,000, he had the Savoy's courtyard flooded, and the walls decorated with depictions of St. Mark's, the Doges' Palace, and other well-known Venetian landmarks; he hired Enrico Caruso to serenade his two dozen guests who were afloat in a gondola under huge representations of the Lions of St. Mark's in ice. Nor did Ritz and Escoffier have anything to do with another affair given at the Savoy before the curtain of 1914 fell, a "blowout" at which a man who had broken the bank at Monte Carlo in a series of plays on red at the roulette table ordered a massive feast, all in red. The very lights and hangings of the restaurant were changed to red, the waiters were all costumed in red, down to their gloves; and the thirty-six guests were served only red dishes, including lobster, rare beef, wild duck in Bordeaux, red cabbage, beet salad, a mousse of strawberries, red wines, and so forth, on a red and black tablecloth that was designed as a huge roulette board. Ritz and Escoffier would have thought this was going rather far.

Such was one side of life on the eve of World War I. At the other extreme was the life of the everyday workingman, who in Britain, the most industrialized and prosperous of the European nations, was reported in 1913 as earning an average wage of only about twenty shillings (somewhat below five dollars) a week. "How does a working man's wife bring up a family on 20s. a week?" asked the author of an angry tract; "Assuming that there are four children, and that it costs 4s. a week to feed a child, there would be but 4s. left on which to feed both parents. . . ." Many families subsisted almost entirely on bread and tea,

and one study of the situation in York found that infant mortality in the poorest class was running to 247 per thousand. As James Laver writes in his *Manners and Morals in The Age of Optimism, 1848–1914*, "Perhaps the most shocking thing . . . was the complacency with which this state of affairs was accepted. When some poor old woman died of starvation in an East End attic the verdict of the coroner was 'self-neglect.'"

Still, the position of the working class was not entirely bleak. A 1904 official study found that on an average weekly family income of thirty-six shillings there was an outlay of twenty-two shillings for food, the biggest item by far being meat, followed by vegetables and fruit, cheese, bread and flour, butter, and fresh milk—a great change for the better in terms of

Advertisement for a bourgeois cookbook, c. 1850

proteins over the predominantly carbohydrate diet of Corn Law times. This improvement, gradual as it was, reflected a subtly changing economic balance.

The overriding factor was the "population explosion"—herald of the explosions to come in Asia—which between 1800 and 1900 doubled the number of Europe's inhabitants. Emigration, chiefly to the Americas, under stress of hunger, politics, and economic aspiration, drew off a part of this, but the Old World was confronted with a huge increase in mouths to feed. Fortunately, this burst of population was matched by a vast increase in industry and in food production. As cities became factories, so agricultural producers found new and larger markets for their foodstuffs. Farm machinery raised crop yields on both continents (the Americans McCormick and Hussey had first shown their grain reapers abroad at the London Great Exhibition of 1851). New chemical fertilizers succeeded the

Soup-to-nuts service by the ideal waiter

less productive organic fertilizers. Plant and animal breeding had become a science. European migrants were opening up vast new areas of land in the Americas, South Africa, Australia, and New Zealand to farming and livestock.

Long-distance rail and sea transport helped to revolutionize Western man's daily diet, especially when coupled with a new technology of food preservation. The ancients knew that cooling a food served to postpone decay, and the ever-curious Francis Bacon, ruminating on this point, had experimented with freez-

ing early in the seventeenth century. And, around 1795, the Frenchman François Appert had limited success "canning" foods, subjecting them to very high temperatures and storing them in sterilized glass jars for as long as three months. Yet, as we have seen, common preservation methods were long confined to sun-drying, smoking, salting, pickling, preserving in sugar, and fermenting, with all the loss or distortion of flavor and food values these processes entailed. Beginning in the mid-nineteenth century, however, a great breakthrough occurred. Men as various as the experimental dairyman Gail Borden of Litchfield, Connecticut, the meatpackers Gustavus Swift and Philip Armour of Chicago, the German food processer Baron Justus von Leibig, and the great French bacteriologist Louis Pasteur figured in it. The problem of getting fresh milk to growing urban markets before it spoiled had long defeated dairymen. By 1865, though, some refrigerated milk was reaching London by train, and experiments were under way in France to build ammonia-cooling plants. Nine years before, Borden had obtained a United States patent for a "fresh country milk from which the water is nearly all evaporated and nothing added"—a condensation of milk that was pure, economical, and readily transported. (Pasteur was then conducting studies on the sterilization of milk.)

Meanwhile in the 1860's, the meat-packing industry was established in Chicago, where fattened Western cattle met several Eastern railheads. With the development of freezer freight cars in the next decade, the industry was able to supply Europe with beef from the Western plains and pork products from the Iowa corn country. In 1877 the first frozen mutton was successfully shipped from Buenos Aires to Le Havre. Due to a collision, the voyage took six months, but the meat arrived in good condition. Meat from Australia and New Zealand began reaching England soon thereafter. As one of the major shippers there remarked, "Where the food is the people are not, and where the people are the food is not. It is however . . . within the power of man to adjust these things." A *Daily Telegraph* reporter marveled in 1880 that the

Automated dining for the weary

imports could not "by any peculiarity . . . be distinguished from freshly killed English meat."

In 1863 Baron Haussmann, as part of his grand plan for transforming Paris into a metropolis able to serve the increasing population, had designed the central, hygienic slaughterhouse of La Villette. Pasteur, by developing a method of inoculating sheep and hogs against the dread disease anthrax, vastly improved the practice of animal husbandry as well as public health. Inoculation of cattle, scientific dressing and process-

ing, factory canning of a growing list of products, pasteurizing of milk—all these processes changed the whole configuration of supply from the old days of small, filthy market stalls and dependence on the latest wagon or boatload of what the nearest fields or fisheries had to offer. Underdeveloped nations of Latin America, the Middle East, Africa, and the Orient did not—and in large measure still do not—participate in these advances, a fact which made their own population explosions the more critical.

Along with new methods of food production, handling, and distribution in the West, there also came into being the gradual mechanization of the household. This, too, had its profound effects on food customs, and ultimately on the structure of social life. Until about 1830, cooking throughout Europe had depended on the age-old open hearth and the wood-fired oven—cumbersome installations demanding an immense amount of arduous labor. All was well so long as labor was accessible and cheap. Then came the "red-hot monster," as Dickens called it, the iron range, with its more compact and efficient utilization of wood or coal fuel. An even greater labor-saver, a crude version of the gas range, had been patented at the beginning of the nineteenth century, and an improved model was shown at the Great Exhibition of 1851, but except in hotels, it did not come into use until the 1880's when coal gas became widely available. In place of laying fires and cleaning out clinkers, all one had to do then was turn a handle. The next step was the electric range, first shown in London in 1891. Domestic refrigera-

347

Miss Toklas and Company

*T*he late Alice B. Toklas may not have been the finest chef ever to wield a spatula, but she certainly fed the most interesting collection of diners of her day. As cohostess of Gertrude Stein's Paris salon in the first decades of the 1900's, Miss Toklas met almost every great and potentially great artist and writer of the modern movement. Dancers, critics, royalty, and Iowans also appeared at the door on Rue de Fleurus, hoping to be invited to one of the celebrated dinners. Between callers, she gathered notes for *The Alice B. Toklas Cook Book*, which became as much a collection of anecdotes and musings about her famous friends as of recipes; it was written in a witty and crisp style that makes it far more widely read today than the brilliant, arcane works of Miss Stein. Miss Toklas' recipes were often as eccentric as her appearance—the sketch below by Roger Baker captures the peculiar integrity of his friend. A recipe for hashish fudge suggests just how wicked the maiden lady could be. Except for telling the reader where to buy the forbidden ingredient, her directions for making fudge are as precise as anyone could wish, but there are other recipes as impressionistic as *Bass for Picasso*. "Before coming to Paris I was interested in food but not in doing any cooking. When in 1908 I went to

live with Gertrude Stein . . . she said we would have American food for Sunday evening supper . . . the servant would be out and I should have the kitchen to myself. So I commenced to cook the simple dishes [of] California. . . . My repertoire . . . expanded as I grew experimental and adventurous. One day when Picasso was to lunch with us I decorated a fish in a way that I thought would amuse him. I chose a fine striped bass and cooked it according to a theory of my grandmother who had no experience in cooking. . . . She contended that a fish . . . once caught, should have no further contact with the element in which it had been born and raised. She recommended that it be roasted or poached in wine or cream or butter. . . . I covered the fish with an ordinary mayonnaise and, using a pastry tube, decorated it with a red mayonnaise, not colored with catsup—horror of horrors—but with tomato paste. Then I made a design with sieved hard-boiled eggs, the whites and the yolks apart, with truffles and finely chopped *fines herbes*. . . . when it was served Picasso exclaimed at its beauty. But, said he, should it not rather have been in honour of Matisse than of me."

tion, another boon, had appeared in the 1860's, as had first attempts at a mechanical dishwasher—an indication that there was already a "servant problem."

At the country house of Longleat, seat of the Marquesses of Bath, the normal complement of indoor staff at the turn of the century ran to forty-three, from house steward and housekeeper down to lamp boy. At Chatsworth, the 273-room palace of the Dukes of Devonshire, the entire house staff ran to a hundred or more shortly after World War I. The wage of a good butler or cook in London in those years appears to have averaged £50 annually—in addition to which there was, of course, room, board, and such "fringe benefits" as guests' tips, kickbacks from suppliers, accepted access to the ale and wine in the master's cellar. All this soon changed. New York's lofty Mrs. Hamilton McK. Twombly, daughter of William H. Vanderbilt and granddaughter of Cornelius, the former ferryboat owner who had become a railroad magnate, was one of those to upset the pattern when in 1917 she hired the Escoffier-trained Joseph Donon to be chef of her mansions at a salary rumored at $25,000. By the 1920's a highly trained cook or butler in a well-to-do private house on either side of the Atlantic could command a salary many times that paid before 1914—too much, it soon appeared, for all but the most prosperous. The between-wars generation needed and wanted to rid itself of the tyranny of the servant. The triumphant end result in America was the technocratic, all but servantless house, its kitchen processes simplified by blenders, mixers, pressure cookers, and automatic cooking controls, its staple foods duly packaged, branded, and often premixed or precooked by great corporations with their own dietitians and recipe writers, and the family's food reserve from the supermarket laid down safe and sound for months to come in the arctic recesses of the freezer.

The proprietor and chef of one of the most prestigious restaurants of recent decades, Alexandre Dumaine of the Hôtel de la Côte-d'Or in Saulieu, France, remarked to a visiting American gastronome one day that "Frozen food is dead food," and took his guest along to watch him carefully test and buy only the freshest and finest of produce in the local market to prepare for that day's luncheon. Another great French *cuisinier*, the late Fernand Point, worked in the same fashion, searching for perfection from stall to stall and from one *vignoble* to the next for his restaurant, La Pyramide, in Vienne, where an air of intimacy quite removed from the flamboyance of Ritz and Escoffier prevailed. These men were the ultimate refiners. Nothing, according to the skilled taster Joseph Wechsberg, was ever quite so perfect as Point's gratin of crayfish tails. One leaves La Pyramide's great chef with a poignant picture of him gathering of a morning some thirty bunches of tiny watercress from the riverbank for a purée to delight his few guests.

It is easy—perhaps all too easy—to wish the revival of traditional individualized cuisine such as that found today only in the finest European restaurants. It is easy to mock the modern condition, with its bland efficiency, its producers' promises of "uniform quality guaranteed," and its ultimate offense, the precooked "dinner" consumed by millions from tin containers, without so much as the small pride of one's own bowl or platter, while gazing raptly at the latest Western. Yet such abasement of cookery has been accompanied also in our time by its internationalization, and in a larger sense, by its democratization.

The American housewife, long supplied with good advice, but only recently with a more sophisticated audience for her ministerings, has risen to the occasion by adding all manner of highly specialized, semiprofessional equipment: French omelette pans, Dutch cutlery, Italian pasta presses, Chinese *woks*, Spanish paella pans. Abroad, such American "specialties" as tunafish salad, hot dogs, hamburgers, milk shakes, steak, and corn on the cob had migrated with the G.I.'s and the tourists. Canning and refrigeration had also aided the commingling of Western and Eastern influences. Caspian Sea sturgeon, Malossol caviar, Bering Sea crabmeat, and Aus-

Aubrey Beardsley's sketch of "The Fat Woman"

tralian kangaroo tails could readily reach Kansas City, just as North and South American beef could be moved, for instance, to Istanbul. Scotch grouse, once air freight was established, were to be found among purveyors and restaurateurs in New York only a day or two after the Highland hunting season had opened, just as Hudson River shad roe became available at Paris and London branches of Prunier's soon after the first March nets were cast off Tarrytown. A few hours' flight could bring the fresh-caught makings of a bouillabaisse from Marseilles to Le Pavillon.

Once fully launched, the process of global interaction of tastes was not to be stopped. Results were sometimes astonishing. In Moscow it became a fad in some official circles to abandon the traditional drinking of vodka straight and to adopt the capitalistic habit of the cocktail—mixed, often, in an electric blender, an innovation which was itself a Western import. One such Muscovite cocktail, named *vostorg* ("delight"), consists of a frappé of cognac, cherry liqueur, lemon juice, cherries, and ice. At the same time, the West was taking to vodka with such enthusiasm as to drive traditional producers of gin and whiskeys to near panic.

Westward in the Philippines, whose indigenous culture had been dominated by Spaniards for 350 years, then "liberated" by the Americans at the turn of the century, then overrun again by Japanese and truly liberated by the Americans after World War II, West and Orient met in extraordinary disarray. Though the archipelago had originally attracted Europeans for its spices and native fruits, a dinner given in the early 1960's at the presidential palace in Manila in honor of the returning General MacArthur began with canned American fruit salad. A correspondent writing for the *Saturday Review* spoke of Manila as looking "like a sprawling, unwieldy city in the United States. Its traffic-clogged avenues are blighted by billboards proclaiming American merchandise in high-pitched Madison Avenue jargon; sleazy drive-ins offer 'colossal' hot dogs, hamburgers, and other gastronomic imitations."

Postwar Japan served a breakfast of bacon and eggs, along with the traditional morning fare of seaweed wafers, rice, and bean soup. A branch of Maxim's opened in a basement under Tokyo's Ginza complete with Toulouse-Lautrec posters and copies of French china and silverware; young Japanese preferred to drink Scotch rather than *sake* and eat *hottu doggu* rather than the traditional sliver of raw fish called *sashimi.* Hamburgers, steak, *crème caramel*, and ice cream were served on Japanese dining cars, themselves somewhat of an innovation since Japanese travelers had traditionally taken their own food aboard.

France's national institution, the café, fell into catastrophic decline, with some thirty thousand of these establishments closing their doors in the last decade, from the famed Select and La Rotonde in Paris to innumerable zinc counters in the back streets of Lyons and Marseilles. Such voguish establishments as "Le Drugstore," with its American sodas and high-speed sandwiches, overtook some. The increasing home comforts provided by television, refrigeration, and central heating overtook others. The

prolonged two-hour lunch favored by the business and professional classes, often followed by a brief snooze before returning to work, gave way to a quick platter at the "snack bar." (Indeed, under President de Gaulle inducements were offered officials who would cut

Pristine waiters before the dinner hour

down on their luncheon time.) In the Marne valley, which for so long held sacred the slow and painstaking production of some of the West's finest cheeses, a factory opened that according to *The New York Times* "turns out cheese in a fast, continuous strip, like a steel mill." Machines were devised in Brittany to produce crepes on an assembly line; another in Besançon to fabricate the long, slim French loaf in an endless ribbon, chopped off in short lengths for the consumer. America created the supermarket, but Paris went a step further and computerized it. The *Super-Marché de Poche*, set up in 1967, was the first successful completely mechanized food establishment, in which one could see but not touch packaged samples of the food sold (Frenchmen have always had a weakness for probing everything on the market stalls); the customer, gathering a punch card for each selection, turned them in to a clerk who transmitted the order to a computer for toting up the bill; thereupon, the order was transmitted to the stockroom where duplicates of the merchandise on display were bagged for taking home.

The elite string of hotels, like those Ritz had commanded, have been overtaken by Hilton, whose International division as of 1968 operated 47 hotels in 32 countries. Built by Conrad Hilton, who got his start as the operator of small-town hotels in Texas, the chain provides cornflakes and U.S. Prime steer beef to guests around the globe. To order a breakfast of waffles and deerfoot sausages at the Istanbul Hilton as prepared by a Turkish cook who has never laid eyes on such strange fare before, can lead to surprises. And in London the high-rise Hilton monolith that now dominates Hyde Park, far from insisting on American foods, features—of all things—a Polynesian dining room.

Who influences whom when it comes to dining? A distinguished French chef of our day, René Verdon, White House chef under President and Mrs. Kennedy, abruptly resigned his position when under the Johnsons a "kitchen economizer" was hired and Verdon was ordered to use frozen vegetables. Yet another leading French chef in America, Pierre Franey, trained at Drouant's in Paris and celebrated as chef of New York's distinguished Le Pavillon restaurant for two decades, resigned his position in 1960 to become *chef de cuisine* of the Howard Johnson chain of some 785 roadside eateries, along with 18 Red Coach Grills, and their retail packaged foods division. He has since developed "quick-frozen gourmet foods" such as beef Bourguignon, whose recipe for 13,000 servings calls for $2\frac{1}{2}$ tons of cubed beef, 600 pounds of mushrooms, 700 pounds of onions, 60 gallons of Burgundy, and 465 gallons of sauce. Franey foresees a time when Howard Johnson's will even serve caviar.

Great Britain has also invaded Germany—in a fashion hard to believe. In 1967, as if striking at the heart of the greatest beer-producing country in Europe, the Watney-Mann brewery of London opened the Victoria, an "authentic" British pub in Düsseldorf, and the Sir Winston Churchill in Paris. There are even plans afoot to establish pubs in Florence and Madrid.

Yet all this lively interchange might also be transitory. Who can tell? Despite all the advantages of nature, science, and imagination available to man, there has been present at the tables of the world a haunting knowledge of hunger and insufficiency. Fully half of mankind, it was established by United Nations experts in 1966, was inadequately fed. In another fifteen years, they predicted, there will be an additional fifteen billion mouths to feed. "Half the world's children of preschool age," as Drew Middleton summed up in *The New York Times*, "are so undernourished that their physical and mental growth is retarded and mortality among these children in the underdeveloped countries is 60 times as great as in more advanced societies."

Those who enjoy a good table cannot quite escape the thought of this.

THE BANQUET YEARS

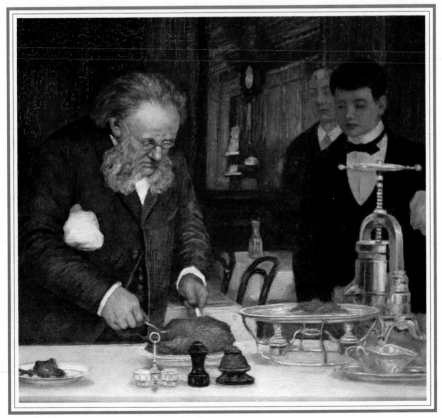

Frédéric, proprietor of the Tour d'Argent in Paris, preparing its famed duck, c. 1890

Absinthe-minded

Harper's Magazine, APRIL, 1889

Toward the *fin de siècle*, music halls like the Folies-Bergère were the most egalitarian of Parisian institutions, catering to those with "overworked digestions and underworked intelligences . . . foreigners, shop assistants on the spree, and little ladies on the make." Undiscriminating audiences relished the nightly fare of sentimental ballads, dirty jokes, and risqué dances. The barmaid, however, in Edouard Manet's painting of the nightspot opposite, has long been inured to the performances on stage as well as off, and waits impassively as a customer chooses a bottle. People in search of more solitary dissipations could drink absinthe at a local café such as the one above. Introduced to France about 1850 by soldiers returning from Algeria, the wormwood flavored liqueur quickly became a favorite of the decadents. Absinthe reputedly doubled the potency of anything taken afterward; overindulgence could cause blindness, delirium, madness. It was outlawed in 1915.

COURTAULD INSTITUTE GALLERIES, LONDON

To get their jobs les forts *carried 440 pounds on their heads. Their uniform was the broad-brimmed hat which kept the blood of fresh-killed carcasses from dribbling down the neck. Their trade was moving the markets' produce from farmers' carts to stalls like that in the 1898 photo at left, then back onto wagons for delivery to retailers like the butcher opposite, who poses with his family, his employees, and a canopy of well-dressed meats.*

"The Belly of Paris"

Les Halles, condemned now to make way for sky-scrapers, stands on a site which since the twelfth century has been the central market place for all France. The present markets, ten giant iron and glass sheds, were begun under Napoleon III, following the sort of aesthetic-cum-political brouhaha of which only Parisians are capable and after such far more revolutionary designs as that in the inset above were rejected. Les Halles was, in fact, only one of dozens of wholesale food markets designed during the nineteenth century to accommodate the needs of Europe's burgeoning cities, but it has always had a special charm. Add to its architectural interest the bustle of merchants and roustabouts, the ambrosial smells of flowers, fruits, and fish, the brilliant colors of bloody meats and fresh vegetables, and most particularly the onion soup served at neighboring cafés, and one has a last glimpse of Paris' famed late-night-to-dawn tourist spectacular.

By the late 1800's the tea package had given birth to mass marketing complete with brand names and chain stores. It was time for advertising, and as these posters demonstrate there was no lack of talent to produce it. On the facing page, at upper left, two maidens promote sales for a local vintner. Haughty despite their dishabille, they shout, "Down with the middleman." To the right is an ad for the "only working baby bottle with its own guarantee." At bottom, Fouquet and Company, today a thriving restaurant and delicatessen, promises firstrate merchandise, which it still delivers. On this page, clockwise from left, a swaying housemaid, a nattily dressed chorus, and a strong man push two flavors of tapioca, chicory coffee, and the only broth "conserving the flavor of fresh meat."

359

Finishing touches are added in the dessert room.

Bushels of oysters are shucked in the ice room.

In the cold pantry butter and aspics are molded.

All That Glitters

Napoleon III's new imperium had to sparkle—the nation that called it into being expected no less. The head of state willingly obliged by spending lavishly on travel, clothes, and entertainments. To be sure, all that glittered was not gold; that had been stolen during the uprising of 1848. But the new electroplated table-ware would hardly be noticed by the guests above, gathered in the Galerie de Diane of the Tuileries for a ball in 1869. Led by Napoleon and Eugenie, they take their customary tour of the tables before dining. Meanwhile, the food, brought up by dumb-waiter from the elaborate kitchens, left, turns lukewarm *à la française*.

361

A la Carte

Dufy's water color celebrating the liberation of Paris, 1944

Gauguin's colonial satire, c. 1900

Renoir's juggling chef, 1878

Before the nineteenth century, diners had to find their way through dinner without a written menu. It took the Parisian restaurateur to introduce the *carte* to polite society. Since it was to be decoration as well as guide, noted artists were often called on to execute the illustrations, sometimes for money, sometimes in exchange for supper. Renoir prepared menus for his favorite patrons. Toulouse-Lautrec, himself a gourmet, sketched menus for meals to which he was invited. Even Gauguin in his Tahitian retreat gave banquets complete with anticolonial menus. Production of such ephemera in our own century has been rare, but a day of national joy could still inspire the remarkable display of artistic-gastronomic enthusiasm opposite.

Toulouse-Lautrec's modiste, *1893*

Disgorging the sediment

Inserting the cork

Fastening the cork with string

Bottling the Bubbles

The crew poses with the top-hatted owner and two "nurses," workmen entrusted with turning the bottles.

The inhabitants of Champagne had known for a long time that the wine of their region underwent a second fermentation in the spring which transformed it into a sparkling delicacy, but they had to wait until the late 1600's when Dom Pérignon made a cork that withstood the pressure built up by gases in the bottle. Further experiments taught local vintners to blend the products of different vineyards and to add a little sugar before the spring fermentation to encourage the bubbles. Ever since Champagne presented its gift to a grateful world, the pop of the cork has signaled a celebration. These engravings of workers in Pierry accompanied the musings of one ardent admirer in an 1855 issue of the *Illustrated London News*. "A *souchet* of flounders—a *compote* of pigeon—and a salad of strawberries. Well, one may struggle with such a repast. . . . This is Ida's birthday, and she must be toasted as becomes the lady of my heart . . . the

only draught worthy of such an honor—a bottle of champagne iced to a degree. This bumper I drink in silence. How grateful—how delicious! Remove those grosser matters, and leave me alone with this sublimated liquor—created for love's libations. What other draught born of the grape goes direct to the heart like this and in a moment makes the pulse beat quicker? What pleasant memories are associated with this reaming glass, remembering as we do the silent tongues it has made eloquent, and the anxious hours it has converted into mirthfulness. Who has not led some bashful maiden down to supper and thought the task a bore until a glass—perhaps two—of this elixir has converted her into the sweetest prattler that was ever listened to? Or who has not seen some scornful lady that has slighted the heart devoted to her through a whole program of quadrilles and polkas, smile at last when humanized by a *tazza* of champagne?"

Securing the wire cap

Putting on the tinfoil

Wrapping the bottle in paper

365

Fête Champêtre

"The world was a ripe peach and we were eating it," wrote Sir Osbert Sitwell about the "smart set" reigning during the 1920's. The "ripe peach" would rot in their hands in the next decade, but in the years between the war and the depression, the beautiful people moved in a surrealistic whirl of gaiety and brilliant conversation, exotic costume and exquisite food. To them the *fête champêtre* came as naturally as it had to their hedonistic predecessors in the courts of the Louis'. In the painting at right Kees Van Dongen, psychological portraitist of the age, has caught all the kaleidoscopic color of a picnic at a French estate. The party is just getting under way—the sun is high in the summer sky, flirtations are still at the hand-kissing stage, and the champagne supply seems limitless. What better way to launch *le weekend*?

366

Hôtel de Paris

Monaco has long been a meeting place of the monied and titled. The caricaturist of the twenties, Sem (who appears at bottom on the lady's left), sketched notable patrons at play in the famous hotel's dining salon. Each year's drawings were compiled as a "souvenir" of the Monte Carlo high season, but they were not without malice. At left, for instance, a well-known count has a drink with the mysterious "Lady M," whose back is discreetly turned.

The Enduring Art

Claude Derain's homely still life above focuses on cooking implements not unlike those found in the Egyptian pyramids or the tombs
of ancient Etruria. Edouard Vuillard's lithograph opposite catches the
mood of relaxed satisfaction of a woman cleaning up after the family
dinner. Both works, executed in this century, suggest the timelessness
of the culinary adventure. Only the details have been changed: the
faster pace of life has brought about a demand for lighter, less elaborate meals; technological changes like the improved stove and running
water have taken most of the drudgery out of cooking; rapid transportation, canning, and freezing mean that almost all ingredients
from albacore to zucchini are widely available. Any aspiring gourmet
now has the means with which to experiment, with the result that our
era boasts more fine cooks than ever before—and an enormous
brotherhood of knowledgeable eaters to appreciate their productions.

ACKNOWLEDGMENTS

The following is a list of picture credits for front matter and text. Page numbers appear in boldface type.

Front cover Biblioteca Ambrosiana, Milan; Scala **4** N.Y. Public Library, Prints Division **6** Studios Josse-Lalance **12** Romain Robert **13** Louvre, Paris; Tel-Vigneau **14** Valeriano, *Hieroglyphica*, 1586, N.Y. Public Library, Rare Book Division **15** American Museum of Natural History, New York; Lee Boltin **16** By Permission of the Trustees of the British Museum **17** Louvre, Paris; Giraudon **18** Metropolitan Museum of Art, Harris Brisbane Dick Fund, 1957, New York **20** Archepiscopal Museum, Ravenna; Anderson **21** Museo Nazionale, Rome; Boudot-Lamotte **22** top, Roger-Viollet; bottom, Courtesy of *Life* Magazine; Frank Scherschel **24** Younger, *Gods, Men, and Wine* **25** By Permission of the Trustees of the British Museum **43** By Permission of the Trustees of the British Museum **44** Metropolitan Museum of Art, Fletcher Fund, 1938, New York **47** Museo Nazionale, Naples, Anderson **48** Musée des Antiquités Nationales, St-Germain; S. Guiley-Lagache **51** Brooklyn Museum **52** Museum of Fine Arts, Boston; Gift of H. P. Kidder **54** Gabinetto Fotografico Nazionale, Rome **76** Archives Photographiques, Paris **78** Folger Shakespeare Library, Washington, D.C. **79** Rheinesches Landesmuseum, Bonn **81** George Whicher, *The Goliard Poets* **82** Bibliothèque Nationale, Paris **85** Bibliothèque Nationale, Paris, Service Photographique **86** Montagné, *Larousse Gastronomique* **87** *Kuchenmeisterei*, 1490 (facs. ed.), N.Y. Public Library, Rare Book Division **88** By Permission of the Trustees of the British Museum **89** By Permission of the Trustees of the British Museum **90** Lehner, *Folklore and Odysseys of Food and Medicinal Plants* 118, 124 *Opera Di M. Bartolomeo Scappi*, 1643, N.Y. Public Library, Rare Book Division 120, 122, 123, 125 N.Y. Public Library, Prints Division **126** Sotheby & Co.,

London **127** Graf Eltz **129** Nat'l. Portrait Gallery, London **130** Stow, *Survey of London*, 1633 **133** Victoria and Albert Museum, London. Crown Copyright **156** De Bry, *East Indies*, Pt. 4, N.Y. Public Library, Rare Book Division **157** De Bry, *East Indies*, Pt. 4, N.Y. Public Library, Rare Book Division **158** Metropolitan Museum of Art, Rogers Fund, 1913 **159** Museum of Fine Arts, Boston; Heeramaneck Collection **160** Library of Congress, Washington, D.C. **162** Smithsonian Institution, Freer Gallery of Art, Washington, D.C. **163** By Permission of the Trustees of the British Museum **164** By Permission of the Trustees of the British Museum **165** Dufour, *Tractatus Novi de Potu Caphe; de Chinensium The; et de Chocolata*, 1685, N.Y. Public Library, Rare Book Division **167** By Permission of the Trustees of the British Museum **168** Dutertre, *Histoire Generale des Antilles*, 1667–71, N.Y. Public Library, Rare Book Division **169** Dufour, *Tractatus Novi de Potu Caphe; de Chinensium The; et de Chocolata*, 1685, N.Y. Public Library, Rare Book Division **190** Smithsonian Institution, Freer Gallery of Art, Washington, D.C. **191** Royal Ontario Museum, University of Toronto **192** Art Institute of Chicago, Kate S. Buckingham Fund **195** Bibliothèque Nationale, Paris; Service Photographique **196** M. H. de Young Memorial Museum, San Francisco; Roy Leventritt Collection **199** Fine Arts Gallery of San Diego **200** N.Y. Public Library, Prints Division **202** Courtesy of Inosuke Setsu, Tokyo **203** Seattle Art Museum **224** Louvre, Paris; Giraudon **225** National Museum, Stockholm; Giraudon **226** Bibliothèque Nationale, Paris; Service Photographique **227** Bibliothèque Nationale, Paris; Service Photographique **228** American Philosophical Society, Philadelphia **230** Bibliothèque Nationale, Paris **231** University of St. Thomas Art Department, Houston **232** Bibliothèque Nationale, Paris; Service Photographique **233** Archives Photographique, Paris 235 Bulloz 236 Giraudon 237 Carnavalet; Bulloz 262 National Museum, Copenhagen 263 Musée Municipal de Lakenhal, Leyden 264 Mattioli, *Commentaires*, 1578 265 Wendy Buehr Collection 266 Museum Fur Volkerkunde, Basel 267 University of St. Thomas Art Department, Houston 268 Pinto Collection of Wooden Bygones 269 N.Y. Public Library, Prints Division 270 Liptov Museum, Ruzomberok 271 Liptov Museum, Ruzomberok 272 Metropolitan Museum of Art, Rogers Fund, 1927 273 Museo de Artes Decoratives, Barcelona 274 Anne S. K. Brown, Military Collection 275 Picture Archive, Jewish Seminary, New York; Frank J. Darmstaedter 302 Courtesy of Ronald A. Lee 305 By Permission of the Trustees of the British Museum 306 By Permission of the Trustees of the British Museum 307 By Permission of the Trustees of the British Museum 308 Marshall B. Davidson Collection 309 Cleveland Museum of Art, Gift of Mr. and Mrs. Warren H. Corning 310 N.Y. Public Library, Prints Division 311 N.Y. Public Library, Prints Division 312 Morris, *Portrait of a Chef* 314 Metropolitan Museum of Art, Harris Brisbane Dick Fund, 1953 315 By Permission of the Trustees of the British Museum 339 Bettmann Archive, New York 340 *Guide Michelin* 343, 345 Studios Josse-Lalance 344 Collection Robida, Paris 346 Bettmann Archive, New York 347 Bettmann Archive, New York 348 Virgil Thomson Collection 350 The Tate Gallery, London 351 *Yellow Book*, July, 1894 384 Antique Co. of New York, Inc., Incorporating the Antique Porcelain Co.

Grateful acknowledgment is made for permission to quote from the following works:

Andrieu, Pierre, *Fine Bouche*, copyright © 1956 by Pierre Andrieu and Editions Causse. Published by Cassell and Company Ltd., London.

Apicius, *The Roman Cookery Book*, translated by Barbara Flower and Elisabeth Rosenbaum, copyright © 1958 by George G. Harrap and Company Ltd., London.

Bickerdyke, John, *The Curiosities of Ale and Beer*, published 1965 by Spring Books, London.

Cheng, F. T., *Musings of a Chinese Gourmet*, copy-

right 1954 by F. T. Cheng. Published by Hutchinson and Co. Ltd., London.

Clair, Colin, *Kitchen and Table*, copyright © 1964 by Colin Clair. Published by Abelard-Schuman Ltd., New York

Diaz del Castillo, *The Discovery and Conquest of Mexico*, copyright © 1956 by Farrar, Straus, and Cudahy, New York.

Drummond, J. C., and Wilbraham, Anne, *The Englishman's Food*, copyright © 1957 by Jonathan Cape Ltd., London.

Herodotus, *The Histories*, translated by Aubrey de Selincourt, copyright 1954 by Penguin Books Ltd., London.

Higham translation, *Oxford Book of Greek Verse*, copyright 1930 by The Clarendon Press, Oxford.

Jacob, Heinrich Edward, *Coffee*, copyright 1935 by The Viking Press, New York.

Lach, Donald F., *Asia in the Making of Europe*, copyright © 1965 by University of Chicago.

Lopez, Claude-Anne, *Mon Cher Papa, Franklin and the Ladies of Paris*, copyright © 1966 by Yale University, New Haven.

Mitford, Nancy, "Madame de Pompadour's Staircase," *History Today*, Volume IV, No. 1, 1954. Published by Bracken House, London.

Montagné, Prosper, *Larousse Gastronomique*, copyright © 1961 by Crown Publishers, Inc., N.Y.

Montaigne, *Essays*, translated by E. J. Trechman, copyright 1935 by Oxford University Press, New York.

Petronius, *The Satyricon*, translated by William Arrowsmith, copyright © 1959 by William Arrowsmith. Published by University of Michigan Press, Ann Arbor.

Plumb, J. H., *Sir Robert Walpole*, copyright © 1956 by John Harold Plumb. Published by Houghton Mifflin Company, New York.

Pottle, Frederick A., ed., *Boswell in Holland 1763–1764*, copyright © 1956 by Yale University. Published by McGraw-Hill Book Company, New York.

Rugoff, Milton, ed., *The Great Travelers*, Volume 1, copyright © 1960 by Simon and Schuster, Inc., New York.

Seranne, Ann, and Tebbel, John, eds., *The Epi-*

373

*The editors wish to express their deep gratitude to the
institutions and individuals mentioned below for their
help in providing pictorial material and for supplying
information and advice.*

Wine consultant: Pierre Bennerup, New York

Historical research: Mrs. Helen Prince, New York

Photography: London—R. B. Fleming and Co.
Ltd.; New York—Century Photo Service, Inc.,
Max Steinbook; Oliver Baker Associates,
Geoffrey Clements; Paulus Lesser Photography,
Inc.

Napkin illustrations on page 333 drawn by
Cal Sacks

Ing. Paolo Agnesi, Imperia

Bayerische Staatsbibliothek, Munich

Bibliothèque des Arts Décoratifs, Paris
    René Salanon, Chief Curator

Bibliothèque Nationale, Service Photographique,
Paris, *Madame Le Monnier*, Chief Curator

Bibliothèque Royale de Belgique, Brussels
    Martin Wittek

Mrs. Jane Horton de Cabanyes, Madrid

Carnavalet Museum, Paris

Germanisches Nationalmuseum, Nuremberg
    Dr. Bernward Denekee

Hamburger Kunsthalle
    Dr. Otfried Schroeder

Jewish Theological Seminary, New York
    Frank J. Darmstaedter

Kunsthistorisches Museum, Vienna
    Dr. Erwin M. Auer, Director

Arpag Mekhitarian, Paris

Metropolitan Museum of Art, New York
    Miss Ellen Franklin
    Miss Nora Scott

Michelin & Cie., Paris

Musée d'Art et d'Histoire, Geneva
    Madame Anne de Herdt

Musée d'Art et d'Industrie, St-Etienne
    Madame Yvonne Allemand

Musée de la Manufacture Nationale de Sèvres

Musée Municipal de Lakenhal, Leyden

Museo Nazionale, Naples
    Dr. Giuseppe Maggi

National Museum, Copenhagen
    Miss Fritze Lindahl

National Museum, Stockholm
    Dr. Pontus Grate

National Palace Museum, Taipei
    Dr. Chiang Fu-Tsung, Director

New York Public Library
    Astor, Lenox, and Tilden Foundations
    Mrs. Maud D. Cole
    Mrs. Philomena C. Houlihan
    Miss Romana Javitz
    Miss Elizabeth Roth
    Lewis M. Stark

Osterreichische Nationalbibliothek, Vienna
    Hofrat Dr. Hans Pauer, Curator

Rijksmuseum, Amsterdam

Rosgarten Museum, Constance

Dr. Roudinesco, Paris

Georges Sirot, Paris

Miss Bianca Spantigati, Rome

Mrs. Maria Fossi Todorow, Florence

Max Willibald, Erbgraf zu Waldburg-Wolfegg,
    Schloss Wolfegg, Algau

INDEX

Page numbers in italic type indicate that the subject is illustrated.

376

SAVOY THEATRE, 341
SAXONS, 77
SCANDINAVIAN COOKERY, 262
SCAPPI, BARTOLOMEO, 121, 148–49, 148–49
SCHILLER, FRIEDRICH, 88
SCHORGER, A. W., 168
SCIPIOS, 50
SCOTTISH COOKERY, 16
SCYTHIANS, 48
SEALS, used as food, 82
SEAWEED. See Water Greens
SEM, 369; sketches by, 368–69
SENECA, 54
SEPTIMUS SEVERUS, 44
SERRES, OLIVIER DE, 124
SERVANTS, 238, 242–43, 242–43, 245, 305, 311, 318, 349; in China, 195, 196, 197; in England, 133, 305, 305; in Flanders, 278, 278; in France, 235, 242–43, 242–43, 245, 246–47; in Japan, 216, 216–17, 218, 218; medieval, 87–88, 88; Renaissance, 121; in Russia, 297, 297
SEVIGNE, MADAME DE, 230
SEYMOUR, ROBERT, 329; painting by, 329
SHAKESPEARE, WILLIAM, 131, 132
SHEEP RAISING, 15, 26, 50, 80, 82
SHELLFISH, 13, 44, 271; crabs, 50, 350; crawfish, 46, 233, 349; lobsters, 50, 58, 345; mussels, 46, 76; oysters, 44, 51, 56, 125, 238, 271, 313, 324, 360; shrimps, 197
SHEN NUNG, Emperor of China, 191, 201
SHETLAND ISLANDS, 82
SHILLING COOKERY, 312
SHUJA, Shah of Persia, 167
SHUNSO, 215; painting by, 214–15
SICILY, 43, 52, 76
SIGISMUND, abbot, 79
SIMOND, LOUIS, 315
SITWELL, SIR OSBERT, 266
SLAVS, 76
SMOLLETT, TOBIAS, 310, 313
SNAILS, 44, 197
SNAKES, used as food, 191
SOBIESKI, JOHN, King of Poland, 170
SOCRATES, 42, 43, 53, 64
SOMMAIRE TRAITE DES MELONS, 118
SOPS, 85
SOUBISE, PRINCE DE, 232
SOUP KITCHENS, 271
SOUPS, 13, 86, 194, 227, 236, 262, 263, 268, 271, 341; bisques, 224; broths, 84, 194; Chinese, 191–92, 194, 200; chowders, 84; consommés, 26, 342; minestra, 191; purées, 85, stocks, 225
SOYER, ALEXIS, 307–8, 312, 312
SPAIN, 16, 17, 25, 51, 63, 75, 77, 82, 158, 193, 272, 290–91, 290–91
SPARTA, 25, 48, 49, 50
SPICE TRADE, history of, 9, 155–65, 169,

172, 172, 179; map of, 172, 173
SPICES AND SEASONINGS, 17, 19, 33, 45, 46, 48, 57, 57, 63, 77, 78, 79, 87, 159, 166, 293, 350; anise, 86; basil, 158; bay, 86; caraway, 86; cardamom, 157; cinnamon, 17, 84, 86, 157, 161, 162, 172; chili, 15; cloves, 17, 86, 159, 162, 163, 164, 172; coriander, 19, 50, 193; cumin, 45, 50; dill, 86; fennel, 14, 50; garlic, 24, 125, 196, 291; ginger, 17, 19, 82, 157, 159, 161, 162, 164, 172, 202; mint, 19, 34, 50; mustard, 228; nutmeg, 17, 159, 162, 172; paprika, 273; pepper, 17, 156, 157, 159, 161, 162, 172, 172, 228; saffron, 17, 82, 85, 157, 158; sage, 86; salt, 17, 45, 50, 51, 58, 80, 82, 84, 86, 228; sesame, 24, 82, 163, 193; thyme, 24
SPOONS, 88, 130, 144, 144, 196. See also Eating Implements
SQUASHES, 15, 186, 193, 370
STEEN, JAN, 260, 262, 278, 286; paintings by, 260, 279, 287
STEIN, GERTRUDE, 348
STEWING, 13, 85
STEWS, black broth of Sparta, 50; bouillabaisse, 350; chaudemer (fish stew), 84, 234; goulash, 262, 273; haggis, 16; hotchpotch, 85, 262, 263; in Middle Ages, 84; ragouts, 44, 85, 224
STOCK. See Soups
STOVES AND OVENS, 13, 233; brazier, 291, 291; brick hearth, 61, 85, 290, 290, 347; Chinese portable, 198; Egyptian, 28, 28–29; electric, 347; gas, 347; iron range, 347; wall ovens, 85, 87, 113, 113; woodfire oven, 347
STRABO, 17, 157
STUFFINGS, 18, 50, 86
SUET, in food, 16
SUETONIUS, 49
SUGAR CANE, 86, 158, 168, 168
SULLY, DUC DE, 124
SUMER, 17, 20, 22, 22, 23, 24
SUPER-MARCHE DE POCHE, 351, 352
SUPPERS, 230, 231, 232, 343
SWEETENERS, honey, 18, 19, 22, 24, 34, 42, 46, 50, 51, 77, 84, 85, 86, 170, 293; sugar, 84, 157, 158, 163, 193, 296
SWIFT, JONATHAN, 304, 305
SYBARIS, 48
SYMPOSIUM, Plato's, 42, 43
SYMPOSIUM, Xenophon's, 43
SYRIANS, 34, 34

T

TABLE LINENS, 118, 121, 128; matzo covers, 275, 275; napkins, 53, 123, 258, 332, 333; tablecloths, 88, 105, 123; tea caddies, 202, 202

TABLEAU DE PARIS, 232
TABLEWARE, 53, 56, 118, 121, 123 130, 133, 133, 140, 144, 213, 213, 224, 224, 225, 225, 231, 231, 250, 250–51, 258, 258–59, 286, 293, 293, 302, 302, 304, 308, 308, 309, 309, 334, 334. See also Porcelain
TACITUS, 50
TACUINUM SANITATUS, 113
TAILLEVENT. See Tirel, Guillaume
TALLEYRAND-PERIGORD, Charles Maurice de, 237, 238, 257, 257
TALMUD, 25
TAMERLANE, 167
TAOISM, 190, 192, 207
TAPIOCA, 168, 359
TAVERNS. See Inns and Taverns
TEAHOUSES, 201, 202–3, 217, 217
TERTULLIAN OF CARTHAGE, 56
TESSERAE (ration cards), 70
TEUTONS, 76
THACKERAY, WILLIAM, 332
THAMES RIVER, 82
THEARION, 43
THEATRE DE L'ODEON, 92
THEOPOMPUS OF CHIOS, 49
THICKENERS, 85, 225–26
THREE SISTERS, 275
TIBER RIVER, 42, 48
TIBERIUS, Emperor of Rome, 46
TIEN-HSI CHENG, 198
TIREL, GUILLAUME, 85, 85, 90
TOKLAS, ALICE B., 348, 348
TOLSTOY, LEO, 275
TORTOISES, 22
TOSCANELLI, PAOLO, 155
TOULOUSE-LAUTREC, HENRI, 363; water color by, 363
TRAJAN, Emperor of Rome, 63, 70, 71
TRANSCAUCASIA, 23
TRES RICHES HEURES, of the Duc de Berry, 94–95, 95
TRIER, 77
TRIMALCHIO, 54, 55
TRIONFI, 152, 153
TROY, 16
TRUFFLES, 44, 113, 113, 118, 166, 225
TUBERO THE STOIC, 47
TUILERIES, 360–61, 361
TUSCANY, 51, 119
TUSSER, THOMAS, 83
TUTANKHAMEN, King of Egypt, 31, 36
TWICKENHAM LODGE, 129
TWO BOOKS OF COOKERIE AND CARVING, 131
TZU HSI, Empress of China, 197

U

UNITED STATES COOKERY, 349, 350, 351, 352